Life Skills

What Your Schools Forgot To Teach You
You
Volume I

By

Meena Kukreja, M.D.

authorHOUSE™

1663 LIBERTY DRIVE, SUITE 200
BLOOMINGTON, INDIANA 47403
(800) 839-8640
WWW.AUTHORHOUSE.COM

First published by AuthorHouse 07/19/05

ISBN: 1-4184-8711-2 (e)
ISBN: 1-4184-8712-0 (sc)

Library of Congress Control Number: 2004095514

Printed in the United States of America
Bloomington, Indiana

This book is printed on acid-free paper.

THIS BOOK IS DEDICATED IN HIS NAME

"LIFE SKILLS: WHAT YOUR SCHOOLS FORGOT TO TEACH YOU" IS A BOOK CONSISTING OF TWO VOLUMES

WHERE IT STATES IN THIS BOOK TO READ THE CHAPTER IN "LIFE SKILLS", IT IS REFERRING TO THE SECOND VOLUME.

© 2002 - 2005

Table of Contents

Chapter 1.   BODY HYGIENE

Wake up early in the morning daily and develop a body clock. Go to the bathroom every morning to pass your stool and so develop a body clock.

Do not read magazines or books while passing stool. This is how you develop constipation. You must sit, or squat, push your stool out, clean your rectum and get up. It should not take more than three minutes.

Brush your teeth daily in the morning and at night. Take a bath every morning. Make sure that you wash your genital and rectal areas. You do not have to wash your hair every morning.

Women having their monthly cycle must not be treated as untouchables. But they must have less physical hard work.

Waste material from body, as in pads, and contraceptives must be wrapped before they are put in the garbage pail. They should never lie exposed. They should preferably be kept where they cannot be seen. This is hygiene, modesty and decency.

Change your underwear (panties, bras, undershirts) daily after the bath. Change your socks daily. Do not wear panties that have single cord in the back instead of covering your buttocks. Besides being immodest, the cord can cause irritation of the anal area and cause an abscess. Do not spend more than fifteen minutes in the bathroom.

Contrary to current practice, it is not necessary to use a deodorant under the armpits. You are rubbing a chemical against a sensitive area repeatedly. Talcum powder works just as well. Do not use dyes and chemicals on your body until

you are eighteen years old. Remember that you are growing, and your cells are multiplying. This is not the time to use dyes and chemicals on your bodies. We do not know which of these agents can cause cancer or lifelong allergies or hair loss.
Until you stop growing, use lotions etc. sparingly.

It is not good to use air fresheners or air sprays for the same reason. They are chemicals. They can cause asthmatic attacks and lung damage. Open a window instead. Do not live or work where the windows cannot be opened. Fresh air is the best remedy for killing germs and is good for your lungs. Similarly, drying clothes in the sun is good, cheap, and kills bacteria.

Pray in the morning after coming out of the bathroom. Pray in the evening before preparing your evening meals. You can say any prayer. Read the chapter on prayer. This is charging you. You would not leave home without charging your cell phone, so why not charge yourself?

On the weekends, see that your nails are trimmed. Nails consistently covered with polish cannot breathe and become weak and brittle. See that your ears are free from wax and your belly button is free from dirt. Do not poke sticks in your ears or belly button. Use a small cloth or tissue dipped in oil instead. Dry with regular cloth or tissues. Change your bed sheets and towels weekly and in between if you dirty them.

Take out the night before all clothes that you will need for the next day. Then you will not be running around in the morning looking for things. Remember that if your clothes attract more attention, people will not be able to focus on what you want to convey. Prepare your school bag and lunch the night before.

Be organized. Put your things in a systematic order in the same place. You will save a lot of time looking for things. Being a teenager does not mean that you can live like a pig and be messy. Use the weekends to organize your shoes, drawers, closets and your room, as well as to do your laundry, fold your clothes, and put them away.

Understand that the school only teaches you about the environment around you. Side by side with the school, you need another education to prepare you for life. The teenage years are the time to learn good habits of neatness, organization, and self-discipline to prepare for adulthood. Otherwise you will be a failure.

Do not eat or force your children to eat once they are full. There is a center, called satiety center, in your brain that tells you when to stop eating. If you keep ignoring this center, you will grow obese. Once a child is full, remove the plate. Understand that the children will eat a lot during periods of growth and will eat much less while they are not growing. This will occur in cycles. Do not eat around the clock. Eating or munching all the time means that your stomach must produce acid all the time to digest the food. This leads to acidity, gastritis, and other stomach problems. Your stomach is designed to need a gap of three hours to digest the food and push it forward. Have three meals a day plus a snack around four. You should always have breakfast. Eat lots of vegetables and grains. Drink six glasses of water a day to flush out the poisons in your body. There should be no soft drinks or soda with breakfast, lunch, or dinner. Your body needs water. Eighty percent of your body is water. Do not eat junk food more than once a day, preferably at a snack time. Please note that breakfast or dinner is not a cereal bar. It should consist of a meal with grains, fruits or vegetables as freshly cooked as possible. Eat and drink in moderation. A body toned with self-discipline works far better than one that moves under whims and fancies. Rinse your mouth after meals. Dabbing with a napkin is not good enough. Wash your hands before and after eating. People who have low blood pressure need to increase their salt intake.

Do not give babies food low in salt or sugar.

You do not have to eat meat in order to survive. Remember that the strongest animals (the gorilla, the bear, the elephant and some dinosaurs) are vegetarians.

You should fast once a week, during which you have no meat. You eat your breakfast, but your lunch should consist of only fruits and vegetables, lemonade, and juice. It teaches you self-control. This fasting should not be done if you are traveling, are a woman expecting a baby, or are ill.

Exercise all your joints every day. Read the chapter on exercises. Walk every day. Do deep breathing exercises at least five times every morning and night.

Make sure you get adequate rest. You should have a break for an hour at lunch. You should spend some time of it resting. People should not use the lunch hour to work, attend conferences, lectures etc. At mealtimes, your stomach should be getting the blood supply to digest the food, not your brain.

Sleep is imperative for your body to live and to function at its best. Sleep is the time when the body repairs damages, catches up with production of vital ingredients to nourish the body and restores energy. It also helps you to work through your problems, pain and depression. People without adequate sleep get irritable, lose concentration, and fall ill. Do not disturb a person sleeping unless it is very urgent. You can cause the body damage. At home, do not do your work at the expense of another person's rest. Do not have loud music late at night, because people need to sleep and charge their bodies. Do not have loudspeakers at night for the same reason. Teenagers need more sleep and will usually catch up on the weekends.

You should never have loudspeakers for your prayers. Your God is not deaf.

Do not sing your prayer out loud if other people in your home are sleeping.

Do not take sleeping pills if you cannot sleep. Do not panic that you are not able to sleep adequately. Each person needs sleep of a different duration. It can range from four to eight hours. It will also change at different stages of life and from time to time, depending on what is happening around you and where you have been. If you cannot sleep, read a book, watch television or do some chores. It is okay to stay awake for a night or so. But do not sleep the next day. Wait for your regular hour to sleep during the next night. You will eventually get back into your regular pattern. Do hard physical work or exercises. The person who works hard physically has no trouble falling asleep. He falls asleep the minute his head hits the pillow. People who say they have not slept for many nights still catch naps at different times. The body will catch up on its needs. Lack of sleep can be caused by difficulty falling asleep or waking up in the middle of the night. This can also be due to depression or worry.

Care about your innocent animals and refuse to use anything on your body for which they had to be tortured or killed. Learn how your make up is tested. Refuse to wear anything for which children had to slave.

Chapter 2. EXERCISES

After the age of twenty, you must move all your joints through their full range in at least seven repetitions once a day. If you do not, you will suffer from frozen joints, painful muscle spasms, contracted joints and muscles, or inability to rise, walk, or function to your optimum level. You will lose your flexibility. After all, youth is flexibility.

The following are basic exercises to keep your joints flexible and are not to be confused with strengthening exercises. These exercises can be done in standing, sitting or lying positions, depending on your strength. When the optimum position is preferred, it will be so mentioned. All exercises should be done in about seven repetitions, once a day. You can start by doing them in three repetitions daily and then gradually build them up to seven times. Advanced people go up to ten and then twenty. No exercise should be done when you are tired or if it causes pain. People with specific illnesses should consult their doctors for any contradictions to these exercises.

Before any exercise is begun, it is essential that you do deep-breathing exercises. The optimum position is to lie on your back and have your arms by your sides. Your legs should be stretched out. Take a deep breath in as long as you can. Imagine that you are directing the breath almost to the bottom of your spine. Then put your lips in the shape of an o and breathe out saying the sound of o. Why are you saying this sound? Because it allows better control over your breathing and you can exhale in a measured way for a longer time. Repeat seven times.
Visual tapes of these exercises can be ordered.

Neck

1.Bend your neck forward so that your chin touches your chest or is as close to it as possible.
Now bend your head back as far back as you can.

2. Turn your head to the right so that your chin touches your right shoulder. Then come back to the midline and stop with your face forward in midline. Now turn your head left so that your chin touches the left shoulder. Again, come back to the midline.

3. Tilt your head so that your right ear touches your right shoulder. Come back to the normal position in midline. Then tilt your head so that your left ear touches your left shoulder. Again, come back to the midline.

Sitting position
All the above exercises can be done in the sitting position.

Lying position
You can do exercises 3 and 2 while lying on your back.
Exercise 2 can also be done lying on the stomach.
Exercise 1 can only be done when you lie on your side.

B. Shoulders

1. Lift your shoulders and rotate them forward seven times and then backward seven times.

2. Pretend that you are jumping rope. Swing your left arm in a forward circle with your elbow straight seven times, and then in a backward circle seven times. The circle should be as wide and as high as you can make it. Then swing your right arm in the same way.

3. Put your arms by your side, keeping your elbows straight. Bring your hands up over your head and make them meet.

4. Put your right hand behind your neck and your left hand behind your back and try to meet them. Now reverse them so

that the left hand is now behind your neck and the right hand behind your back. Reverse them again.

Sitting position
All the above exercises can be done in the sitting position.

Lying position
Exercises 1, 2, and 3 can be done in the lying position on one side using the opposite arm. In exercise 3, bring your arm up all the way, so that it lies over your head.
Exercise 4 can be done in the lying position on your stomach.

Everyone should put their hands behind their heads with elbows flat on the bed while they lie on their backs. This should be done using no pillows. This should be done for five minutes before sleeping and after waking up.

C. Elbows and hands
1. Bend your left elbow and straighten it. Repeat on the right side.
2. For this exercise, the optimum position is to sit with your elbow bent and your forearm stretched out on the table. Turn your palm facing up. Now put your palm facing down on the table.
3. Rotate your left hand in a circle clockwise seven times and then anticlockwise seven times. Repeat with the other hand.

Sitting position
All these exercises can be done in the sitting position.

Lying position
All these exercises can be done in the lying position.

D. Back

1. Stand with both arms raised. Now bend forward as far as you can go down. If you cannot bend anymore, start swinging your arms sideways and you will go down further. Hold for the count of three. When you come up, first lift your head up, and then arch your back as if you are coming out of the water. Now come up with your arms up. People who are doing this initially are advised to hold a table or wall with one hand and bend forward with the other arm stretched out.

2. Stand with your right arm raised. Now bend as far to the left as you can. Your left hand should get as close to the left knee as possible. Repeat seven times. Repeat on the other side.

3. Put your hands on the waist. Do not move your hips. Turn to the left as far as you can, looking over your left shoulder. Come back to the midline. Now turn to the right. Repeat seven times. This exercise is best done in the sitting position. It cannot be done in the lying position.

Sitting position
All these exercises can be done in the sitting position.
No. 1 can be done sitting on your knees.
No. 2 can be done sitting and bending sideways until your elbow touches the bed.

Lying position
Exercise 1 can be done while lying on your side.
Exercise 2 can be done while lying on your back.
Exercise 3 cannot be done in the lying position.

E. Stomach

1. Stand with your arms raised up. Slightly spread your feet. Touch your left foot (or as close to it as possible) with your right hand. Do it seven times. Then touch your right foot with your left hand.

2. Lie on your back, knees bent and feet on the floor. Bend forward and touch your knees with your hands. Hold for the count of seven. See if you can advance to the next exercise.

3. lie on your back. Keep your hands behind your head. Bend your left knee. Touch your left knee with your right elbow and vice versa.

Exercise no. 1 cannot be done in the sitting or lying position.

F. Hips

1. Hold the table and squat and stand up. When you advance, keep your arms crossed across your chest as you do this without support.

The following exercises for the hips are best done in the lying position.

2.Lie down on your back. Lift your left leg as high as you can. Hold it for the count of seven seconds. Bring it down. Alternate with your other leg.

3. Lie on your left side. Lift your right leg up as high as you can with the knee straight. Hold for the count of seven. Bring it down and rest for the count of three. Repeat seven times. Turn and lie on your right side and repeat with your left leg.

4. Lie on your stomach. Keep your knees straight. Lift your left leg up. Hold for the count of seven seconds. Repeat seven times. Repeat on the right side.

5. Lie on your back. Keep your left leg straight on the floor. Bend the right knee and place the foot on the floor. Bend the knee inward seven times. Then put the bent right knee outward on the floor in a froglike position seven times.

G. Knees

1.Squat and stand up seven times.

2.Stand on your toes and then on your heels seven times.

3. Stand with your feet apart. Now shift your weight to the left, bending your left knee sideways. Come back to midline. Do this on the right leg. Come to midline. Repeat seven times.

4. Hold the wall in front of you with both hands. Keep one leg in front and bend it slightly. Keep the leg behind straight. Now move your weight forward, bending the front knee and keeping the back knee extended. Release and repeat. Do this on other side.

5. Stand. Bring your right foot up behind you, as close to your right buttock as possible. Repeat seven times. Do this on the other side.

6. Sit on a chair and stand with your arms crossed across your chest. If you cannot do so, hold onto the arms of a chair and stand and sit.

7. Sit on a chair. Bring your left foot up and place it on the chair near your left buttock. Put your foot back on the floor. Repeat seven times. Do this on the other side.

8. Sit on the chair. Hold your left leg out in front of you with the knee straight out. Hold for the count of seven. Put the leg down. Repeat seven times. Repeat on the right side.

9. Lie on your back. Hold your left knee with both hands and bring your knee to your chest. Straighten your leg. Repeat seven times. Do this on your right side.

10. Lie on your back. Keep your left foot on the floor with the knee bent. Slide your foot as close to the buttock as you can. Straighten your left knee. Now repeat with your right foot.

11. Lie on your stomach and bend your left knee until the heel touches your buttock or is close to it. Keep the right leg straight on the floor. Reverse this. Repeat seven times.

Exercises 1–4 can only be done standing.
Exercise 5 becomes 11 when lying down.
Exercise 7 becomes 10 when lying down.

You can do an exercise similar to no.4 by getting on your hands and knees and shifting forward and back.

Exercise 8 can be done lying down by being on your back and raising your left leg up in air with your knee straight and counting to seven. Repeat on the other side.

H. ANKLES
1.Stand on your toes and heels alternately.
2.Sit and rotate your ankles first clockwise seven times and then anticlockwise seven times. This exercise can be done in both sitting and lying positions.

Chapter 3.   YOU DO NOT LIKE TO EAT

Saying that you do not like to eat is the same as saying that you do not like to fill your car with gas/petrol. Your vomiting after eating is the same as putting gas in the car and then removing it. How do you expect the car to run? The car may conk out. How do you expect to function?

Your brain cannot live without oxygen for four minutes. It gets damaged. The brain also needs food to function. Prolonged food insufficiency causes a decrease in your reasoning and logic. It also lowers resistance to illness. It can also hasten your departure from this world. When you have insufficient food (perhaps as you deliberately wish to declare war on your body), you will become irritable and unable to concentrate. Your interpersonal skills will suffer. Your body is sending frantic signals that all is not well and is hoping against hope that you are not too dumb to ignore them. It is trying to warn you that by staying thin, things will not get better.

An immature person hates his body because he is too thin, too fat, too short, or too tall. He will do things to the extreme. He will spend hours exercising or not eating. This obsession with his body will take over all the signs of an addiction. His personal life and family life will suffer as he turns into an awful person.
An immature person focuses on his body in order to make up for the lack of a personality, or because he has an inferiority complex, or he knows only this way to handle life. A person who is bulimic hates either his body or his mind.
But no one has ever liked a person because she is size six.

An immature person has no map for the road of life.

A mature person is comfortable with his body and himself. This is because he is not lost. He has found his map for the road of life. He will stay healthy. A mature person knows that the first thing that matters is character with honesty toward oneself. It means sitting down and considering whether what one considers important is really important. The mature person always wants to be at his physical, emotional, mental, and spiritual best.

This he will achieve:
by getting adequate sleep;
through self-discipline;
by getting up early at a fixed time;
by maintaining adequate food intake;
by making sure he gets breakfast every day to neutralize the twelve-hour buildup of acidity in his stomach;
by seeing that meals do not consist of fortified milkshakes but are food with grains, vegetables, and fruits, and should be eaten three times a day;
by having a snack between lunch and dinner;
by exercising three times a week;
by taking time to rest in the day;
by meditating;
by taking a break from work at lunch;
by praying every morning and so charging his/her batteries;
by balancing his life between work, study, family and friends and
by becoming a nice person for his family to be with.

Please note that you cannot be a good friend if you are not first a good person to be around with your family. You will never be happy. This is because good manners start at home and then progress outward.

So, take the first step toward maturity. Be friends with your body. Be comfortable with who you are. Make your aim to be healthy instead of being thin. Do not try to be what others are. Forgive yourself if you make a mistake. Do penance by helping others. Focus on others instead of yourself. You would not worry about what others think of you if you knew that they were too busy with their own insecurities to think of you.

Any therapy that does not include advice is not therapy. Even a friend who listens to your problems will try to guide you.

Chapter 4.   WE ARE EQUAL

A white horse is not considered superior to a black horse. We judge it by its other qualities.

A white rose is not superior to a red rose in our eyes.

Yet one man was considered to be superior to another merely by the color of his skin!

Think of the horrible cruelty performed throughout history based on this twisted logic!

And we call ourselves intelligent beings!

By kindergarten, and throughout every grade after that, it should be mandatory to teach children that people look different, but that "different" does not mean inferior.

As a doctor, I can tell you that when we operate on black, brown, or white people, we find that underneath the skin, everything is of the same color!
If the brain is gray in a white person, it is gray in a black person. If the liver is brown in the Brahman, it is brown in the untouchable. The heart and blood is of a red color in the white, brown, and black people. Everything beneath the skin is of the same color and same number: the muscles! the nerves! the bones! the organs!

Also similar are the intelligence, the emotions, and the hopes and fears!

Is it not then crazy that genocide has been committed simply over the color of the skin, or that we hold our superiority because of the color of our hair or eyes?

We would never say that a brown horse is superior to a white horse or that a red rose is superior to a yellow one. Yet, we have applied this insane logic to mankind and have committed unbelievable acts of cruelty and slavery because of it.

If all you learn in life is that people who look different are equal, you are ahead of a vast number of people.

Respect people who look different. Open your heart and homes to them, and you will be blessed. Do not make fun of someone who has difficulty speaking your language until you master his.

Respect someone who has a different religion. All religions lead to the same God just as all sunlight leads to the same sun.

Do not kill over religion. You insult your God.

Never consider a human untouchable. You damn your soul.

Never consider yourself as belonging to a superior race. You damn your race.

If someone in your group hurts another because of his different looks or beliefs, it becomes the responsibility of everyone in your group to make restitution to the people hurt. If you cannot find the people affected, make restitution to other people of their race in their name. But restitution has to be only in the amount to help him recover from his physical wounds or to be resettled. If someone was killed then the restitution has to be to help his family survive until the children can grow up to be bread winners as well as to fix a pension plan in his name . If however whole towns are wiped out, then the only restitution you can do is to help build up an industry or a town. However this cannot be done if the race that was hurt then starts afflicting others.

The only way you, the soul, can advance is when you regard yourself as an equal member of the human race. You are here on this earth to advance. Do not make this birth unproductive.

Chapter 5.   WHY SHOULD YOU SPEAK THE TRUTH

You should speak the truth because:

When you lie, you acknowledge that you are scared of the other person, and so that makes you weak.

When you lie, you usually have to add more lies. That can lead to chaos in your personal life. To handle this chaos, you spend unnecessary energy and so become weak. As you use up this extra energy to do so, you become nervous, irritable, and frustrated and become weak. Your personality becomes fragmented.

Your brain, like the computer, is used to storing information as facts. By constantly changing a fact that the brain knows and by asking it to speak something else, you need to add extra memory space. For this, it needs additional energy. So, you become weak. It is as if you tell your computer that the color of your hair is red. Now to send that information to someone, all you have to tell the computer is to forward it. But if you want to lie to someone, you will have to spend extra work telling the computer that this person must be told that your hair is black.

When you lie, you are not proud of yourself, and that makes you weak.

Should you lie if a person's life is at stake? If the person has not hurt humanity, the answer is yes. This is because a higher morality steps in. This is why you should always listen to your conscience. Other than that, you should speak the truth.

By stating a fact, you can look at the person in the eyes. You have nothing to hide, so you do not lose energy. You stay strong. You need courage to tell the truth sometimes as you may have to face displeasure or painful consequences. But courage does develop.

When you tell the truth, you get the trust and respect of your fellow men. A man is to be respected by his moral stature and never by the money he makes.

By telling the truth, you attract people who are also thinking the truth, and you can set into motion a force that no army can withstand. Gandhi practiced truth and freed his nation. Mandela refused to tell a lie in order to get out of prison. The result was that a country became free and these people became giants.

You do not say, " It is not that I wanted to lie. It is just that I could not bear to tell you the truth. I thought I would lose you or cause you pain etc". The fact remains that you showed things to appear, as they were not. Thus, you are a liar, and a cheat, and you have betrayed someone's trust. Your character does not deserve to be treated with love or respect. A trust once broken, even in the name of love, can never be regained.

What would you rather have, a man or a woman who loved you but was a cheat or a person who was so honest that you had nothing but admiration and pride for him/her? Remember that a man or woman who lies or cheat once will do it again. You should look for a person who sticks to his/her principles regardless of the consequences.

You may be the richest person in the world, but if you are living a lie, you will feel trapped. That is why Christ said that the truth will set you free.

Our spirituality can only be aroused when we are not hypocrites.

When we tell the truth, it is the first step to getting in touch with our inner self and making contact with God.

Chapter 6.   PRAYER

Prayer strengthens the spirit and allows it to carry on in discouragement, and suffering. It gives hope. It makes tranquilizers and antidepressants unnecessary.

It gives peace. It gives you great power. But, to receive this power, you must not lie, cheat or harm others. You must help others, because only then is your hand open to receive.

But there are people who do great wrong and yet pray daily? They do not pray. They just mechanically repeat sentences. They have shut out their conscience.

In order to pray you cannot hurt or kill innocent people because you want a better race, because you feel superior to them, because you want to do it in the name of your religion, or just because you want to exterminate them.

You cannot pray if you hurt people because they have a different color, language, religion, or culture.

You cannot pray if you harm persons or beings dependent on you.

You cannot pray if you torture or kill animals for sport or experimentation.

You cannot pray if you torture children, or bring them suffering.

You cannot pray if you lie, or cheat others.

You cannot pray if you sacrifice animals in the name of religion.

Your prayer will not be heard.

Cruelty and Bigotry cannot coexist with prayer.

There is a prayer when you speak and there is a prayer where you listen and receive your power. You do not have other thoughts then.

Pray twice a day, morning and evening. Bow with respect before and after you pray.

All religion leads to one God. When people differ from this, it is as if each person is proclaiming that the sunshine in his house is the original sun. He does not realize that the sunshine in all the different houses comes from the same sun. If you pray to "your God", you prayer will still be heard, just like all the sunshine leads to the same sun.

Someday there will be temples with different sides representing different religions, but the center will be empty to represent one God.

If you do something wrong or hurt someone, you should do penance before you pray; or as you pray, you must agree to do restitution and penance. If you cannot make up to the same person, find a person in similar circumstances. Hear his pain caused by actions like yours. Help him/her. If you cannot do so, make restitution to the community in cash or kind.

Pray every morning before you start your day:
Our Father, Hallowed be Your name.
I stand before You and thank You for what I have.
I shall not hurt nor torture living beings.
I shall not hurt, nor kill, in the name of color, race or religion.
Give me intelligence, and the knowledge of right from wrong.
Help me to Care, Share, and be absolutely Fair.
Help me to conquer Anger, Greed, Lust, and Fear: fear of pain, fear of failure, fear of rejection, fear of death, and fear of life.
Help me to practice Truth and Justice. Give me Strength and Courage.
Give me Hope and Faith: faith that no matter how I suffer I do not lose my moral values, faith that I can present my suffering

for the betterment of someone else, faith that You will always hold my hand.
Help me to show Love and Compassion to those less fortunate and release the Joy and Peace within me.

You can use any prayer you are fond of.

Another prayer is:
Oh God, Who is my father, my creator, my caretaker.
I greet you with deep reverence.
You are Truth,
You bring light into the darkness of my mind,
I worship your true form, whatever it is,
Take my mind and put it on the right path.

There is a prayer where you ask for inner joy, intelligence, peace, power and strength. Read the prayer of the highest development in "What makes a good human being?" in *life Skills*.

Sit silent for a few moments. Be still to be connected. Do not think of other things .
How do you keep your mind free from thoughts? By focusing on your breath.

Speak of the Lord with respect. Do not use His name frivolously.

Spirituality is the path of the soul to God. It is not doing whatever makes you feel good. It is achieved by self-discipline, by following moral laws, by meditation and by prayer.

Pray twice a day, morning and evening at the same time. A child by one year of age should sit, stand or kneel with you in prayer. See the prayer of a small child. Bow with respect before and after you pray. Do not pray only when you need something or are in trouble. Why should He listen to you then? Do not put conditions in your prayer.

God is not deaf. Your prayer must be done quietly. It should never be done over loudspeakers. Your prayer should never disturb another person's rest.

Pray daily. It prevents panic attacks; give clarity of thought and peace. It is your pipeline to strength, courage, faith and hope.

You do not leave home without charging your cell- phone, why not yourself?
A bulb has to be connected to a power source in order to light up. The stronger the voltage, the brighter it burns. The more resistance to it, the less the power. Has anyone seen electricity? No. We can only see the effects of electricity. For a very long time no one even knew electricity existed. The more resistance you offer to God,, the less is the flow of power from God to you. Anger, hatred, greed, cruelty, selfishness, lust and deceit cause great resistance to the flow. We have to be connected to get out inner energy, our inner strength. The more we are connected, the more inner strength we have. We have all seen people with more force, and ones with hardly any. It is up to you to make the connection.

A man without this connection has a very high chance of:
just existing,
being depressed,
feeling helpless and
being immoral.

A prayer has to come from a sincere heart in order to be heard. Like electricity, it has to be insulated. It has to be insulated from anger, hatred, greed, cruelty, selfishness, lust and deceit.

A prayer has to be in a language that we can understand.

Pray together at least once a month in your churches, temples and synagogues.

There can be no alcohol or drugs in religion because religion demands complete clarity of mind.
There can be no slaughter in religion because religion demands that we respect all living things.
There can be no free sex in religion because religion demands morality, decency, and self- control in order to reach God.
There can be no wars, nor cruelty, nor hatred in the name of religion, because religion preaches compassion and love.

Respect all religions.

Understand that most of your pain is inflicted by man and not God . So, do not say, "God, why are You doing this to me." He is not. But God can give you the strength to bear the pain. However, you have to ask for help.

Understand that the bad times teach us, but the good times test us. But we must be open and ask, "What can I learn from this". If you have pain in your heart from your past, you cannot drown it in drugs or alcohol, even though you try for years. But you can ease it by reaching out to others with a helping hand and then praying.

You do not have to stand in lines for hours to see His picture. That is just His picture. God is everywhere.

You do not dress and undress idols and say you took care of God. You can only reach Him by praying to Him and doing service to others in His name.

You do not have to pray to His messenger. You can pray to Him directly

Remember that to hurt or kill in the name of color or religion is the lowest kind of depravity. To be silent while others do so is sinful.

While the State can separate itself from religion, it must not remove prayer and morality. Removing prayer leads to the formation of an immoral society with self-destructive behavior. What prayer should be used in school? The prayer that was used for the longest time with the universal name of God in the prevailing language of the school.

All the five religions should be described in school.

Take time in the day to admire what God has created.
Do a good deed frequently in cash, or kind, in the name of God. It will come back to you.

The highest faith is interfaith and the highest spiritual act you can do is to help someone of another faith.

You are a soul in a body, and not a body having a soul. You are here for a limited time to see how much you, the soul, can develop. This can only be done by listening to your conscience and by doing the right things. It is by being completely honest, moral, decent, courageous and compassionate to all living things. You will be ultimately judged only by your greed, cruelty and immorality.

Of what good is your beautiful house if you care not about the welfare of animals, your neighbors and your environment? You might as well be a mummy in a beautiful museum.

One does not just exist. One forms beliefs to guide one through life; and your beliefs should be: honesty, morality, modesty, decency, courage and compassion.

Do not tolerate leaders who accept immorality, immodesty and indecency in the name of broadmindedness or progressive thinking. These are leaders who are too weak to stand for what is right, or too greedy filling their pockets.

Do not ever say that we must follow the laws even if they are wrong. According to this logic, not one of Hitler's men did anything wrong because he was " following the laws' of his time. According to this logic, people could still be slaves or be fed to the lions, as those were the laws of that time. The tax on tea put by the British in Boston should have been right because the British were the government at that time.

History has shown us, that in every country, unfair and immoral laws were made by people in power. It takes courage to speak out against a law when it is wrong.

History has shown us, again and again, that it was only because of the few courageous people, who spoke out against the immoral and unjust laws, that wrongs could be righted. Laws are often made by people with personal insecurities and bias, who blindly make a law because of some loopholes or because of pressure of personal gain or from powerful industries.

THE FIRST RULE FOR A LAW IS THAT IT MUST BE MORAL AND BENFIT PEOPLE, CHILDREN AND THE ANIMALS.

ABOVE ALL LAWS ARE THE LAWS OF YOUR CONSCIENCE, MORALITY AND COMMON SENSE.

Chapter 7.   THE PRAYER FOR MY CHILDREN

Though my children come through me,
they are not of me.
I take care of them in Your name.
I do nothing to them, which would make me feel ashamed in
front of You.

They, each, come with their own bags
of happiness and sorrow;
of destiny and life span.

I thank You for my
time given with them,
and now I leave them
at Your feet.

PRAYER OF A SMALL CHILD

Dear God,

Please help me to share my toys and things.
Please help me to care, share and be fair.
And if things do not go my way, please help me to handle it
well.
And fix my boo boos. Amen

Be silent for a moment to say anything in private.

Chapter 8.   DO YOU HAVE A RIGHT TO MAKE MISTAKES?

"I made a mistake. I have a right to do so. I am human". Only a fool will whine that he has a right to make mistakes. Or, it will be the cunning person who wants your permission to keep making mistakes and ruining your life. This includes the politician.

The person who states that he has a right to make mistakes does not want to learn.
He or she does not want to be scolded nor punished when he does something wrong.
But mistakes cause pain to oneself and others. Life is too short to have so much pain. You have no right to have others suffer from your mistakes.

When you say that you have a right to make a mistake, it is as if you are saying that you have a right to walk blindfolded and keep falling, while all along, the rest of us had the ability to remove your blindfold and prevent you from breaking your hip. All the energy you used to keep guessing where to put your next step while walking blindfolded could have been used in things that are so much more important!
Do you call that being intelligent?

You have no "right" to make mistakes. You only have the right to make as few mistakes as possible, and to be ashamed of them when they occur. It is one's duty to get as much information as possible and listen to as much advice on the subject as possible. Only when there was no information available and one took the best possible course of action that could be taken, should a mistake be condoned.
Even then, penance must be done.

The wise person knows that mistakes cause pain to oneself. What is worse, our mistakes cause needless pain to others. Mistakes ruin relationships, careers and businesses. They can cause loss of love, trust, respect, money and life. The wise man does not want this. He wants minimum pain in his life. He does not want to waste his time reinventing the wheel. So, he will learn from the teachings of others. He will also learn from the mistakes of others. Thus he will minimize making his own.

With mistakes, there has to be accountability. If you made a mistake, you must be held accountable. You accept your responsibility, are ashamed and apologize. You resolve not to do it again and you try to mend what was damaged. You try to mend relationships. You accept the blame and the punishment. And you do penance. You make up for your actions.

But :
1. You do not fight back.

2. You do not lie. You do not tell the blamer that his accusation is not true when it is. You are honorable when you admit honestly that you did what you did. The other person begins to admire your courage and honesty.

3. You do not tell the accuser that it is all his fault: if only he " was a different person, had behaved otherwise, was there when you needed someone, gave you the freedom needed, had not upset you the way he did" etc, this would not have happened. This is nonsense! You alone are responsible for what you did. There will be no passing of blame. This type of philosophy should be banned from being shown on the soap-operas.

4. You do not say that you are human and have a right to make mistakes.

5.You do not blame the accuser for reacting the way he is toward your action,
" Why are you making a big deal about it? Why do you over-react? Why do you walk away? So I made a mistake!" This is a sign of being manipulative.

He is reacting the right way. A human being reacts the right way from inside. He has a right to be hurt, shocked, insulted, cheated and outraged. You are compounding your mistake by telling him that he is too unintelligent to react the right way. It is you, who is not handling your mistake honorably. It is you, who is destroying this relationship and is going to lose him. These are the sure ways of losing other people's love, trust and respect.

Never lie.
Never counter- attack when you are accused.
Never blame the other person for reacting the way he is.
These are the signs of a selfish, manipulative person.

If you did something that he is accusing you of, but you are hotly denying it , that does not change the fact that:
1.you are lying and
2.that you believe that he/she is stupid enough to fall for it.
Do you think that the other person does not realize that? Do you think that he is going to like you on either ground? It is the person who is honest who can still save the relationship.

If you say that it is he/she who makes things unpleasant, or being with him is unpleasant, or what he does is unpleasant, then you have just attacked his personality on unjustifiable grounds. Why would he ever want to be with you? You are going to lose a relationship

You are forced to go on a trip with someone and you threaten that you will make it unpleasant because you are going against your will. That makes you inhuman.

If a person agrees to your compromise of a trip for only two weeks from the original three, and you immediately ask it to be cut down to one week, then you do not want compromise, you want power. You have shown that you are unethical. The ethical person will stop when he gets what he bargained for and not see if he can push one further.

If you later meet him and act as if you do not understand what happened and you thought you were going on the trip for the two weeks, that makes you a hypocrite and manipulative. Why should you be surprised that he leaves you? There is nothing honorable in your character.

The honorable person will agree to the invitation without a fuss, request if it could be cut down to two weeks, thank the person and resolve to make it a pleasant trip for both. This is acting as an adult.

If a past mistake is being mentioned, you do not say, "the deed is done. I cannot undo it, so why talk about it". It is important that the past is brought up to show a pattern. What you have to say is, "I am sorry. It shall not happen again".

Understand that this is not a battleground where you are trying to save yourself from an attack. You are trying to develop into a better person and are correcting your flaws. It is the person with an inferiority complex who considers it a personal attack if his mistake is pointed out.

You do not say, "Well, you behave like you are telling me to. I will not change". If you have decided to continue behaving as you did, then you are responsible for the consequences and deserve them.

Never act with your parents as if they are your equals. Never fight them on equal grounds. There are things that they can see that you do not have the maturity to even understand right now. If your parent says that he/ she wishes you were dead, do not go around telling others how shocked you are at your parent's cruelty. We all know that you did something to pull that anguished cry from your parent's heart.

You never blame your past or how you were brought up as an excuse for your present sins. Many people all over the world have been brought up in far more horrifying situations than yours, and have still emerged decent, honest and honorable. Go to the third world countries and you will find honesty and nobility even among the begging lepers.

Your past does not affect your present unless you decide so and unless you wish to use it as a crutch. A leader should never try to hide behind that excuse if he does not want to earn the contempt of others.

You do not say " I need therapy in order to find out why I acted as I did." This is a cop out. You are not a puppet that is being pulled by mysterious strings.

After the age of eighteen years, a man or a woman is responsible for his/her actions. He acts, having decided to give in to his greed, lust, addiction, dishonesty or cruelty. He, and not his past, is responsible for every step he takes. His conscience is with him at every step. He actively chooses not to listen to it. The fact that he is contrite only when he is caught speaks volume towards his guilt.

Are you going to tell God " I need therapy to know why I sinned "? God is going to tell you that the excuse is not acceptable. He gave you a brain and will power. And he made you accountable.

You do not say, "I was a victim". You are not a victim if you are over eighteen, if you could walk away, if you could pick up the telephone and call, and if you are not mentally retarded. You cannot hide your guilt behind this sentence.

You do not say that you made a mistake because you were struggling with your identity. There is never an identity crisis. You are who you are as a worker, as a spouse, as a child, as a parent and as a citizen. All this contributes to your identity and determines who you are. Your identity is not determined by a place.

What you are struggling with is your conscience as you chose to prefer a deviation as a source of pleasure and entertainment. There is nothing admirable about that. What you chose as entertainment is not your identity.

When you are caught, or if you happen to get the morality to stop your sin, you need to act like a decent person and:

1. Acknowledge that you made a mistake/sinned.
2. Accept responsibility for your mistake/sin.
3. Be ashamed.
4. Apologize.
5. Accept punishment.

If no punishment is offered,

1. You must make restitution to those hurt.
2. You must do penance.
3. If you hold a position, you must resign that very minute. You do not resign a few weeks or month down the road. You cannot

be allowed to make or pass any more rules or laws. You lose all rights to any privileges.

If you are over eighteen you must do penance. Giving up something you do not like, or doing something you want to do, is not penance. It is hypocrisy.

Penance is achieved:
by doing something you do not like, or
by giving up something you like, or
by doing service to community.

At home, you can:
Take over house work for the next few weeks,
take care of people beyond your time allotment,
stop watching television for a week or so,
give up a favorite activity,
give up a favorite food for some months,
meditate,
help someone,
do community service,
fast for a day per week for so many weeks,
and do this with humility.

If you are a politician or hold a high/public office and made a mistake, you must resign immediately. Do not wait even for a day. Your mistake is more grievous.
This is because:
your mistake affects a large number of people.
Secondly, it is a betrayal of the people's trust in you.
Thirdly, your actions influence many people who may want to imitate you.
Do not compound your mistakes by struggling to stay on. That shows your greed for power.

You must make a public acknowledgement.

You must privately pray for forgiveness.

You must help those wronged. If you cannot help those wronged because they are gone, you must help those in similar situations.

You must do six months of work divided between three months for animal welfare and three months of community work.

If you have wronged society and are a public figure, you must pay a fine towards charity. Half of whatever money you make on your books must go towards charity.

You cannot hold a public position for five years.

Chapter 9.   SHOULD YOU TAKE TIME OFF TO FIND YOUR SELF?

The only person who would take time off to find himself is one who is lost.

The only person who is lost is one who has no map for the road of life. It has to be the person who has had no development, or who does not have any faith or religion. He does not know what his beliefs and values are or what rudder he should use to cross the channel of life.

You do not find yourself by climbing mountains, crossing rivers, traveling to countries or taking risks.
You do not find yourself by going away from home and living by yourself. The movies are lies.
You do not find yourself by neglecting your duty to your parents and family. In fact, it is only by staying with them and doing your duty; by learning from their experiences and wisdom; by controlling your impulses and desires; by going to your religious books for wisdom; by asking the wise people questions, and pondering over answers, that you " find yourself" –what your faith is, what your values should be, what your goals should be, what you should and should not tolerate, what should be your foundation as a human being, socially, financially and spiritually. It is by doing self-study at the end of the day, and the week, and by asking that you did the right thing that the answers come into the mind.

You run looking for the kingdom when the kingdom is within you. Every religion gives you very clear cut guidelines, defining who you are, why you are here, what is the purpose of life, what should be your moral values and goals, and how you should get your power regenerated. So, for you to say that you are lost is like a person standing in the middle of water and saying he is thirsty.

The person with faith, beliefs, moral values, character and goals knows how to behave in any situation. This is why religion and prayer has to be taught side by side with education so that a person does not suddenly stop and decide that what he is learning has no bearing on how he should behave in life, and that he is still empty and depressed. So, he has to take off valuable time off to look for the answers that he should have known at a much younger age.

Go to the chapter on "where is your map for the road of life" and "what makes a good human being". Go to your religious books and you will find your way.

Chapter 10.   WHERE IS YOUR MAP FOR THE ROAD OF LIFE?

You would not travel in an unknown territory without a map. You certainly need one for the road of life. It is important that you write it down and study it. Your map eventually determines your character.

Your map should have the following:
1. Your "self-worth".
How important do you think you are? Your self-worth should never depend on the size of your chest or the shape of your thighs. Your self-worth depends on the inner you. You are made by God. This alone makes you a highly valuable being. If you have patience and are caring, if you are fair, if you are moral, if you are helpful, and if you are responsible, then you are invaluable.

Once you realize your worth, you will not listen when people tell you that you are stupid or no good. You will not accept abuse. You will demand to be treated with respect or will leave a relationship. But if you have low self-esteem, people will abuse you and you will have a life filled with pain.

You should realize that you are complete in yourself and therefore are not scared of living alone. You do not become complete in a relationship. You only share your whole self in a relationship.

2. Your "source of power".
You would not leave home without charging your cell phone. Why not charge yourself with a prayer to God? It is better than any anti-anxiety medication, tranquilizers, or antidepressants. It is a great source of strength. It helps you handle panic attacks.

It prevents you from making mistakes. Pray twice daily. Also, get strength from religious books.

3. How much "you value your health and brain".
If you are concerned about being optimally fit, you will eat the right food, take the right meals and do the necessary exercises. You will stay away from addiction. You will not eat too much or too little.

4. Your "education".
This will determine how you will support yourself. Even if you just want to get married, you must be able to support the family in case your husband falls ill. So, you will have to decide what sort of education you should have.

5. Your "values and beliefs".
This includes your sense of what is right and wrong. Read the chapter "What Makes a Good Human Being" in *Life Skills*.
What are your fundamental beliefs?
What line of morality will you refuse to cross?

Your values should require that:
You will speak the truth, You will be honest.
You will keep your word.
You will be courteous.
You will not throw pearls before people who will not appreciate them.
You will offer excellence.
You will be cheerful.
You will dress well and live in neat surroundings.
You will be alert if something puzzles you or makes no sense.
You will not waste your love on those who do not value it.
You will not flit from man to man, or woman to woman, but will choose your mate carefully.
You will not live where you are not respected.

You will not be lazy.

You will support yourself. After twenty-three years of age, you will not take money from your parents to live. Once earning, you will give your parents money instead.

You will offer your parents home in their need and in their old age.

You will be the same in good and bad times. Understand that it is the weak character that becomes cruel and obnoxious when he feels powerful, but polite and depressed when the chips are down.

You will conquer anger and fear.

You will believe that true power is not had by demeaning others, by controlling others, by manipulating them or by having wealth.

True power comes from having no fear and being calm inside.

You will care, share, and be fair to humans and animals.

You will live to your highest physical, mental, emotional, and spiritual level.

You will practice modesty, decency, and morality; and

You will do balancing.

You will balance:

your education, with physical development,

your education, with spiritual development,

your education, with "life skills" (these teach mental and emotional development as well),

your education, with home skills (cooking, cleaning, sewing, repair, neatness, organization and child care),

your education, with skills of self-defense,

your study with recreation,

your recreation with friends, to recreation with family,

your social skills with friends, to social skills with family,

your work, with your family life,

your duty toward your work, with your duty toward your parents, siblings, spouse and children.

All these are your values and beliefs.

6a. Your "social support" in terms of relatives and friends and what good terms you keep with them. Or are you going to be antisocial?

6b. Your aim to be "involved in social causes".
Will you allow your leaders to practice injustice, immorality, and destroy family values and decency in the name of freedom?
Will you allow your leaders to take God away from society or prayers from school?
Will you allow schools to teach alternate lifestyles to your children?

7. Your "sources of strength" that will keep you away from antidepressants:
your character, your beliefs, your prayer, your religion, and your God.

Chapter 11. FUNDAMENTAL BELIEFS

The highest faith is to respect all faiths.

The highest love is to be able to love people who are different from you in color, race, caste or creed.

Conquer anger, greed and cruelty to all living beings.

Make sure that the animals on our planet are treated fairly and humanely. Join an animal welfare organization.

Care, share and be absolutely fair.

Practice modesty, decency and morality.

Know that a man must be valued by his moral stature and wisdom, and never by the money he makes.

Ultimately, man will be judged by his greed, cruelty and immorality.

These beliefs should be taught in every home and school.

Chapter 12.   BEING BROADMINDED

"The greatest thing a democracy has to fear is licentiousness".

To allow anything, the society must follow one rule:
"It shall do no harm to our children, our women, our society and our moral development".

It is for this reason that for centuries, society emphasized modesty, decency and morality. Today our leaders have closed their eyes and are breaking every rule themselves. The price we are paying in terms of attacks, rapes and "family pain" is awful.

Broadmindedness does not mean that you remove the word modesty, decency and morality from the dictionary and from your life.

Broadmindedness does not mean that women can greet men by embracing them.

Being broadminded does not mean that you can be immodest in speech, clothing or action. It does not mean that your speech can include obscene languages involving bowel movements, sexuality or depravity.

Broadmindedness does not mean you crack indecent and sexual jokes around the house, or allow sexual magazines to be read.

Broadmindedness does not mean that you can wear immodest clothes revealing your breasts, cleavage, buttocks, cleft or any part of genitalia, or that you can walk around in your bras and panties.

Broadmindedness does not mean that you perform suggestive or provocative dances.

Broadmindedness does not mean that you can show nudity, sexuality or obscenity in magazines, shows or movies

Broadmindedness does not mean that we allow drug companies to advertise products that affect sexuality, genital organs or menstrual periods on televisions, computers or magazines.

Broadmindedness does not mean that we display bras in open market.

Broadmindedness does not mean that we display contraceptives in open in stores.

Broadmindedness does not mean that talk shows should allow vulgarity, obscenity or discuss wife swapping, topics of sexual behavior or sexual jokes, topics about breasts, genitalia or arousal.

Broadmindedness does not mean that hotels, ships, planes, airports, transport stations and magazine stores can sell or display pictures, magazines, performances or movies that show nudity, sexual acts, sexual jokes or innuendoes, stories or pictures. They cannot have areas for nudity.

Broadmindedness does not mean that we display the titles of "sex" on our billboard magazines or pictures.

Broadmindedness does not mean that we allow public billboards advertising sex parlors or allow the parlors to exist within towns

Broadmindedness does not mean that schools and colleges should allow pornography, sexual acts or nudity in magazines, books or shows on campus in name of free speech. Education should always be taught in an atmosphere of restraint and morality.

Part of education is self- control of impulses and desires, restraint, self-discipline, decency, modesty and morality. What we teach and practice about morality, or the lack of it, will have a profound effect on society and on each one of us.

Just as you do not wish to allow drugs or hate- filled literature on campus, you do not allow nudity, sex or pornography. These are as addictive and as destructive to family and social life as drugs. Broadmindedness does not mean that we allow colleges or universities to teach our children immorality, sexuality or homosexuality. Such universities should be shut down.

No school should teach alternate lifestyles in the name of broadmindedness.

Broadmindedness does not mean that boys and girls should be allowed to occupy the same building for living quarters or dorms; or be allowed to stay out late with no check- in time at night. Every one of these rules was in effect in the fifties. Every one of the rules has been tossed aside in the name of broadmindedness.

Boys and girls must stay in separate buildings and visit each other only in visiting lounges, not in each other's room. There must be fixed times for them to be back in their buildings.

Broadmindedness does not mean that we allow swapping of wives or girlfriends. This is immoral.

Broadminded does not mean that we confuse nudity with art. Showing of genitals and breasts does not make a thing more beautiful. Those who say that it does are hiding the fact that it arouses their lust.

Broadmindedness does not mean that we allow pornography to be allowed into our country. Like drugs, it must be banned.

Broadmindedness does not mean that we forgive a person for his present sin because of the way he was raised in the past. All over the world, people have been brought up in much more horrific ways and yet have emerged decent and honorable. After eighteen years of age, it is your duty to listen to your conscience and be accountable for all your actions. Your brain has the power to chose right from wrong irrespective of your past life.

Broadmindedness does not mean that we forgive a person when he cries that he was the victim. You are not a victim if you are eighteen years of age and above, if you could have physically walked away, used a telephone and are not mentally retarded.

Being broadminded does not mean that we equate entertainment with sexual excitement or sensuality. Being broadminded does not mean that we take away the innocence of our children and youth.

Broadmindedness does not mean that we allow male nurses and male technicians to handle females. This violates the modesty of women. We have problems of male doctors molesting women. Think of the male nurses and technicians putting their hands on the private parts of women. The State must insist that women are only treated or tested by female attendants.

Broadmindedness does not mean that one accepts homosexuals, transvestites. pedophiles and people having sex with animals as normal. We do not permit this behavior in society.

Broadmindedness does not mean that we separate the personal life of a leader from his professional life. A leader has to set an example. What great men do, the masses will follow. Anyone in the public eye affects the public by each action of his, private and public. Therefore, a leader must be as clean in his personal life as he is in public.
The character of a public man is of profound importance.

What sort of madness is this, that in the name of broadmindedness
I should accept abnormal over what is normal?
I should accept immodesty over what is modest?
I should accept indecency over what is decent and
I should accept immorality over what is moral?

Broadmindedness does not mean that we can say that we will let immoral people live their lives and we will live ours.

With immorality, as with evil, you can never live and let live because immorality and evil will take over your society, your children, your homes and your lives.

Chapter 13. ADDICTION

Addiction is a situation :

In which you become a slave to your passion;

In which the more you have of something, the more you want;

In which you need a higher dose to get the same euphoric feeling;

In which your sense of right and wrong is destroyed, as is clarity of vision;

In which all sense of moral responsibility is lost;

In which others get hurt as selfishness, cruelty, and immorality creeps in;

In which the family is destroyed and society can be hurt; and

In which you are ultimately destroyed.

Medically, things give you a feeling of euphoria and ecstasy only by stimulating certain centers in your brain.
But these centers can be stimulated to a higher euphoric degree by a different way, a fact that every master- of- self knows.
But for this, you need self-discipline; you need self–control; you need to speak the truth; you need to give; you need to care, share and be absolutely fair; you need to meditate and you need a teacher.

Only by controlling your desires, can you achieve fulfillment of your desire for the ultimate happiness.

Chapter 14.   STRESS

Stress was present on the day the caveman walked out of his cave to hunt a dinosaur for lunch. He did not know if he would eat or be eaten. He did not sit down and cry that he had stress. He did not run to his doctor and said, "I have stress so I have all medical problems." He accepted his life and went and did what he had to do. That is probably why he survived.

All over the world people are hungry. Some are beggars . Some are lepers. Some fight famine and war . They do not know whether that they will live to see the next day. They do not cry they have stress. They do what they have to do under all that pressure but accept it as a way of life.

Yet, you in the developed world, you who have every amenity, you who have no famine and who takes luxuries as amenities, you cry the minute things are not what you want and say that you have stress.

Who told you that life would be a rose garden and that you would have a silver spoon in your mouth all the way? Have you forgotten that life comes with good times and bad times and that you get both as a package deal? So why do you accept one and not the other? You do not complain when you have the good time. Why do you complain when you get the next package?

Your ancestors crossed the prairies and fought a revolution without crying "stress"
Just because life is not what you want, just because you are studying, just because someone around you got sick or is dying, just because you have to take care of your children or have to meet a deadline does not mean that your body cannot handle it . Did it not handle it when the caveman went to hunt a dinosaur?

So please stop whining. Accept the fact that you have to undergo good times and bad times and that it is the wise person who can take the bad times with peace, with acceptance, with equanimity, as a challenge and as an unavoidable part of life. It is a sign of maturity and of good development of personality to be able to do so.

After all stress makes life worth living . Just ask any patient in a nursing home for the aged.

Chapter 15.   ANGER

Why should you control your temper?

Because when you are angry, you cannot be happy or have fun.

Because when you are angry, you cannot be friendly.

Because when you are angry, reasoning is lost. You cannot be logical. You cannot make the right decision.

Because when you are angry, you cannot be fair.

Because when you are angry, you cannot be compassionate.

Because anger can only provoke anger or fear in return, not understanding, and therefore this cannot solve problems.

Because when you are angry you may hurt someone, and consequentially, you may hurt yourself.

Because when you are angry, you lose your wisdom, and so ruin shall follow.

It is said in the holy books that a man who cannot control his anger is not a man. He is undeveloped and has no self-mastery. Therefore, he can never enter heaven.

Anger will occur if we have been treated unfairly, and only then is it correctly felt.

Anger will occur if we have done something wrong and we need excuses.

Anger will occur if we are tired or hungry.

Anger will occur if we feel that we have been slighted. But if we have good self-esteem, we would not be affronted easily.

Anger will occur when we are frustrated.

But frustration is part of life, and anger is not the correct response. One must know how to handle frustration and how to defuse the situation.

You do not have to release the anger in order to live well. You have to divert this energy into constructive channels instead of losing it. That is why people feel weak or depressed after they lose their temper.

Do not think that by showing your temper, you become a big man to be admired or impressed by. After all, anyone can be a loudmouthed, arrogant fool. You are to be pitied, because you are letting your emotion control you. Only a bully tries to control others through his temper. And a bully is only to be despised. A wiser man uses knowledge and communication instead. Things do not always have to be his way.

A wise man tries to handle the situation, not control it. He tries to defuse the situation, not ignite it. Being calm never means that you are meek or timid. The more self-esteem a person has, the more he can control his temper. It is a milestone in our spiritual progress. Temper and our other emotions (fear, cruelty, lust, greed, envy, etc.) are like wild horses trying to run amuck. The true "master" is one who has them under his control.

Show temper only to the degree needed.

People with a short fuse are very immature. They are also inconsiderate and cruel. They get upset over little things. Yet another man will let an elephant roll over him before he is perturbed. It shows the different stages of development. The second one also has a far happier life.

When you do not react with anger or fear to someone else's anger, you have progressed.

The movies teach you that the way to handle temper is:
to throw things;
to hit out at everything in sight and
to act calm to fool your victim and then explode in an outburst of cruelty;

The movies show that a macho man is the one who shows a terrible temper.
A macho man is one who looks calm, but burns inside and plot a deadly revenge.

This is true only if you want to ruin your life, peace and happiness.
This is true only if you want to ruin the lives of those you care for.
This is true only if you want to ruin your relationships.
This is true only if you want to end up in jail.

The man who is meek in front of his superiors but comes home to have everyone cower from his temper is nothing but a bully. When this person has to deal with a crisis, he is a coward.

Temper is good only when it raises a person or nation against what is wrong or unjust, and inflames one to correct it or to destroy some one evil.
Every time you get angry, you lose vital energy that you need to do things with or to concentrate by. When you lose your temper, you make mistakes and ruin relationships. You may simmer, scream, hit and murder.

In the brain, the anger center is a primitive one. Its job is to set an explosion in every direction so you cannot think straight.
But the higher centers in the brain can be trained to dampen this center.
You are not being told to hold your temper inside. You are being told to channel this energy and not lose it.

So, diffuse your temper at once using these methods:

a) Do not act immediately. Freeze. Picture your anger as a flame in your head. Picture yourself bringing it under control and extinguishing it. Do not move until you have done so and know that you are in control.

b) Move away immediately from the person who is making you violent, especially if it is a child or an animal or someone weaker. It could be as simple as putting the baby in a crib, where he cannot fall, and moving to another room for a few moments. Go to the bathroom and do ten pushups or watch the television for five minutes or look out of the window.

c) If the person arousing your anger is an adult, leave the house. Walk.
Do not drive. Run. Go look at the sky. Sit under a tree. Talk to someone about something else. Do something absorbing. Do not return until you are calm.

d) If you cannot get away physically because you are at work or at school, get away mentally. Think of other things. Do other things. Talk to people about other things. Read a paper. Go to the bathroom and do five pushups.

e) For a brief second, put yourself in the other person's shoes. Tell yourself that the other person may have a point or reason. Try to understand it. If he hurt you innocently, forget it.
Did he hurt you unthinkingly? Tell him that you are hurt. If he is genuinely sorry, forget it.
If he does not care that he hurt you, or if he says, "So what if I said it," you do not want to have anything to do with him. If you have to talk to him because of work or because he is a relative, treat him with cold politeness. If he is an immediate relative, tell him that you will not be abused.

f) If you are upset, do not enter your home until you have calmed down.

The second most important part of your life, your home life, is beginning. Do not ruin it.

g) If you are angry, make sure that your basic needs of food, rest or sleep are taken care of before you speak or act.
Make sure that you are not near your "victims" when you have taken drugs or alcohol, which lowers your threshold of irritability.

h) Do not get angry over little things. Keep your temper and your vital energy for big issues if you wish for wisdom and peace. Remember that after losing their tempers, people usually feel drained or depressed. This is because they have lost their energy.

i) Do not shout at your wife or children because your boss shouted at you or because you were frustrated at work. Never displace your anger. That is a sign of a bully.

J. If you have to react:
Keep your hands yourself. Act calm to be calm. Aim to become deliberately calm within five minutes by stopping all angry thoughts.

Take five deep breaths and then count to ten, before you open your mouth.

Keep a low voice. You do not have to shout to make a point.

State what is bothering you at that time and stop. Do not bring in anything else.

Your aim is not to show how angry you are, but to make sure this incident does not recur.

Hear the other person completely and quietly without planning your next sentence. Be quiet for another two minutes, as she may have to add some words.

If the discussion starts getting too volatile, postpone it. Say, "I am too upset to discuss it right now." After a few minutes of silence, start talking about something else. Return to this topic the next day.

Distract yourself. Your brain cannot hold two emotions at the same time.
Go for a walk. Do not drive.
Talk to someone else.
Read something entertaining.
Watch television
Play with someone.
Go and talk to a neighbor.
Do something absorbing and intricate.
Do exercises.

But:
1. You cannot hit any object around you.
2. You cannot hit any person.
3. You cannot call names or be verbally abusive.
4. You cannot counter-attack the person getting angry with you.
5. You cannot displace the anger at one person on another.
6. You cannot blame someone else for making you violent.
These are the six signs of a coward.

Never get angry because you assumed something or because someone incited you to. Check your facts first.

When two persons are fighting, they are in the midst of a battlefield and cannot see what is obvious to an observer outside the field.

So, go to an impartial outsider for advice.

There are times when you need to stay away from the person you are angry at for an indefinite period until raging emotions cool down and you can be rational again.

Do not allow your temper to make you resort to revenge tactics. Revenge will corrode your soul and turn you into a brooding monster. Your internal peace is far more important. Channel your energy.

Never make a decision in temper. First, take time to cool off.

Chapter 16.   WHAT IS CARING?

You are not a human being if you do not care about others.

Caring for others is one of the highest developments of a soul. Caring is not the love you feel for one man or woman. Caring is a way of your life with all living beings.

Caring is the opposite of selfishness. Some people are non-caring. They are monsters. They will bring pain to others and themselves.

Caring has to be taught by example by a powerful figure. When taught by a mother who has no importance in the family, it is taken as a sign of weakness.

You must teach your children caring everyday and see that they are doing acts of caring. You must correct them every time they become selfish. Caring starts at home, with your family, your parents, your spouse, your children, your pets, your relatives, your friends, and progresses, as you develop, to your neighbors, your society, the animals and the world.

Caring means that you can put your feelings aside for the feelings of others. Caring means that their pain becomes your pain, and you are happy in their happiness. You are caring when you worry about the welfare of others, their comforts, their rights and their happiness at the expense of your happiness if needed. You are also caring when you try to unite people and families instead of separating them.

But you do not allow them to abuse you. To care for someone who does not care about your welfare is inviting abuse.

You are caring when you keep quiet so others can study or rest.

You are caring when you stop watching your show so that others can watch theirs. Please note that all children should be taught that their shows must be stopped when an older person wishes to see his shows. This is how children learn good manners, self-control, respect and caring.

You are caring:

when you think of how others will worry about you and so give them, the information needed or keep your word,

when you worry how others will manage, be safe, live or handle illness,

when you take time off to be by your parents, siblings, relatives or friends' bedside in time of need and thus show your children what is truly important,

when you put other people's feelings before yours,

when you stop doing what causes pain to your loved ones,

when you do not do what you desperately want to do because you care to be moral, modest or decent,

when you cancel your program and stay home because people are ill so that you can give them water, food, sympathy, help or company,

when you give people water and food because they are unable to do so themselves,

when you get them groceries and medicines because they cannot,

when you take them to the doctor because they are unable to go alone,

when you help them to cross the road because they find it difficult,

when you carry the heavy load so they do not have to,

when you give the help someone needs even without being asked,

when you find a hurt animal and you take care of it,

when you find a person ill on the road and you take care of him and take him to hospital,

when you take care of your relatives when they are in hospital and take time off from work and school to do so,

when you risk your studies or a promotion in order to do so,

when you offer a portion of what you earn to your parents every month once you start earning,

when you take care of your parents,

when you offer your home to your parents when they are weak, ill, aged or in need,

when you offer your home to your relatives and friends in time of need,

when you share what you have,

when you give of your time and skills to help others and,

when you find people deprived from their rights, and you fight for them,

when you care that modesty, decency and morality are disappearing and bring them back,

when you acknowledge that the earth also belongs to the animals and you fight for their rights and

when you are concerned that your society is heading towards self-destruction and you try to turn it around.

Your parents gave you life. To break contact with them, to ignore them when they are ill, to not be by their bedside when they are in the hospital or undergoing an operation shows how selfish and inhuman you have become. Do not say that you have the responsibilities of your children. They are watching you and will do the same to you when your time comes. Your duty is to make arrangements for your children, or remove them from school and go be by your parents and take care of them. It is your duty to take leave from your work, and school, and be by your parent. Otherwise there is no person more selfish and non-caring than you.

To not make sure that your parent, divorced or otherwise, has money to take care of him or her in old age is to be selfish and inhuman. It is your duty to give them money and to offer your home for the rest of your parents' lives.

To quietly let one brother or sister financially and physically take care of your parent and to not do your share shows how selfish and inhuman you are.

To bring a child into this world and to not financially and physically take care of it , or to not give it your name shows how selfish and inhuman you are.

To see someone, or something, in trouble and to not reach out to help because you "do not wish to be involved" shows how selfish and inhuman you are.

You should have not been born. Rest assured that the later part of your life will be full of pain.

Chapter 17.   END OF THE WEEK CHECK LIST

1.Did I take care of my body with hygiene and exercises?

2.Did I keep my surroundings neat and organized?

3.Did I control the impulses and desires that come into my mind?

4. Did I practicing self-discipline physically and mentally? Did I get up at a fixed time? Did I exercise and meditate at fixed times? Did I fast once a week? Did I clean my surroundings before I go to bed? Did I finish what I start? Did I complete what needs to be done for that day? Did I take out my clothes for the next day?

5.Am I polishing my skills?

6.Did I care, share and was I fair?

7. Did I do my duty as a child, sibling, spouse, parent and citizen?

8. Was I decent, modest and moral?

9. Did I do balancing between my job, spouse, children, relatives and friends; or is one getting priority over others?

10. Did I value myself only if others like me? Do I run from men to men or women to women?

11. Did I treat my family, relatives, friends, neighbors and colleagues with courtesy, fairness and generosity?

12. Am I treated with respect and fairness? If not, what am I doing about it and why am I putting up with it? Why am I not leaving the people treating me so? Why am I not getting financially independent?

13.Am I making my financial foundation? Am I dependent on my parents to pay my bills? Why? Do I know what is in my bank this month? Do I write what I spend every day? Does my balance match what I have in my purse. Do I know how much I need to survive every month? How do I get this much? Do I know what I make? Is it enough to pay my monthly bills? If not what am I planning to do about it? Do I have savings to pay for six months if I am fired, or to pay for my illness or for old age?

14.Am I forming a social network of friends that will carry over in my old age and be my social foundation. Do I decide who I will meet each weekend?

15.Am I doing something about the welfare about the animals? Have I joined a group for this?

16.Am I doing something to protect my children from any immorality they are being taught in schools, television and computers.

Am I fighting against sexuality, homosexuality and pornography being taught in schools and colleges? Have I joined a union for this?

Am I fighting against the removal of God and prayer from school and public speech? Is this not interference of freedom of speech that I am not allow to speak or sing about God publicly? Yet I can curse God publicly! Have I joined a union to fight this?

(It is not enough to be good in your home if you do not fight the evils of your society).

17.Am I developing my spiritual foundation? Am I praying twice a day? Am I meditating? Am I removing the blocks to my spiritual progress?

Chapter 18.   HOW DOES ONE HANDLE, PAIN AND SORROW?

Do not be trapped by sorrow.
Read the chapter on frustration and depression in *Life skills*.

Fifty percent of the pain that we have is received by the decisions that we ourselves make, based on how we feel about life, about what we are taught or feel is right or important, about our values, about how scared we are from society.

We also have pain in empathy. This is from the pain of our loved ones as they suffer because of the decisions they make.

Forty percent of pain that we receive is by what others do to us in the name of cruelty, non- caring, greed, abuse, lust or selfishness.

These bad times are not given to us by God. Do not blame Him.
They are given to us by man. So, do not ask why He is hurting you. He is not. Do not say you are angry at the way He is making you suffer. He is not.
What God can give you is the strength to handle the bad times, provided you ask for it. He can help you grow stronger and overcome your afflictions or handle them with peace.

The other ten percent of pain that you have is the bag of sorrow that you come into the world with, together with your bag of happiness. Remember that your child too comes with his own bags of pain and happiness. Read "The Prayer for my children." This ten percent is to give you a chance to grow.

You do not take pills to handle depression. You do not go to therapy to handle this depression.

In the rest of the world people are struggling with poverty, tyranny, cruelty, wars, loss of loved ones and natural disasters. They do not take pills or therapy. Neither did your forefathers. And they had much more to handle than you.

The movies have taught you wrong. You do not blame stress for your problems. Stress is, and will always be, part of life. Otherwise, there is no life on this planet. Each one of us comes to this earth with a bag of happiness. He/she also comes with a bag of sorrow.

So, you come with stress in your luggage. Maturity is that you accept this as part of life. This includes pain that you get from your parents, from your family, from your children, from your relatives, from your friends, from your loved ones, from illness, from loss of loved ones, loss of income, loss of job, loss of reputation, loss of love, loss of basic needs for survival, loss of life, poverty, destruction of home, and property, and facing anger, hatred, contempt and working hard, long hours, fighting in courts, and fighting period.

This is part of your "life-on-earth" package.

The third world accepts it as part of life and deals with it. They do not cry, "I have stress and let me run to my doctor and have some pills to pop in my mouth to deal with this". As a human being, you were not meant to sit in a comfortable house, with a part-time job that you love and be surrounded with loved ones and riches.

Life is a struggle. Let us acknowledge this first step.

The second step is that it is in the struggle that we develop. It is in the fire of adversity that the soul is developed. Through all the pain, the anguish, the terror, the despair, the horror, the sorrow and the depression, if you just hang on and make it, you will emerge so confident, and so strong that nothing can faze you. But you cannot do this if you pop pills in your mouth, take needles or swallow alcohol to numb your self.

The third step is that bad times teach you, provided you stop and ask daily, " what can I learn from this? " The answer may just change your life.

Medicine and alcohol make you weak. They delay the process of resolving pain and sorrow. They do not allow you to complete the adjustment process. They slow your thinking and take the sharpness of thought away. They make you numb. They do not allow you to come up with coping mechanisms. They do not allow you to see if there was something you could have learned from this. They do not allow you to become strong.

Do not whine that your job is stressful. So is that of the soldier in the war. So is that of the fireman's. So is that of the doctor's struggling to save lives. So was that of the caveman's as he stepped out of the cave to hunt a dinosaur for lunch. So is that of each of us as we struggle long, uncertain and unpleasant hours to try to bring food on the table. It is the wise man and woman who accepts this and goes forward uncomplaining.

If you have suffered, you have a choice. Firstly, you can keep thinking about it, burn in pain or hatred, and cry about it again, and again, so that you are trapped by it. You may keep crying about what is gone or what was done to you. You no longer care to support yourself financially. You cannot make clear decisions. Nothing matters anymore. You may not want to live. You cannot then be free to live as you would have if it had not happened to you. Your sorrow has trapped you.

Crying about a thing alone, and with others, is the right way to relieve sorrow. But, if after two years you are still obsessed by it, then you must understand that the more you think about it, the more pain you will get.

It is maturity to not let your personal sorrows affect your professional life. Keep them separate at all times. Make sure that your professional life continues to bring in the income to cover your expenses from day one.

Make sure that your social circle remains intact and you continue to expand it.

Steps to handle pain and sorrow:

1.Pray for comfort and strength.
2. See that you have a source of income to meet your expenses and emergencies from day one. This is imperative. Otherwise, you will add financial worries to your sorrow. You must be financially self-supportive even if you do not want to live. Surely, you do not want to die as a burden on society? Even if you do not want to live more than a week, just earn money for that week. Lack of money may force you to make terrible decisions that you later regret. You may lose your home, your children and your health. When you go to work, you get distracted. You meet other people. You get new waves of sympathy that comfort you. You get new ideas to cope.
3.Become financially literate so that you do not lose what you already have because of your sorrow.
4.Appreciate what you still have, your spouse, your other children, your health and so on. You may lose it tomorrow. I have had parents so wrapped up in sorrow of one child and then they lost their second one.

5.Distract yourself. Give twenty minutes or so to your thoughts of sorrow. Then go read a book, talk to someone, watch television, do gardening or create something.

6.Put aside your pain to help the pain of your loved ones who, too, are suffering. Comfort and distract them.

7.Take care of yourself physically.

8. Have friends to commiserate with. Materially rich countries are poor socially. So, go to self-help and therapy groups. But in countries that are rich in caring and sharing, your neighbors and friends will come and sit with you, day after day, and cry with you and console you. Do not turn them away. Friends and people can enrich your mind and give you different insights on various topics..

9. Do one act of kindness a day. You will feel comforted.

10.Be involved with innocent beings like children and animals. Play with them and take care of them.

Pain comes in so many forms. You may be dying. Your loved one may die. Your child is handicapped or has a catastrophic illness. You may have lost everything you owned. Maybe you were a victim of senseless violence. Maybe your trust was betrayed. Maybe your wish could not be fulfilled. There are so many scenarios.

Understand that the bad times teach us while the good times test us. Fame, fortune and power are the ultimate test to see if we will retain our morality. Or will we think that now that we have money, fame and power, we do not have to follow any rules? Therefore, we can be as indecent, as immodest and as immoral as we want to be. Look around you and you will see that it is true. "Power corrupts and absolute power corrupts absolutely". But the bad times teach us, provided we ask, "what can I learn from this?" In the midst of all the anguish, the despair and the terror, the bad times do teach us, provided that we want to learn.

When you have sorrow, it is as if you stand at a T-junction and can only go left and right. Turn left and you will withdraw into yourself as an angry, bitter, antisocial person who can never smile again. Turn right and you will say to yourself, "What can I learn from this? " The answer could put you on a totally different road. It could change your life. You may become patient, tolerant and develop a very high self-esteem. You may throw away the nonsense and only accept the real values that matter.

When you learn that you may be dying, you may become keenly appreciative about the beauty of the world around you. You may live every moment to the fullest. You may finally sit down and ask," who am I? Why am I here? What things do really matter to me and how can I develop to the highest degree?" You may learn that you still have this source of love and you can still pour it out. You may determine that you will do something that will give you some self- esteem and satisfaction.

If you are dying, you do not turn your face to the wall and shut out everyone.

You still have a purpose in life. Your purpose is to pass on to your family and others the art of handling the last days, weeks or months of you life. After all, they too will get sick and die some day. You have to pass on to them courage and the art of dying with dignity and grace. Courage is to live each day to your fullest potential and in honesty. Courage is to go on when you are afraid or hopeless. In those last days, you may still show some interest in your fellow beings even though you feel that it is no longer important. You may achieve acceptance and you may finally achieve peace.

Even the person who is violently attacked can learn that he must wake up, find his self-respect and never allow this to happen again to him or others. He will analyze his mistakes, then take steps to prevent this and will learn different ways of self-protection as well as a support system. He may work to change himself or the system around him.

If you have a handicapped child, you will still learn a lot. He will teach you to disregard what is not important, and to appreciate what is. He will show you courage and endurance. If you say "why me?" Well, maybe you were considered the best, intelligent, caring parent this child could have and he will suffer less with you around than if he was with others. Or may be you needed to learn something.

If your child, or a loved one died, he had only this much time to live and learn after his previous birth. If he died because of others, than it was an untimely death. Remember that it is not being unfaithful to someone's memory to stop crying for him or to live life to the fullest again. Your child, now in the other world, wants you to do that. Live life fully in his name. He will always be in your heart. Make the world a better place in his name if you wish to have peace. Do good to others to give peace to his soul, and yours, now and every year on his anniversary. Go once to holy places in his name so that he may have love and peace wherever he is and so may you. You must live so that he will be proud of you by being upright, compassionate, by being keenly appreciative of the creation around, by passing love around, by helping another child or person "in his name". He has not been reduced to nothing. He has moved on to another world. If your child died at birth, it was the failure of the vehicle, the body. If my car fails, I cannot drive myself further but I do not identify myself as the car. The soul is still alive.

Or perhaps you want to kill yourself? Will you let one person or one failure destroy your appreciation of the beauty of the world? Will you give that one person or that one failure so much power over you? Can you really be so selfish that you will not care about how much pain you will cause your family as they try to struggle on their own without the help only you could have given? What happens if you are forced to stay in this world without your body and watch their pain?

Say to yourself that if you have to tread this path of pain, you might as well get it over with. The first step is self-discipline. You must get up immediately from the bed on waking up. Do not lay awake thinking of what others did to you. You must aim to get dressed and began work within an hour. Do not think of anything while you are getting ready. This is called mental discipline. Whatever you wish to brood over, do so in the evening.

Have a routine. Go to toilet. Brush your teeth. Wash your face. Take a bath. Put on your clothes. Comb your hair. Put on your make up (always be well dressed), do your breathing exercises. Say your prayer. Be quiet to let Him get through to you. Finish this within an hour. Then go to work and offer excellence.

Know how much your expenses are. How much is your income? Is it covering your expenses? If not, why are you not looking for a second job? What is your goal from the income point of view? Why are you not meeting it? True revenge is to do better than your enemy does.

What you do not do is take anti- depressants, anti- anxiety medications, sleeping pills or other medications. Your depression and your sorrow will not be resolved. And you will end up weak. Your sorrow will only be resolved by talking about it, by crying about it, by sharing it with others, by other people's love, by praying, by your dealing with it one day at a time and by time itself. You do not run to medications.

When you talk about it, when you share your pain with a friend, neighbor, a human being, your pain will be "lessened" by half.

You get much needed "sympathy" that heals your pain.

People will cry with you and worry over you, and you will discover "caring".

You will get much needed "advice" that helps you to either stop feeling sorry for yourself or teaches you to cope or else teaches you how to pull yourself out of your condition.

You will be shown how others went through a similar condition and survived. You will be shown how others went through worse conditions and survived. Thus, you will get "courage".

You will be told how things get better in different ways. Thus, you will get "hope".

By dealing with it one day at a time, you will "break the pain in small parts" so it is easier to handle.

By praying and asking for help, you will get "strength".

In third world countries, people are losing their loved ones, their freedom and their homes. They have to deal with poverty, hunger, abuse, terror and anguish. They do not pop pills in their mouth to deal with this. They handle what comes their way with their character, with their tears, with their prayers, with their beliefs and with their faith in God. That is their strength. Why do you not learn something from them?

It all boils down to how you handled your cross, or if you will, how you carried your bag of pain. Did you carry it with your honor and morals intact? Did you pick up all the pieces you were shattered into, become whole again, and went forward having regained your identity?

Did you do so without neglecting your skills, without being a burden on society, but by being self-sufficient, by helping your fellowmen on the way and at all times living with honor?

Did you overcome your fears and loneliness? Did you become whole again, a person complete, handling his pain, but full of love and curiosity about life?

Or, can you think of nothing else but revenge? Can you think only of hurting others, as you have been hurt? Do you want to pass on the pain?

Or do you stay full of sadness because you can not accept your loss so that you are no joy to be with?

It is also as if you are being asked what you wish to do about your pain. Do you wish to offer your pain so that others may suffer less? Maybe you can offer your pain so that the children will suffer less or the animals? You can offer this daily.

So, you can learn and grow from pain.
You can pass the test by handling it the right way.
You can offer your pain to alleviate someone else's pain

How you deal with anxiety, panic attacks, sorrow and depression is determined by your attitude and beliefs.
How you deal with anxiety, panic attacks, sorrow and depression determines if your character will grow strong or weak.

Only the person who has self-discipline can handle pain, sorrow and panic attacks. Since we will have all these problems at some point in our lives, it is critical that we develop self discipline.

We come here to develop and grow but the choice is ours.

Chapter 19.   AN ABUSER, A BULLY AND AN INFERIORITY COMPLEX

An abuser is a bully.

A bully will cry about the harm done to him and his ancestors but will not acknowledge the pain and suffering that he is causing to others.

A bully cannot care, share or be fair.

A bully only wants his way without logic or consideration of others.

A bully wants total power.

A bully thrives on the fear and submission of others.

A bully will not admit his mistakes. He has no remorse. The only other emotion he feels is fear when the chips are against him.

A bully has an inferiority complex.

A person with an inferiority complex will try to feel superior in the following ways:

by taking needless dares or by showing off;

by trying to make others feel inferior by insulting and criticizing them;

by demeaning the values most important to the victim;

by insulting the victim's friends;

by being polite to those equal or superior to him, but practicing selfishness, rudeness and cruelty at home or toward those weaker than him;

by attacking the intelligence of others ("You are stupid. You misunderstood. What you do is not important");

by applying physical, verbal or emotional abuse;

by intimidating others with his anger;

by respecting only those with money;

by controlling others through deprivation of money;

by controlling others through deprivation of information;

by becoming completely non-caring or
by controlling a victim through isolation and loss of social support from relatives and friends (this is done by behaving rudely to the relatives and friends, or by insulting the victim in front of others).

A person with an inferiority complex will not help his mate in household work.

A bully only feels strong when he has money or can control someone.

A bully will say that since he provides money, the only moral laws are what he wishes.

A bully is a weakling because he has no fundamental beliefs or a map for the road of life. He has no principles. Therefore, when things go against him, he becomes a meek person.

Chapter 20.   ABUSE

There is physical abuse that we are all familiar with.
There is verbal abuse, which involves name-calling and insults of the other person. We can attack his intelligence saying he is stupid or no good etc
And then, there is emotional abuse.

Emotional abuse starts in such a subtle manner that we are not even aware of it and attribute it to the attacker having a bad day. This is because we do not know how to define it. But the attacker is just testing waters to see how far he can get away with what he is doing.

Emotional abuse occurs:
when we are not valued;
when we are cursed;
when our happiness is ignored;
when we are treated with contempt;
when what we say and what we do is not considered important;
when we are told that we are not liked (we are constantly criticized);
when we are insulted privately, and in front of others;
when our basic needs of food, rest, clothing, sleep and recreation are not met (we may be made to stay cold);
when we are not given what we are entitled to;
when we are consistently treated with anger;
when we are left alone to struggle through difficult times (e.g. illness etc), instead of being helped;
when things are done consistently to us that cause us hardships;
When we are kept in the dark as to what our financial situation is, what our assets are and what our debts are;

When we are financially abandoned;
When our mate has an affair and thus breaks his/her contract with us to be faithful;

An abuser will try to attack your intelligence. He will try to brainwash you by saying that you are stupid or that you should not think. He will consistently try to tell you that you misunderstood. Do not believe him.

Abuse can be done to husband, wife, children, parents, animals, humans and countries.

Never accept abuse in order to maintain peace in the family. The price that you will pay in the end will be horrifying.

Never give up your rights because you feel generous or noble. You will ultimately lose his/her respect and your self- respect.

Child abuse
Child abuse occurs:
when a child is beaten, breaking soft tissues, bones or eardrums;
when a child is locked in his room and not allowed to get out or have contact with others for more than a day;
when a child, over ten years of age, is forced to stay hungry for more than a day while there was food in the house; (Younger children must have access to food).
when a child is made to put his body against a hot or freezing surface;
when a child is put in hot or cold water;
when a burning object is put against the child;
when a child is chained;
when a child is hit against the wall or other hard surface;
when a child is hit on his head with a stick;

when an infant or a child up to five years of age is shaken repetitively;

when a child is made to swallow hot peppers or hot food;

when a child is made to stand naked outside the house;

when a child is made to stay outside in inclement weather;

when a child is pushed down the stairs;

when a child is not given access to medical care;

when a child is not allowed to play for some hours daily;

when a child is not allowed to have access to friends and

when a child is not given access to reading material

There is also abuse if a child is not given access to reading, writing and mathematical skills.

Please note that this definition of abuse also applies to women, to men, as well as prisoners of wars, and (with the exception of education) to animals.

The definition of abuse remains the same.

Never give up your children for adoption unless you are ill or dying.

This is not love, nor sacrifice. This is breaking of your covenant to God when you give birth. This is abandonment of a child. Any abandonment of child is not only abuse, but also a violation of its trust and right to have its biological parents. No animal abandons its young.

To do this for money shows how immoral and low you have sunk.

Never sell you children or put them in hardship so you can survive. This is immoral and abuse.

The emotional abuse occurs:

when a child is cursed;

when a child is told that he is unwanted;

when a child is not allowed to participate in social functions and

when a child is not allowed to visit others with the family (A child is not supposed to stay only with friends of his/her age but must mix with people of all ages. This is how social skills develop).

Abuse by child
A child abuses his/her parents :
by treating them with disrespect;
by not listening to them;
by cutting off contact with them;
by violating the parents' rules for home and outside as long as the child is dependent on them, or shares their home;
by violating their moral rules and values;
by cursing them;
by insulting them alone and in front of others;
by not giving them the importance that parents deserve in the milestones of life, such as birth , marriage and death. This is the time when parents pass on traditions. When conceited and selfish children think that just because they earn money, they can design their own affairs, and parents have no say or role in how a ceremony should be conducted, or when parents become reduced to a role of guests in these functions, then that is abuse of parents.
by beating parents;
by not giving them money in old age or need;
by not giving parents his/her homes;
by not giving them adequate space to live in (making them sit outside all day because there is " no room in the house";
by not giving them food;
by making them work;
by making them his/her babysitters and not realizing how tired they become;
by not helping them in their time of need

by not giving them medical care;
by separating them,
by not protecting them from others and
by taking away their money once the parents are retired, or once the child is over twenty- two.
I have seen a ninety-seven year old deaf and blind woman living alone and the daughters justifying it by saying that "she is visited every day". This is horrifying abuse. Any parent over sixty or if not working must live in the children's home and be treated with respect.

Abuse from relatives exists:
if they do not speak to you or your children,
if they do not help you in time of need,
if they do not share your good and bad times,
if they do not comfort you in sorrow,
if they do not fight on your side when you have been unfairly treated and
if they betray your trust.

Abuse of country
The same rules of abuse apply when any human being wants to control another human being or when a country wants to abuse another country.

You control a country when:
1. You make it scared of you.
2. You violate its rules and beliefs.
3. You take away its resources.
4. You make it weak.
5. You make it isolated.
6. You use propaganda to confuse it.

If a country is abused, it must follow the same rules of fighting abuse.

It must publicize the atrocities that are being done, so that the world opinion can shift against the abuser. No abuser likes his actions to be made public.

It must appeal for sanction against the abusers.

It must build a network of support.

It must hide or develop its resources or prevent them from going to the enemy.

It must build up the morale of its people by counterpropaganda and by resistance.

Chapter 21.   WHEN ARE WE ABUSED?

We are abused:

When we do not have self-respect.

When we do not have a map to guide us on the road of life.

When we have formed no codes of values. We do not know what we will accept or what we will not tolerate.

When we have an inferiority complex.

When we accept the belief that we are stupid and are incapable of understanding our problems or their solutions.

When we keep complaining of the way we are treated but do nothing about it.

When we follow our whims and fancies so that we are rocked every which way by them like a boat without a rudder.

When we have no goals or aims.

When we have no self-discipline or self-control.

When we are in denial and have no clarity of vision. We keep hoping that the other person will realize that he is wrong and will change.

When we ask other people as to how we should behave, instead of thinking of the pros and cons of a situation and making the decision ourselves.

When we are silent in the face of injustice.

When we do not try to become financially literate and financially independent.

When we are afraid to take risks for what we believe in. We are afraid to move out, to live alone, to be independent, to take a stand, or to fight back.

When we feel that peace is to be attained even at the cost of our ideals and principles.

When we do not inform the world of what is happening.

When we go back to the abuser without becoming powerful.

Chapter 22.   HOW DO YOU HANDLE AN ABUSER ?

When people abuse you, they lose the right to expect fairness from you. They will take advantage of your fairness to flourish. Do not be fair to them.

The man who is polite when the chips are not clear to him but is cruel when he is on the top is not someone you want to marry. Study the family and see how the other people in power are behaving toward their spouses. Perhaps your would- be spouse is behaving better because he is not sure of you, is lonely, poor or isolated. Rest assured that he will behave horribly when he is in power.

Remember that an abuser wants total control. He will stop at nothing less.
He does this by the following:

1.He takes away the money. He keeps you in the dark about the financial situation so that you do not know what your balance is and what you have. He shows anger if you ask for information about your finances. He insists that you pay for items. What can you do without money?

2. He insults you in front of others. He curses you. He tells you to shut up in front of them. He makes a fuss every time you meet your friends. He criticizes them or says that they are not worthy of you. He criticizes your family. So, you lose the support of your friends and become isolated.

3. He flirts in front of you so that it becomes unpleasant for you to be there.

4.He criticizes you so that you lose your- self-esteem and self-confidence.

5. He interrupts your basic needs of food and sleep so that you get weak.

6. He refuses to help when you are exhausted so that you stay weak.

7. He tells you to leave the house so that you become terrified that you will not have shelter. Do you see how lonely you have become?

8. He contradicts every sentence that you say to the children, and others, so that they can see how stupid you are.

9. He shows his anger, so that you are scared of him. He will also show his anger when you ask him about the financial picture.
10. He insists that he will do what bothers you.

11. He uses the " I am really a nice guy technique". That means that he periodically shows himself to be nice or caring so that you are confused and not clear as to whether he really is a nice man and, if you just tried harder or a different approach, things would be better.

He may show only some of these traits or all of them. He may deny these traits and say that "you misunderstood" thus attacking your intelligence.
An abuser will tell you that since he does not drink or womanize, he is not an abuser. That is not true.

Do you see what sort of a monster you are dealing with? As a spouse, he was supposed to be your best friend. He was supposed to care, share and be fair. This man is your enemy.

The same rules applies when any human being wants to control another human being or when a country wants to abuse another country.
You take away its resources, make it weak, make it isolated and make it scared of you. Then you use propaganda to confuse it.

First, have clarity of vision and do not be in denial.
Secondly, become financially strong and have a network of friends.

1.The first step is to be alert about abuse and never to excuse it because "he had a bad day or is under pressure". A bad day or pressure is no excuse for abuse. He would not abuse his boss or the neighbor if he had a bad day! Do you know why? Because they would not put up with it for one minute. Never tolerate anything that undermines your self-respect. Have clarity of vision. Are you being treated, as he would tolerate being treated?

2.The second step to stop abuse is to inform the world of the abuse and the abuser's name. No abuser likes his actions to be made public. That very fact tells you that he knows that the world will consider his actions wrong.

Know that a bully only understands the language of a bully.

3.Value your intelligence and instinct above all. Know yourself to be a very valuable person. You are created by God. That alone makes you valuable. In addition, you are caring, patient, kind, honest and hardworking. This makes you very valuable.

4.Where is your self- respect? If he insults you, walk out of the room and refuse to come back until he apologizes.
If he starts criticizing you in front of others, walk out of the room.
If he insults your family and friends, refuse to talk to him.
If he criticizes you constantly, stop talking to him.

5.Follow the rules for fighting.

6.Get financially intelligent. Insist on knowing your financial picture immediately. Learn what are in the bank accounts, pension plans and retirement plans. If he refuses to let you see them, that is an ominous sign that you are dealing with an abuser. A person who loves you will at all times give you free access to the financial picture. This is why every woman from the first day of marriage should make it a religious habit to know her accounts every month and the balance at all times.

7.The next step is to insist that you open a separate bank account with some money to spend in your name alone. If you do not work, ask that he give you a monthly amount to put there. Do not come back until your account is opened and money is placed. Make sure the account is only in your name. If he refuses, see a lawyer. Read the chapter on marriage and finances in Life skills.

8.The next step is to talk to a lawyer to see whether you want to fight this man while staying in the home, how you can keep the home, whether you will lose the home or the children on moving out. Read the chapter on "Separation" in *life skills*.

9. Whom do you go to for help?
Talk to your doctor for help. If the doctor is not willing to be involved then you do not want such a doctor. A doctor has to see that you are healthy in and out. The doctor must call the

police in case of physical abuse whether you want it or not. The doctor should also inform your husband's employer in case of physical or non- physical abuse. This should be mandatory. The employer plays a powerful role as a deterrent. The doctor, as well as the police and the employer, must ask your husband how much money he gives you to use freely per month. This affects your emotional health.

Call your friends and your relatives. It is the moral duty of every human being to take care of abused persons or animals and not send them back.
If you are physically hit, call the police and go to a shelter. Every state should have shelters for abused women. Otherwise, go to your friends or relatives.

If you are in a foreign country, contact your embassy and say that you are being abused. It is the moral duty of an embassy to protect its citizens abroad. They should direct you to the embassy and then give you and your family food and shelter. They should then call your husband. They should give your husband a warning and take away his passport for the time being.
If he repeats his action, he should be returned to his country. Should you wish, the embassy can put you on the plane back to your country.
This ticket can be paid for from your husband's current and future earnings. The embassy should call your husband's employer and inform him of the events.
You should be able to contact the personnel department of your husband's company and it should become mandatory that they inform your employer.
Once contacted, whether by you, the police, the doctor or others, the employer must meet with your husband and warn him that abuse will not be tolerated. It is the moral duty of the employer to see that the character of his employee is good. You

would not employ a thief or a cheat. Similarly, you will not hire a wife- abuser because that shows a non-caring and cruelty in his character that can affect the company in the long run.

Give the employee a warning to mend his ways. Put the information in his personal file. Give his wife a phone number that she can call at the company if the husband again abuses her. Inform the husband that the next call will deprive him of his job. Insist that, the very next day, you see a bank account opened in the wife's name alone and that the next check goes in her name. Insist that you see the account every month for six months and that there is always the balance of one check there. Make sure that the pension plans or any investments are in both husband and wife's names, as they should be once the employee gets married. Insist that the wife comes in to see the personnel. Inform her of what she has in terms of finances and what she can do in case of abuse.

This is the moral obligation of an employer in any society. The employers play a powerful role as a deterrent in wife abuse. Their roles must be emphasized. They must have a policy for wife- abuse.

Your employee cannot say that this is his private business because once he has abused a human being; it becomes everyone's business.

No abuse can be considered a part of personal life.

A man who abuses his wife will abuse his children.

It has to be mandatory that the police, the doctor, and the employer must file a report with the state for wife abuse. These parties play a powerful role in preventing wife abuse.

If the husband is having an affair, this also violates the sanctity of a married life. Friends, the doctor or the police must be informed. Either party can document it in file and should be able to forward it to the family court with your permission.

When you are abused, or if your husband is having an affair and he refuses to mend his ways, you should be able to file a complaint against the abuser in the family/domestic court immediately. Laws should pass that this should also be done automatically once the police or your doctor forwards your file to the court.

The court should then automatically file a restraining order stating that your husband cannot be near you or the children until the court hearing.

Laws should pass that a second letter from the court must go immediately to your husband's employer stating that his employee has committed abuse, and that, until further notice, all paychecks will be split in equal amounts between husband and wife. The wife's check should be sent to the court address in her name until the court gives further orders. She will pick up her check there. All these require laws.

The court hearing should be scheduled within a week and must include statements from the neighbors, the children, her doctor, friends and police.

The husband can admit his guilt and pay the fine, which shall be turned over to his wife. He will be responsible for any fees paid by the wife. The lawyers should be those paid by the state and the court should not charge any fee.

His wife has the option to file for divorce.

His employers should be ordered to continue to pay the split paychecks for one year. All pension and investment in the company should be immediately split in half and the contributions continue at fifty percent to each account. At retirement, the wife's portion should be turned over to her personally in front of a witness.

Please note that it has to be mandatory in every state that a wife's portion of pensions and investments cannot be turned over to the husband by her signature. It must be given to her in front of a witness.

If the husband is self- employed, the court has to appoint a bookkeeper who will see that the paychecks are split in half and given to the wife and the husband separately and that all investments and pension plans are spilt in half. This should be filed together with the past year's internal revenue tax returns every year with the court. The wife can appeal any time for the records to be reviewed.

Why is it necessary to do this?
This is because the state values the importance of a family unit as a vital building block of the society. This unit must be protected.
If the husband wants to flirt, use all his money for himself or mistreat his spouse, he has no right to be married.

These two actions of information to the employer and the division of paychecks are powerful deterrents to a man. They will prevent physical violence significantly. If you are not married, you cannot be protected thus.

10. The next step is to get a job immediately with whatever income you can make. Despite the anguish, the terror, the despair and the shame, it is crucial that you become financially independent as fast as possible. Do not sacrifice money for the sake of the children. This will hurt them in the end.
Appoint someone who can watch over them and tell you if they are suffering. Then go to work.

The very first thing one has to ask an abused, separated woman is' "how are you going to meet your expenses?"

In a cloud of pain, and distraught over the loss of her home, family and children, shaken by the cruelty of her husband, this will often be the last thing on her mind. Her whole world has crashed around her. Tragically, everyone, including the psychiatrist, will not ask this crucial question.

But it has to be the very first one asked by friends, colleagues, social workers and psychiatrist. "Show us how your income is going to cover your expenses". It just may prevent her from being on the streets.

If the woman receives some money from her husband, it should be put away for an emergency. She must go to work.

This is why, before a woman leaves, she must be able to answer the question as to how much her monthly expenses are, how she plans to meet them and who will take care of the children while she works. You cannot just run away blindly because you "have had it".

11.The next step is to build this income steadily so that it meets your expenses and still gives you some savings. Hold two jobs if necessary

You must develop financial resources even if you have to leave to get them from him through a divorce or through court. Do not give up your rights.

12. Side by side, you must develop your circle of friends. Despite your loneliness and fears, do not have any love affairs at this time. Know that men will try to take advantage of you in this period because they know that you are very vulnerable right now and they will start with sympathy. Do not be alone with men. Tell your problems only to female friends. Do not discuss it at work. Get social support. Make friends. Build your resources and contacts. Meet your friends every week.

Know when to leave.

When you move out, the problem becomes public knowledge which is the first necessary step.

The very first time a man hits you, leave immediately. If he is dangerous, wait until he is out of the house or call the police. The bully will whimper like a child and apologize. Do not forgive him. His behavior is unforgivable. If you want to give him one more chance, you still have to leave and not return for six months until you are sure you that can make it on your own and are financially self-sufficient.

Know that in marriage, you are supposed to be the best of friends. He has just behaved like a deadly enemy.

Why would you be so stupid as to trust a deadly enemy?

It does not matter if he puts food on the table or gives you the money to buy clothes. You work just as hard for that food and clothes. The only difference is that he gets paid for his services and you do not.

Think of how much he would have to pay if he hired someone to do the cooking, grocery shopping, cleaning, or being a chauffer and a public relation officer. That is how much you are worth. You owe him nothing if he treats you with disrespect.

Other than physical abuse, do not leave a marriage blindly until you are financially self-sufficient and you build a private network of social support.

If he insults you verbally, calls you names, or emotionally abuses you, tell him that you will not be treated so, and will only give him one more chance. He cannot treat you the way he would not want to be treated.

The second time he abuses you again, get a lawyer and file papers for divorce. If you think he will get physically violent, leave the house.
Do not look back.

15.Where do you go?
You can go to your parents, relatives, friends or the police station. It is the moral duty of every human being to give shelter to any being that is being abused.
Parents, if your child comes to you physically, mentally, verbally or emotionally abused, it is your moral duty to give her shelter, protection and financial support.
Do not send your child back. It is immoral to say to the child that she must stay in abusive surroundings until she is dead. That belief encourages men to behave like monsters and that is immoral.
It does not matter that your son-in-law has a good standing in the community, is rich and provides your daughter with a nice home, food on the table or money. Nothing justifies physical violence, mental cruelty or emotional abuse. It is your duty to take the child and her children in.
All relatives, and society itself, must give support to this woman.
People who tell the woman to "forget the past and start again" are putting her life in danger. They are encouraging the abuser to continue his way of life. An abuser will only learn if he is punished.

It is the duty of the society to provide shelter to such a person if she has nowhere else to go. It is the duty of relatives and friends to provide her with shelter, food and financial support.

For relatives to be considered relatives, they must keep contact with you, and your family. They must be fair.

They must share your good times and bad, must be someone you can turn to in times of need, must help you in cash or kind, must not betray your trust, must help you fight for your rights, must be willing to be involved and must treat you with respect. Otherwise, they are not your relatives.

If you are trapped with this abuser for whatever reasons, bide your time as you look for means to escape, but never lose your sense of self worth and self-importance. As long as you have that, no one can have power over you.

This is not what marriage is about. In marriage, the partners are supposed to be friends and to build each other's esteem and help each other.

It is the duty of the politicians to enact the following laws:
All married people must be given the paychecks in the name of both husband and wife. If you are separated, you should file a letter of separation in the family court that must get your spouse's letter as well. Show a copy of the court receipt at your job. You will then get the paycheck in one person's name.

Abuse from relatives exists:
if they do not speak to you or your children,
if they do not help you in time of need,
if they do not share your good times and bad,
if they do not comfort you in sorrow,
if they do not fight on your side when you have been unfairly treated and
if they betray your trust.

If you are abused by a child who is still dependent on you, it is your moral right and duty to restrict his privileges. You should also be able to stop his education for up to a year as he learns the consequences of his actions.

Do not listen to educators who tell you that you must continue to pay for his school/college so that you can show him that while he was behaving like a monster, "you were always there". This is outrageous. What you are doing is creating a bully who is encouraged to continue his behavior. This is a horrible life-skill to teach him.

It does not teach your child that bad behavior has consequences. He will not grow up to be a good human being. Do not be a weak parent.

If your child is older and self- sufficient, he still has no right to treat with you with disrespect, call you "stupid" or other names, or say that what you did was stupid. He has no right to abuse you physically, mentally or emotionally. Do not have anything to do with such a child. Your self- respect is far more important. He is not your child if he treats you thus, or allows his spouse to treat you thus. For an adult child to take his elderly parents' pension or other money is abuse.

If a country is abused, it must follow the same rules.
It must publicize the atrocities that are being done to it so that the world opinion can shift against the abuser.
It must appeal for sanction against the abusers.
It must build a network of support.
It must hide or develop its resources or prevent them from going to the enemy.
It must build up the morale of its people by counterpropaganda and by resistance.

Chapter 23.   PANIC ATTACKS, ANXIETY AND WHAT MAKES YOU STRONG

Everyone gets panic attacks.

A soldier in a battle can have a panic attack, as may one who loses all his savings. Yet, the Christians thrown to the lions handled their panic attacks. How did they do it?

It is wrong to think that a panic attack or anxiety is a disease. It is a reaction to what life is handing out to us. Do you think that the woman in war is not having a panic attack as her loved one is running for cover? Do you think that she can find any tranquilizers at that time to aid her? People in the rest of the world handle famines, wars, and disasters and do not reach for anti-anxiety medications and antidepressants. Yet, we in the most developed country, cannot even live our day-to-day lives without the crutch of medicine.

So, how do the others handle it? It depends on how you have been taught to handle life. It depends on how strong you are.

Panic is a high form of anxiety. Anxiety is when we are afraid of something terrible that we feel is going to happen, or of dire consequences, that someone will leave us, or that we will not perform well.

Anxiety and peace cannot coexist. Read "What Gives You Peace."

You handle a panic attack not through medicines, but by your character and by your self-discipline.

It is the strength of your personality that will determine how you handle a panic attack. It is your courage. It is your acceptance. It is your faith. Face the panic attacks and determine to conquer them bit by bit. You do this by becoming strong.

How do you become strong?
By your beliefs and faith in God.
By acceptance of what is lost.
By living one day at a time.
By talking to yourself and calming yourself.
By becoming so busy that you are exhausted.
By talking to your priest, doctor or friend.
By praying for help.
By keeping contact with your friends as a support system.
By developing self-discipline and self-control.
By having a time limit of handling it.
By determining to make it work.
By knowing that this too will pass.
By having a plan of what you are going to do when you panic.
By having someone with you at that time.
By having a plan B in case plan A does not work.
By distracting yourself through television, through friends, or through reading.
By being encouraged by those who have gone before. If they could handle it, maybe so can you.
By the love of others.
By not vacillating, by making a decision and following it.

Keeping busy, acceptance, distraction, friends, determination, and faith are key factors.

What makes you weak?
Wavering is a weakness.
Not knowing the right timing is a weakness.
Being hooked onto the past is a weakness.
Running after people who do not care for you is a weakness.
Needing the approval or sanction of others is a weakness.

You should be ashamed to say that you cannot work because you are having a panic attack. It is equal to announcing that you are a very weak person who is trying to cop out of responsibilities.

Know that the ultimate power that a person has is having no fear. It can only come with faith.

Chapter 24.   THE ART OF MAKING A PERSONAL DECISION

Answer the following questions:

1. What are my goals?
2. Am I making this decision with my emotions or with my mind? Is there another way to do this?
3. What are the benefits to me by this decision?
4. What am I risking by doing this in terms of abuse, education, money, reputation, breaking the law, job, loss of time, relatives, and friends, etc.?
5. Can I survive this risk?
6. How much time am I willing to put into this venture?
7. What is my back door if I fail?
8. Do I have the money to support me in this decision?
9. Do I have the money to support me if I fail?
10. Who are my supporters?
11. Who are my competitors or antagonists?
12. How will this affect my personal life in positive and negative ways?
13. Is what I am doing modest, decent or moral?

Chapter 25.   KNOW WHEN TO GIVE UP

In any venture, know when to fight and when to give up.
You should give up:
when you have no further resources;
when people refuse to listen to what is fair or logical;
when the other party is abusive or immoral;
when every opening is blocked;
when you have knocked in vain at every door for help;
when a future opening is nonexistent; and
when you cannot meet your needs and expenses.

Chapter 26. SILENCE

One should not be scared of silence but learn to reap the enormous advantages derived from it.

We have become afraid of silence.
We think that we cannot work, think, eat, or sleep unless there are people talking to us on the radio or television, or there is music playing. We cannot even take a walk unless we have a headset with music or we are on a cell phone talking to someone.
This destroys our potential.
Our brain cannot hold two thoughts at the same time.
Outside sound is a sensory input to our brain. The brain has to process it for us to enjoy it. It needs to use some power to do this, but that takes away from the full power of our brain on work or thoughts.

This is fine in work involving physical labor. But, this is dangerous in work involving thinking, learning, and concentration.
When we get a stimulus of sound, we can get distracted at work and make a mistake. When we hear another sound, we can never give our full concentration to the problem at hand, even if we are professionals.
So, it is important that there is no radio or music in workplaces where intense thinking is involved, for example, in libraries, in places of learning, at a secretary's desk, in dispatchers' offices, with firefighters and policemen, at nurses' desks, in critical-care units, in emergency rooms, at the doctor's desk and in places of illness because it irritates the ill at times and saps their strength, and nobody can hear their cry for help. Voices should be kept low and soothing in such places, and people working here are not supposed to call to each other across the

hall and certainly not talk over the head of the person trying to review records or making a phone call. If a doctor or minister walks into a patient's room, the radio or television should be shut off by everyone in that room as a consideration.

People waiting for an appointment can read to pass their time.

We must not overlook the vast importance of silence.

It is only in silence:
that we can really think,
that we can examine a problem and come up with an answer,
that we can prepare for what is ahead of us,
that we get in touch with our intuition,
that we can get in touch with our true feelings,
that we can work out our relationship,
that we can work out our response to our losses, temptations or fears,
that we can form new strategies,
that we can get a sudden insight or inspiration,
that we can create,
that we can lead our souls to a higher development,
that we can release new energies, and
that we can get in touch through true prayer with our God.

A prayer that blares out over the microphone disturbing your neighbors cannot connect you to God.

Chapter 27.   THE SILENT SCREAM

Listen carefully, and you will hear the silent screams of thirsty animals and birds whose water supply is cut off by building fences around the ponds. (I am assured that there is no law against it. As if there has to be a law to prevent a town from being cruel. As if the laws of your conscience are not enough. As if your moral sense is not enough.) Listen to their cries as their ponds are turned over to public parks.

Listen carefully, and you will hear the silent screams of animals as they watch their homes being destroyed by greedy builders, and no one is humane enough to say, "Stop. Leave them some land to live on. Where will they go?"

Listen carefully, and you will hear the silent screams of animals as their parents are run over by careless, speeding drivers. Their bodies lie on the road every day, and we coolly ignore them. If human bodies were being run over and lying around like this, we would be outraged.
No driver is fined, and no license is taken away. A driver will not stop to allow an animal to cross the road. It is as if nothing is more important than we are.

Listen carefully, and you will hear their screams as you joyfully plunge ahead and go on an animal hunt. No animal will hunt for sport. It will hunt only to eat. Yet, we humans are so degraded that we cannot have fun unless we injure, maim, and cause pain to an animal, or we destroy its family.

Listen carefully, and you will hear their screams as their nails are torn off, their ears and tails cut off, their wings cut off, they are boiled alive, they are carried or held tied in agonizing positions, or they are branded with a burning iron just to please us.

Listen carefully, and you will hear the silent screams of animals, as they are tortured beyond endurance in the name of science and experimentation.

Their bodies are burned, cut into pieces, and made holes into, and their eyes experimented with. They are given electric shocks. They lay with wounds, unable to turn, in agony, and we watch with no emotions. We are scientists.

What sort of barbaric monsters are we?

We do not insist that our schools teach children to be kind to animals. We have no clubs in schools that speak for animals' rights. Why?

Are our educators so non-caring?

We are outraged if an animal has a bowel movement on our lawn. The animal does not even have a right to have a bowel movement or pass urine. We punish it when it does so. It is allowed to do so only when we take it for a walk. Would you be able to control your urine and only pass it when I tell you to do so?

Is it more important that your lawns be manicured and untouched, and you be a shriveled, cold, heartless human being?

Or will you listen to the silent screams of the animals and fight for their rights?

The moral fiber of any society is judged by its treatment of animals.

Chapter 28.   ANIMALS

This planet was given to the animals and humans. Man cannot be a cancer destroying everything for his own needs.

Animals are your fellow creatures. Helping animals is vital for the development of your soul. God himself will not forgive your cruelty to them.
Protect them. Protect their environment. Give them the environment they need.

Make sure that your schools have clubs for the protection of animals.

Never use electric shocks to control animals. It is the utmost cruelty.

An animal has a right to run free, to jump, to play, to be curious, or to explore. As long as it does not hurt others, leave it alone. It is not supposed to be on a leash all the time. It has a right to use its voice.

Never hurt them in the name of fun or sports, if you wish to be considered a human being. An animal never hunts for fun. It only hunts to eat.
Are you then lower than it?

Do not kill them for clothing. Never torture them for beauty or other products. Refuse to wear such products. Any company using animal products must allow you to visit their site anytime. If they refuse to do so, they are hiding their cruelty. Do not use their products.

Never torture an animal for experimentation. They have the same feelings of pain that you and I have. Torture yourself first to see how it feels. If you find it barbaric, think of them.

Do not panic that you will get diseases from animals. Your chance of getting diseases is a thousand times more from humans, yet you live among them.
In other parts of the world, people are not scared of living around animals.
Neither were your forefathers, and they lived long enough to bring you into existence.

Animals should be allowed to walk or run free as long as their owners are around.

Even animals you eat should be kept in natural and humane surroundings.
It is your responsibility to find out how they are kept annually.
Visit such sites. If the owners have nothing to hide, they will not stop you.
Make sure that the animals are:
Not kept tied up, but have freedom to walk about and even run, and play with their own kind.
Are not kept in overcrowded conditions.
Are not force fed.
Are not given medications.
Do not see other animals being slaughtered in front of them.
Do not have their young ones taken away from them before they are weaned.
Are not carried while tied up in a painful manner.
Are not kept hungry or thirsty.
Are not beaten or tortured.

Do not eat babies of animals.
Do not eat animals that just had babies.

Do not eat animals that are boiled alive.

Society should not put rules on what pets we can or cannot have, or who we can or cannot feed, or who we can or cannot touch. If we find a stray animal, we take care of it to the best of our ability and resources.

We do not drive away animals and birds because their sounds or their droppings/soil bother us.

Animals that we use for our trade are to be kept in the most humane conditions, given food and water, never overburdened, and given adequate rest. They should not be beaten, whipped, or poked in sensitive areas. They should not be given electric shocks. You are not here on this earth to exist but to live in the most caring manner possible.

Animals cannot have their babies tied away from them. The babies must be free to drink the milk first. How greedy can you be if you take the babies' milk for yourself?
Animals should not be turned out when they have outlived their usefulness, but must be taken care of in their old age.

How inhuman and cruel can we be when we enjoy the excitement of racing animals and whip them and pump them with medication to feed our excitement; when we make animals fight just for our pleasure, or when we hunt animals for sheer pleasure? By hunting, we cause animals pain and death, and break up families just so we can be excited for a few moments.
Why are we so barbaric and low?
All such sports should be banned if we want to advance.
Do not make them perform in show after show. They need rest.
No animal should perform more than once in two days and not at all if it is sick or acting listless.

Do not inject them with drugs to make them perform.

Do not tie an animal's mouth. It controls its heat from its mouth by panting.

Always drive carefully. Do not run over animals. The scene of animal carcasses on the road always shows how barbaric we are.

Do not take away their ponds and lakes. Ponds should not have railings or fences put around them so that the animals cannot drink or so that the ducks or geese cannot climb on to the grounds.
Do not use the land that birds or animals migrate to.

Always be a member of an animal society like Green Peace or PETA or ASPCA.
Any land given to builders by the town must have the approval of these humane societies.

Animals should stay in their natural surroundings. In every town, there should be set aside at least twenty square miles for animals to exist in their natural surroundings, and vehicles should not be allowed to speed around it. The roads must be on bridges so the animals can walk underneath. Do not grab their land in the name of greed.

Pets must not be separated from each other if the owners separate or divorce. One owner must have both, or the parties can alternate taking care of both.

PETS
If you have pets:

Do not mutilate them in the name of beauty.

Do not neuter them for any medical reason. As a doctor, I can tell you that all these medical reasons apply to man too, but no man will neuter himself. It does not change their behavior and is simply a profit-making device.

Always keep your pets in twos at least. Let them have their own company to play with. Do not leave the animal alone by itself while you work all day.
If you can, let them have their family.

Never, ever keep it confined to one corner of the room. Get a toy instead.
It has to have the freedom to move around the house.

Exercise it daily.
When you take the animal for a walk, make sure the leash is long enough for it to sniff around. The animal is not just supposed to walk with you. It has to be allowed to be curious, explore, and sniff around. Do not keep walking as it sniffs. Does it not wait patiently when you stop to talk to someone?

Feed them twice a day. Puppies may need more frequent feeds. Make sure they have access to water at all times. Animals do not get dry food . They can eat table food.

Do not keep them locked in cages at home or while you work. That is inhumane. Would you like to be cramped in a six-foot space for the whole day?
If you have to keep the animal in a cage for a short period of time, make sure the cage is two and a half times the length of the animal. It should be able to turn in the cage. The cage should be at least two and a half times the height of the animal, even higher for monkeys and birds.

It is cruel to keep a bird in a cage. The sky is its world. Why do you want to imprison it for your pleasure? Is not that being selfish? Do not clip its wings.

Do not shave an animal's hair in winter because it is matted. It still keeps it warm.
Always put function before beauty.

Never be angry at an animal or hit it for passing its stool or urine.
You could not pass your urine and stool only when I told you to. Do not rub its nose into its feces. An animal should never be punished for passing urine or stools. It should be able to pass urine at least every four hours or when it has to. Do not feel proud that your animal can stay so long without passing urine. You are damaging its bladder. Always make a corner in the kitchen or someplace that the animal can use if it has to go immediately.

Would you survive if you could only be allowed to pass urine and stool when I took you for a walk twice a day?

Do not make a fuss over animals' feces or droppings on your grounds.
They are manure for the soil. Pick up the feces if it bothers you. If all you can think of is the appearance of your lawn, your selfishness is extreme and you might as well have not been born.

Do not lock an animal in a garage and go away on a trip.
Do not lock an animal in a basement.
Do not keep a single guard dog. Do not keep it chained all day.
Do not leave an animal in a car for even a few minutes without opening the windows.

Do not pollute their environment with trash so that the animals cannot exist.
Never tease an animal. Do not cause it pain and suffering.

Do not use electric fences.
Do not ever use electric shocks to control an animal.
Do not use collars with prongs.
Stoning, whipping, or beating an animal is a crime.
Do not purchase newborns until they are weaned.

Stop if an animal is trying to cross the road. Let him get across.
Places where animals frequent must have an overpass so that cars can go on the top and the animals can cross below.

Never get an animal as a pet and then abandon it for any reason.
This is cruelty. No animal abandons its owner.
Are you lower than an animal?

An animal requires lots of time and training.
Do not purchase babies of animals because they look cute or because your children want them and then abandon them once they are too much work.
No animal will ever leave you. Why does it have more morals than you do?
If you have a pet, it is yours until death.

Do not allow animals to be subjected to pain, suffering, cruelty, and torture in the name of science or greed. Would you allow pain and cruelty to be practiced on your children if it helped research?

No person who fights with companies or institutions doing this should ever be punished for this humane act. Ask the politicians if this is not a humane act. A law should be passed enforcing this called the Animal Humane Act.

Politicians must visit companies and institutions doing research. They must be shown on television doing so and observing what is being done to these animals before they stand for election. Ask your politician if he has visited such places. Ask him if he is animal friendly.
Do not vote for him if his answer is "no."

People who hurt animals have lost their conscience and become inhuman.

Cruelty in any form is still cruelty.

Chapter 29.   IS MONEY RELATED TO INTELLIGENCE?

Intelligence is a quality that we are born with. It is not linked to education.

Many uneducated people are much more intelligent than educated ones. This is a fact worth remembering. Education only gives us learning and some knowledge, and therefore skills to make money. But intelligence is something very different and does not depend on your degrees.

There are many types of intelligence. There is:
the quickness of grasp,
the ability to analyze a situation,
logical thinking,
problem- and obstacle-solving,
mathematical intelligence,
the ability to create experiments and support hypotheses,
the ability to invent,
concentration,
memory retention,
linguistic (the ability to learn languages) and
the ability to have insight, foresight, and creativity.

Anger and arrogance block intelligence.

Intelligence is never related to how much money you make. Anyone can make money. With education and self-discipline, you can make more. A rich man is not necessarily an intelligent man. The wisest men were not rich and did not run after money. Christ was not rich. Neither was Socrates. Buddha, the son of an emperor, left his wealth.

Only a fool tells his wife that because he earns money, he is more intelligent than her; and so can be the only one qualified to make all the decisions. A fool gets threatened by having someone wiser than him around. But a wise man surrounds himself with the most intelligent people. One is only comfortable with one's own level.

When you have money, your intelligence is tested in the following ways:
Are you now going to think:
That you can break all moral laws?
That you can break government laws?
That you can violate modesty and decency?
That you can violate customs and traditions?

The children who say that because they are now earning, they can do "my own thing" (they do not have to listen to anyone and will devise their own weddings, funerals etc.), have become totally selfish and brainwashed by money. They have reduced the importance of their parents to that of a guest. Birth, marriage, death and other milestones are occasions when parents pass down the traditions of society. These traditions hold society together. not only in the present, but also from generation to generation. The wise person knows this. He also knows that when each person does what he feels like, the society gets fragmented and he himself becomes isolated and loses social support that is meaningful in the long run. The only traditions that should be changed are ones that are cruel. No tradition should be changed because of your whim or fancy. You are guilty of hurting society.

Chapter 30. FINANCES

To be financially wise is crucial for your survival.

The first step is to make sure that your income meets your expenses and leaves something for saving. You must have a goal as to how much you will accept as income.

The second step is that you must know what you have in your bank accounts every month.

The third step is that your balance must match that of the bank to the penny.

The fourth step is that every day you must write what you spent as cash and this must balance the cash that you have in your wallet.

The fifth step is that you must always have money to survive three to six months without a job.

The sixth step is that if you have been left money by rich parents then your goal should be to double it.

The seventh step is that you stay away from loans as far as possible.

The eighth step is that you should not have more than one credit card and that every time you use it, you write the amount in your checkbook on a separate sheet just like you write your checks. You must set a monthly limit on how much you will spend. Every night you should total it to see that it does not go beyond the amount.

The ninth step is that you must save one third of every dollar you make.

The tenth step is that you must give ten percent every month to charity.

Know your bills:

Heat, electricity, telephone, television, car's monthly payment, car insurance, car gas for the month, home payments, monthly groceries, any annual insurance payments divided by twelve, plus x amount for extra expenditure and y amount for emergencies.

This is your total bill and your income must exceed this.

If you give cash, ask for a receipt

At the end of the day, write what you spent in cash and what income you got Know the total amount of money you have at the end of the day

Checks

You must balance your checkbook every month with the bank statement. Every day you should subtract whatever check you write and add what ever deposit you made.

1.write your expenses in the same order every month. e.g. mortgage, electricity etc.

That way you will not miss any payment.

2.Write checks in consecutive order

3.If a check is void write that check consecutively in the next available line and write void in explanation.

That way you will remember which check was void

4.Do not try to match your balance with the receipt you get from the bank in the middle of the month, as some checks may not have cleared.

Match only when you get your bank statement but know your balance at all time

5.When you get your bank statement:

A. See if the checks that had not cleared last month did so this month. Mark the ones that have not and put them on the "not cleared" sheet.

B. See that all checks of this month in your checkbook match those in your statement. Mark those that are not present in the statement. These are checks that have not cleared. Put them also on the "not cleared" sheet. You will need to keep money in the bank for their clearance.

C. Add all your checks that cleared from last month with:
a. the checks that cleared from this month,
b. the service charge and
c. the automatic deductions taken by the bank (for example by your credit card).
This is your expense and should match the expenses shown by the bank

6. In the bank, you have your balance from the last month.
Add all deposits you have made this month to this balance
Add any interest you got.
This is your income.

7. Add to this the total amount of checks that did not clear this month
This is your actual income at present and should match you bank income.

8. Minus your total expense from your actual income and you will get your balance. This should match the bank balance to the penny.

Always keep money in other separate accounts for education, emergencies or big items you are planning to spend on. What you earn must cover your expenses and have some additional for a rainy day.

Your wife must have as free an access to your account as you do. Do not try to control your wife by denying access to the money.

Chapter 31.   GREED

Greed is the addiction to money.

When you have greed, you will not follow any ethics in order to make money.

You will order unnecessary meetings, materials, inspections, or tests or consultations.

You will steal each others' workers, secretaries, or contracts.

You will demand and take kickbacks.

You will deliver poor-quality work.

You will take bribes to perform the work that you are paid to do.

Your work will have contamination, impurities or imperfections.

You will not give money to run the household.

You are a capable breadwinner yet you insist that your wife work and then hand over the money to you. Your plan of getting rich is through your wife's labor.

You will neglect the upbringing of your children in order to make money.

In times of illnesses or accidents, instead of being humane, all you can think of is the money involved or lost.

All you can think of is a bigger house, a newer car and a grander way of living; and you are willing to compromise all your principles and cut anyone's throat if he gets in your way.

You do not care about the pain that you will leave around you in your family and society as you follow your aim.

You refuse to share your money with anyone. To you, money is power. The only money you give is when you have to achieve your aim or where you can impress others.
Any one of these points is greed.

Inside you, there is no peace and happiness. You act as a hypocrite with others. The more money you have, the more you crave it.

Read the chapter on addiction.
Any addiction destroys the individual and our society.

Chapter 32. MONEY AND MARRIAGE

Money is the number one cause of fighting in marriage.

A man who is mature and has no inferiority complex wants his wife to know as much as he does about their financial status. But the man with an inferiority complex views money as power and refuses to share it with his spouse. He will allow her to work, but all money has to be turned over to him. She is intelligent enough to earn it, but only he is "intelligent" enough to decide how to spend it. However, if he earns the money, then the rule becomes twisted to say that since he has the intelligence to earn it, then only he has the intelligence to spend it, and he must be treated like a lord for feeding and clothing others.

If she earns more than him, it is "our money." If she earns less than him, it is "his money." So, what he is saying is that "our money" is "my money" and "my money" is "my money." This can be reversed if the wife has the inferiority complex. This is wrong. This is a point of view that you must clarify before marriage.

Marriage vows are to care, share, and be absolutely fair.

The marriage is a unit of two people combining their time input and resources and becoming one unit. If a man says that since he earned his money, it belongs to him alone and only he can decide how and when to spend it, then he should not get married. He should live alone. He should not reap any benefits of marriage. The woman elects to stay at home for the benefit of the family and the children, but she works hard, and what she does is invaluable. What she does keeps the marriage alive. But she is a partner, not a servant.

If you do not earn equally, you cannot be expected to contribute equally to expenses.

All money is to be shared. Someday the state will honor the value of the marriage union, and all paychecks given to married couples will be in both the names of the husband and wife. All money information, the assets and the debts, is to be completely shared by the husband and wife on a weekly basis. No decision to spend major amounts should be taken without discussion between husband and wife.

Neither husband nor wife should spend it on his or her siblings without discussing it with each other. Both should support their parents in old age.

Chapter 33. FRIENDSHIP

Treat your friend as you wish to be treated by him.

Care about him.

Share his joys and sorrows. Be there in times of need, in illness, in death.

Do not betray his trust. Do not steal his job, goods, employee, friend, fiancé or spouse.

Do not criticize him behind his back.

Keep your word to him.

Be responsible and dependable.

Defend him. Never listen to those who tell you not to be involved even if they are your superiors. It takes moral courage to be involved.

Protect your friend, his property and his family in time of danger. Give them shelter and take care of their needs.

But be honest and fair. It is your job to correct him if he acts unfair, cruel or immoral. Do not stay with him if he continues to do so.

Friendship or therapy does not mean that you just listen when your friend or patient is grieving. There is something terribly wrong about a patient having to be in therapy for years to learn to handle his mistakes or pain.

True therapy and true friendship means that:

you listen to his problems,

you give advice and

you inquire how the patient or friend is doing financially so that he is not neglecting his livelihood and compounding his problems.

Thus, you have:

1. Let him cry out his problems (vent his grief).

2.You have made sure that he can financially support himself. (He is not going bankrupt).

3. You have sympathized (offered support).

4.You have pointed out that other specified people have gone down this road and survived (offered hope).

5.You have pointed out that other people have had terrible misfortunes and made it (offered courage).

6.You must also point out advice and solution as you see it, even if the topic is death (offer solution or coping mechanism).

Any listening without advice is meaningless. We would much rather take advice and go on our way then spend years going around in circles trying to see why we did what we did. Even that answer could have been had in the first week.

These points are practiced in villages and cities around the world with success in places where one has not even heard of a psychiatrist.

What you do not say is that "everything will be alright". This is another meaningless phrase created by the movie industry. Everything will not be all right. You do not know that and when you comfort another person, you will not tell lies. What you can say is that "this is awful, and I pray that you will have comfort and strength to get through this. How can I help? I hope everything will get better. God willing, everything should get better".

Chapter 34. RELATIONSHIPS

Relationships should be built on honesty, trust, self-control, and never on cruelty and manipulation. But, because this can be one sided, you never shut your brain and become blind in trust. You must protect yourself as well. Only then can you see that the relationship is perhaps more valued on your side than his/hers.

Those who say not to question them and not to think are your worst enemies. The person who really loves you always wants you to think, be aware, be intelligent, and know how to protect yourself. So, make sure that you know what your economic situation is at all times and that nothing is hidden from you.

Do not believe in putting out equal money for expenditures if you are not earning equally.

Regardless of whether your house or gifts were donated to your partner, all assets should be in both names if this relationship is to survive.

Do not stay with someone who wants you to earn while you are trying to protect and raise young ones.

Do not have a relationship with a person who is living with someone else even if he/she says that it is a mere formality or he/she is forced to do so. True love for you should make him/her leave that person and marry you.

Do not become intimate with a person while he is married as you wait for a divorce. If he wants you to wait for a divorce, then he should wait for intimacy.

See that the person finds out in the very beginning whether you will be acceptable to his/her family and introduces you to them. Your relationship will eventually be with the whole family and not with just one person. Your relationship should never make you rude and non-caring to the rest of your family or make you ignore your responsibility to them. The partner is good for you only if he/she tries to bring the family together and not tear them apart.

Understand that you never grow strong because you stay with someone. You always grow strong yourself through your own awakening inside.

You do not stay with someone so you can change him/her, because you will never be able to do so. Instead, you will have a life of pain.

You never have a relationship by trampling over someone else's heart, or by stealing another person's mate.

Understand that "men will play at love to get sex, while women will play at sex to get love."

You can protect yourself only if you have some moral beliefs and principles and learn to face the fear of living alone. A man is not afraid to live alone. A woman sometimes makes the mistake of thinking that she is only half until she meets a man. It is not true. You are two complete people sharing your qualities.

You do not walk away from a relationship saying it is over whenever you are angry, unless you want to develop mental problems. You are allowed to walk out only in a case of abuse. You do not walk out saying, "What am I getting out of this?" You are not supposed to be getting anything out of this except the knowledge that this is a relationship with good and bad times, with times of suffocation and times of contentment; and that you have to care, share, and be fair, and sustain this relationship. The commitment to the relationship does not depend on how you feel about it from day to day.

You do not live with someone while waiting for the wedding date. Doing so is equivalent to a woman saying that she does not care about protecting her rights and the rights of her children. Doing so is equivalent to both parties saying that they do not care for morality or the values of society.

Why then should they be given the protection of society in terms of police, finances, pension etc.? You first get married then live with someone. Marriage is a lifelong relationship that has been cemented and protected by society's approval. It protects the woman and her children. If you live in a society, you cannot ask for its benefits, e.g., police protection, and yet feel that you owe the society nothing in return. Then you should go and live in a forest. You should always sustain the society by conforming to its values unless what the society is doing is immoral. Even if you feel that your conscience is clear, your actions should follow the mainstream of society's approval. You cannot say that what you do is your business. It is like a wave saying that its movement will not create a ripple effect in the ocean. Your actions will affect society.

The only thing that you marry ultimately, the only thing that will determine whether you will be happy or sad, is character. The only thing that matters in any relationship or friendship is character. And because the apple does not fall far from the tree, your partner will show the family's character at some point.

Just as you can induce radioactivity in a material by putting a radioactive substance near it, so your partner will revert to the family character if a family member comes to live nearby. This can be dangerous in families with a history of abuse. It is far better that you help such families from afar.

The things that destroy any relationship are selfishness, non-caring, betrayal of trust, lack of respect and cruelty. To give a person, with these traits, another chance is asking to be kicked again. Go by his/her past actions. Do not go by future promises. Character does not change overnight. It only changes when it receives an adverse action as a consequence, not just the "threat" of the action.

If you only value your family, you will have no friends.
If you only value your friends, you will have no family.
The crux is balancing and being fair to both.

Children, who think that only their friends matter, and that family life is second to their social life, ultimately lose the family life. Just as you weave the network of friendship by ongoing dialogues and creating pleasant memories, so equal importance should be given to time spent with your family, and the extended family, creating pleasant memories and forming a rich network to extend over the years to support you.

All family functions get priority over visits with friends.
A visit by a rare friend gets priority over regular family affairs.
A visit by a rare family member gets priority over affairs with friends.

You do not step over your moral boundary with relatives and friends. You do not flirt or have games with physical contact with the spouse of your relative, with the relative of your spouse, or with the girlfriend or boyfriend of your friend.

Chapter 35.   WHEN ARE WOMEN AND MEN NOT EQUAL?

Generally, men are physically stronger than women. For this reason, heavy manual jobs in any area should be restricted to men.

Men and women have different organs and thus are designed for different roles.
A man cannot bear a child. Only a woman can do so. For this reason, no one should expect her to perform equal to a man or at her full capacity when she is bearing a child. She should be given a lighter load and given time off in the third trimester.

Only a woman can feed the child with her milk. For this reason, she should be allowed to not work in the first year of the child and allowed to feed and nurture it.

A woman gives birth and nurtures. Her primary role is caretaker of the family and the children. She passes down the values and beliefs to her children. Taking care of children is never quality time. It is immense quantity time. A man's focus is primarily on his work for which he is willing to spend long hours away from home without any guilt. He is anxious to move up the ladder. In every animal species, the mother rears the child because she is designed to do so. The child must never be played with in court battles and shunted from home to home every few days or weeks. This is a very unstable influence on the child.

The custody of the child must be given to the mother unless she is mentally or physically ill and incapable of taking care of the child. Even if she marries, the child should stay with her.

A man gets aroused by the body of a woman. This is the way nature designed his body. For this reason, male nurses should not take care of female patients. We are having problems with male doctors examining females and are passing laws for a chaperone to be present at the time of examination. Think of the male nurse who is bathing the female patient, touching her body and passing her bedpan!

Being treated by a male nurse violates the modesty and decency of a woman.

For the same reason, electrocardiogram technicians and x-ray technicians should only be female for female patients.

A woman cannot say that if she can control herself when looking at a man's body, so can he. The two are not equal! A woman's hormones are different from that of a man's, even chemically. For a woman to go around baring her breasts and wearing provocative clothing is asking to be attacked because we do not live in a society where men are castrated. You cannot ignore nature.

Chapter 36.   RULES FOR FIGHTING

Do not hit. Do not throw things. Do not break things.

If you feel like doing any of those things, freeze. Ask for time out. Put the discussion on hold. Go for a walk. Do not drive. Read a book. Watch television. Go talk to someone else. Put the baby in the crib where it will be safe from you.

Wait until your emotions are under control. Once you put the argument on hold, you still have to keep talking on other subjects. That is what you would do in an office.

Before you resume the discussion, remove other stress factors like fatigue, hunger or shortness of time.

Stick to the point at hand. Do not drag in whatever else bothers you. State, "We are sticking to this topic."

Do not bring in past mistakes unless they are related to the current point.

Do not attack the intelligence of the other person.

Do not attack the relatives as well.

Your aim is not to pass the blame but to see that the point does not happen again.

Do not insist on a thing just to show that you are the person in charge. There has to be a reason for the point to be agreed to.

The point of discussion cannot compromise basic needs of sleep, rest, food, money, consideration, fidelity or morality of the other party.

There will be no insults, no name-calling and no demeaning of the other party or his/her relatives.

Do not speak at the same time. Give each other turns.

Hear the person completely. Even if you think what he/she is saying is completely wrong, listen to what is being said. Do not shut the other person out completely and start concentrating on what you are going to say next.

Do not use the language of the bully.

The bully uses sentences like, "If you want to have relations with me, you will have to give in," or "You are making me angry," or "I do not care," or "I will/will not do this even if it bothers you," or "End of the discussion" (when the bully is losing).

The bully will, during almost every argument, say that you misunderstood or are confused. This is a common trick to attack your intelligence.

The bully will call you names and say that you are stupid.

The bully shouts, throws things, breaks things, slaps, punches, drags, or beats. You do not want to have anything to do with this person ever again, even if he/she apologizes, even if he/she cries. Understand very clearly that this person is your enemy, even if he brings the food to the table.

Immediately start looking for a way to escape. Become financially independent.

If you are fighting, and the other party starts shouting or name-calling, walk out of the room. Say, "We will discuss it when we can do so in a civilized manner." Bring the topic up after a few days.

Sometimes the discussion has to be held in front of a third party because your partner will behave more reasonably and civilized in front of a third person. Also the third person can bring up a point that you both may not have thought of.

Chapter 37.   MANNERS

Good manners start at home and then progress outward.

Get up when a woman or any person deserving respect, senior to you in age, authority or knowledge comes in.

It is the height of good manners to be on time.

Stand up if a teacher or a judge comes into your room.

Stand up if you are visiting a patient and the doctor enters the room. Turn off the television or radio.

Stand up if you have made an appointment to see someone and that person enters the room.

Smile and look at the person who comes in and greet him.

Greet a person and ask how he is before you start stating the reason of your visit or call.

Do not call a person by his first name unless he or she gives you the permission to do so. Until then address the person as Mr., Mrs., Miss and the last name or sir /madam, or uncle or aunty or brother or sister.

Do not ask," who is this?" on the phone. Say" who is calling or whom am I speaking to?"

Do not ask, "What do you want" Say "what can I do for you?"

Say, "please" before a request. Say "thank you" after a service done.

Let a lady, elderly, a weaker person or a child go before you. Open the door for them or offer them your seat.

Do not interrupt someone who is talking to you. Wait until he finishes. If he interrupted you, but is senior, let him finish first. Do not tell him that you were talking first.

Do not walk in and start talking if two professional people are discussing something. Do not walk in announcing what happened to you without caring to see if the other people are already talking. Always walk in quietly at work.

Do not talk across or over the head of a person who is doing mental work or is studying or reading.

If someone is reading, do not talk loudly or start talking about your personal life.

Offer others to get in the car before you

Greet a new neighbor and ask if they need assistance

Do not chew gum while working or if you are at an appointment.

If someone asks you for help, do not criticize them, insinuating that they are stupid or slow or cannot remember what they were shown before. Tell them how to do the problem without any comments. Repeat if necessary the same way.

If anyone eats at your home, stop what you are doing, and go and sit with him or her while he or she eats.

Offer, to everyone around you, whatever you are eating or drinking before you start.

Do not hold a formal conversation on phone while eating.

When somebody you know comes to your house, greet him or her. Offer them a seat. Do not keep them standing. Offer them something to eat or drink.

Spend sometime with the guest even if he or she is a guest of your relative. Do not run off to your room or run off with your friends or to your telephone or computer. It is a skilled art to be able to make conversations with people you do not know and to make them comfortable.

When the guest leaves, come down or up from wherever you are and see him off.

Mealtime is not for one person to eat alone while the rest watch television or sit in their rooms. This is true even if you have had your meal. Always go and sit with the person who is eating until he finishes the meal.

Do not eat your own meals and expect your in-laws or parents to cook their own. This is selfishness. Similarly, do not wash your own dishes and expect your in-laws or parents to wash their own. Then this is not a home. If you wish to have dinner then it is your job to see that everyone has dinner.
If you clean dishes, you cannot just clean up your plates.

One person does not work while the others sit around. Offer help. Have division of labor with your equals. You do not offer division of labor with your parents or parents in laws. Never let an older person work while you sit around.

When you leave a home , look around you to see if you can help with something before you leave. Put the dishes or chairs away. Clean up the table . Tidy up the room.

When you get up in the morning, do not first get on the phone to make a social call. Your first duty is towards your family. Smile, say good morning, complete your body hygiene for the morning, sit with them, laugh and talk with them as you would with your friends, make plans for the day with them, have breakfast with them and then make your social calls.

When you come in the evening, greet your children, spouse or other family members with warmth. Leave the answering machine on and give your undivided attention to them for the first half an hour. This is not the time to criticize. Do not say, "leave me alone, do you not see how tired I am or I need time alone to myself". You would never say this when you reached your office. Your family is more important.

Meal times should be family times to renew your connections.

Always treat your parents with respect. Never call them stupid or other names. Never tell them that what they did was dumb. Never tell them to shut up.

Do not call seniors "old men" and "old women." Treat them with respect. They have some things you lack completely. These are called wisdom and experience.

Do not let your elders work while you sit around. Get up and help them.

Do not ever make fun of elders or scold them.

Make sure that your senior relatives get access to their relatives and friends, as well as have some type of entertainment.

Parents, do not treat your children with contempt. Be considerate.

Offer to help when you are a guest.

It is far more impressive to be courteous and considerate, than to be aggressive and loudmouth.

Do not walk in front of your family like a general. Walk with them.

Open the doors and let others go before you.

Offer help if someone is carrying something heavy or needs assistance to cross the road.

Let a pedestrian "walk" across. Do not drive so that others run for their lives. Do not run over animals. It is murder.

Let another car go before you.

Do not answer a beeper or a phone while you are in the middle of an appointment. Shut it off before you go in. Do not answer it if you are with a customer; or you are the customer and have reached the cashier; or if you are in the middle of a small store where you are interrupting everyone; or if you are talking to a doctor, a policeman, lawyer or any professional person.

Manners and Hospitality

Honor and welcome your guests. Make them feel welcome and comfortable. It is a sign of development and maturity.

In many countries, poor as the people are, a guest is considered a visit from the Gods. Surely, you can show some graciousness. Smile and be courteous at all times. Do not ignore them or not talk to them.

Do not ask or expect people, who come to visit you to cook, clean or do chores in your house.

Do not fix alternate days to cook and clean with them even if they stay for a long time.

Do not ask that the room your guests stay in is neat to your taste. It is their room for the time being. Leave them alone.

Do not be upset if the house is not at its usual neatness. You do not live in a museum. Your graciousness is far more important.

Do not state nor display a board stating, " These are the rule of my house". It is the height of rudeness.

Do not cook only for yourself and expect your guests, relatives, in-laws and parents to cook for themselves. This is selfish and rude.

Do not treat sisters/brothers-in-law older than you as equals in terms of asking them to do chores. You do not ask people senior to you to do chores.

If your guests are sleeping in the day or night, be quiet and do not disturb them. Do not insist that they get up.

Do not expect them to take the bed sheets to the laundry before leaving. This is your job.

Do not jump up every time a guest uses something in the kitchen and clean the place. Do not say, "Do not touch this". Relax. Clean it up at one time.

Do not ask your relatives or guests to clean the bathroom if they have used it.

Do not ask your female relative to do any cleaning that you would hesitate to ask from a male relative of the same status. In fact, you should not ask your guests to do any cleaning.

True hospitality is to take care of your guests as you would take care of your own family, cooking for them, cleaning after them, spending time with them chatting and buying items for their needs. And one must do it graciously.

Do not say that your own family is priority. That means that you are still selfish.
If the guest has come after some time, the swimming or other items planned in your own family do not get priority and should be subject to change.
If relatives have come to visit your brother etc, or if there is a family function, you do not go away sight seeing. That is highly rude and selfish. You take your family to visit the guests and thus teach your child family values.

You do not take money from a relative for staying at your place for a long time unless he has a full time job and offers it.

If your parent or relative is dying, you do not say "call me after the nurse declares my relative to be dead". If you are called, you should be on your way there. When someone is dying, you do not sit in the next room. You should take turns to sit by the dying person's side. Do not leave the dying person alone in your house.

As a guest you should make sure that your visit is not a burden and that you make it pleasant.
Bring gifts when you visit someone after a long time. It can be fruits, food items, plants, flowers etc. Do not go empty handed. You can bring something for the children alone or something for the house.

If someone brings you something in a bowl or plate, do not return it empty. Always fill it with some thing to eat.

Help in the kitchen. Do not relax, watch television, stay in your room or go to bed while the host/hostess is cooking or cleaning up but work side by side with them until the work is done. This is unless you have done a night shift or heavy work and are exhausted. Then help when you are fresh.
Help in any other way you can in the time you have, be it in advice, listening, repair, babysitting etc.

Do not keep your hosts up at night by keeping the radio or television on while they are sleeping. Do not disturb their sleep. Say your prayers quietly.
Do not leave the light on if they are sleeping in the same room.
Do not start making a noise in the morning, disturbing their sleep.
Whatever you have to do, do it quietly. Do not sing in the bathroom or sing your prayers aloud.

Do not spend excessive time in the bathroom. Do not read in the bathroom. Get out of there as fast as you can. Other people have to use it too.
Clean the sink every time you use it so there is no hair or stuff. Empty the garbage daily from the bathroom.

Make sure your surroundings are neat before you leave for the day or permanently.

Bring some groceries, fruit, or flowers for the house occasionally. Alternatively, bring toys or balloons for the children. See that you help in carrying big items if you are stronger.

Make sure that your speech is not offensive. Do not criticize or make fun of or insult the home, the people, the city or the country. Do not insult people that your hosts or their guests like.

Do not insist that people do things your way. Do not do something the hosts do not like.

Do not discuss religion, politics or other items that can send everyone into an intense argument.

Do not dress in a way that shocks your hosts. If they do not wear shorts in the city, do not wear shorts. Remember, "In Rome, dress as Romans do".

Do not dress provocatively. Be modest. Do not use heavy perfume. Do not wear dirty clothes. Do not stay in the clothes you slept in. Take your daily baths and at all times dress neatly.

Do not flirt with the people in the house.

Offer to take the guests out to a dinner or movie.

Do not embarrass your guests by your lack of manners or by your offensive behavior.

If you bring many people from the village because someone is ill in the city, it is your job to ask your host how he will manage to put everyone up.

It is your duty and the duty of everyone in the group to help with the expenses. It is your duty to take as much food items from your homes or the stores as you can. It is your duty to help the hostess with as much work as you can. Do not be a burden.

If you plan to stay for a long time and have a full time job, offer to pay some money monthly.

Always be modest and decent.

Good manners help others feel comfortable around you.

As you mature, you change from caring only for yourself to caring about your family, to caring about your guests, to caring about your neighbors, to caring about your society, to finally caring about the world.

Read inter-personal skills in *Life-Skills*.

Chapter 38.   MANNERS AT WORK

At work, it is important that one be disciplined. One never has fun at work if it is at the expense of being professional. Being professional means that you have self-discipline.

Be polite.
Your voice must be low so that it disturbs no one.
Never talk over a person's head to another person. Move away to a place where he/she will not be disturbed.
Do not walk in greeting people loudly or start talking as if no one else is in the room. Do not disturb other people by your entrance. Your entrance must always be quiet. Smile your greeting.
If someone states that he is being disturbed, apologize. Do not state that that is the normal tone of your voice. Only an inconsiderate fool will do that.
Do not walk in, remarking on what happened to you. Wait until people are free to be with you. An office is not a place to discuss your personal life. Do it at lunchtime.
Do not walk in and start talking to someone who is already in conference.
Do not talk or ask questions across the room to each other. This disturbs people who are working.
Do not keep passing remarks.
Do not talk to yourself while working.
Your personal calls have to be in a low voice. You are not at work to make personal calls. All calls have to be for minimum time for urgent reasons only.
Never stay on a personal call if someone needs your services.
Never be on a personal call if a customer is in front of you.
Be quiet if someone is on the phone.
Do not use curses no matter how upset you are. If you speak trash, you must be trash. Do not make cheap or filthy jokes.

Dress professionally and not in your casual clothes unless you have permission.

Do not hold a conversation with your colleagues or discuss your personal life in front of a customer.

Do not chew things or blow bubble gum. Do not sing at work unless everyone is doing physical work.

Do not eat or drink in front of a customer.

Do not take personal phone calls in front of a customer.

Do not discuss another customer in front of a customer.

Do not comb your hair, file your nails or put on make up in front of customers.

At work, do not put the radio or television on. You are there to work without distractions. The radio or television can distract your colleagues or customers. This is also a violation of the rights of people with attention deficit disorder.

There should be no radios or televisions in banks, financial institutions, libraries, Intensive care units, emergency rooms, nurse's stations, police stations or anywhere that one has to concentrate.

Make eye contact with the customer, smile, and greet the customer and offer him a seat if he has to wait.

Never imply to your patient or customer that he is forgetful or slow in understanding by your expressions, tone, or words. Do not say, "Let me start again," or "That is not what I said" as if talking to a child. Say, "I am sorry if I am not making myself clear," and explain it in another way.

Never ask for bribes or ask for something in return to expedite the job.

Never sit at your chair and tell the customer that you are on break. If you are on break, you should not be sitting there. If you are on break and the customer walks in, help him.

Never make a person stand in front of you and start talking on the phone. Either tell the person that you will be with him in a moment and finish the call as fast as possible, or if the call is lengthy, put the caller on hold and handle the customer.

Always try to finish the first job and then start the next one.

If a line of people starts forming, give them numbers to be called in sequence.

Work fast and efficiently.

Never ask a person to come back the next day for work or receipt that you can do for him that day.

For nurses at work

Do not keep talking aloud with others about whatever interests you or about your personal life when a doctor walks in. Greet the doctor and return to your work.

Do not discuss your personal life over the head of the doctor while he is reviewing the chart. Go to another room or wait until he leaves.

Do not ignore the doctor and keep talking on the phone with your friend or relative while he stands by waiting. Tell your relative you will call him back later. Greet the doctor and answer his questions.

Do not barge in when the doctor is discussing the case with another nurse and say, "Guess what happened to me today?"

Do not keep talking with others about various topics of interest while the doctor is doing an endoscopy or performing other procedures. Be silent. Be attentive to his needs and let him concentrate.

Do not walk away when the doctor is talking to you.

Do not put the radio on at your station. The doctor is already being talked to by many people. He is pulled in many directions. He needs to concentrate. The care of a patient is at stake! With a talk show going on the radio at the same time, how do you expect him to concentrate? For you to taunt, "Oh doctor, you do not even have the ability to concentrate because the radio is on," is unacceptable.

Nurses in operation theaters, delivery rooms and same day surgery cannot treat these places as their homes and sing, shout across the room with personal stories and crack jokes with each other while the doctor is trying to concentrate, do a procedure, deliver a patient or do surgery. This is rude, highly unprofessional and puts the patient's life at risk. No human being should agree for surgery in a hospital without asking the administrator if they have a code of conduct for the nurses in the surgical areas.

The brain concentrates best with the least number of stimuli bombarding it.

Chapter 39. MANNERS OF TEENAGERS WITH ADULTS

These should be taught from childhood:

When somebody calls you, answer.
If they cannot hear you, get up and go to them.
If you said that you were coming, do so within five minutes.
Do not barge in and interrupt people. Wait until they finish talking.
Do not talk at the same time as the other person is talking.
Do not tell an adult that you were talking first.
Do not treat an adult as your equal.
Look at the person when you are talking to him/her or he/she is talking to you. Be still when you are being scolded.
Do not walk away while a person is talking to you.
Do not grab things. Do not take things while others are holding them.
When you eat something, offer it to others first.
When somebody comes to your home and is your relative, an acquaintance, or a friend of another member of your family, do not go to your room. Greet the person, sit, and make conversation with him/her. Offer him/her food and a drink.
When you walk to a car, look at the driver before you get in. He may need your attention.
When you get out of the car, open the door for others. Check to see if they need help.
Do not fight back. Defuse the situation. Be silent.
Be considerate. Be silent when someone is sleeping.
If someone is concentrating on work and asks to be left alone, honor his wishes.
Be helpful. Look around the house. If there is something that needs to be done, do it.

If your parents or siblings are sick, cancel your plans. Stay at home and take care of them.

You cannot give priority to your own plans over the ones involving family. Family and relatives come first.

Be neat. The teenage years are not the time to live in a mess. They are the time for developing organizational skills that will be critical for your future.

Care, share, and be fair.

Chapter 40.   WHY DO YOU WANT TO SHOW YOUR BODY?

"I am expressing myself."

What exactly are you expressing?

"Who I am."

Are you a different person when you are covered?

"Well, I feel good."

Why do you feel good when you are exposing your body?

"I feel I will only be noticed if I am exposing my body, because when I am covered, I am ugly. I have no talents, or I am so nondescript that no one will ever notice me."

So, you have to do something immodest and indecent in order to be noticed?

"Yeah, that's how the singers do it, right?"

Notice the inferiority complex speaking out.

Notice the influence of the rich and famous, untalented people.

1. Understand that the person who exposes his body is scared that people will not like him if he is covered.

2. He does not know how else to attract attention to himself because he thinks that he is nothing when he is covered with clothes or if he stays decent.

3. He does not know how else to feel important. He is a person with a deep inferiority complex.

4. He feels that the media only focuses on people who show their bodies.

The rich and famous people are those who became so, not because they had a shred of talent, but because they exposed their bodies or did something indecent.

Those are the only type of heroes left.

5. He has not found himself. He has no map for the road of life and is groping to find what works in this society and what will make him feel big.

6. He feels that he owes nothing to his family or society. He does not love them. He does not care about the shame he brings to the family or the damage he does to society. This type of person will not be able to have a loving relationship with anyone. He/she will not have a "normal" family life.

What he does not understand is that he will get noticed, but will get no respect or admiration from others. They will look at him as you look at any weird object. This will further decrease his self-respect. He may have money but will feel empty and loveless. Ask rich people why they are still running to the psychiatrists and why their lives still have pain.

Why did Marilyn Monroe kill herself?

An "indecent exposure invites only a disrespectful response."

Notice that the person who does not go around exposing his body is one who:

is comfortable with himself even if he stays covered in public;

feels important even without shocking anyone;

has values and moral beliefs;

is not lost (he has a map for the road of life; he does not need to find himself);

has goals;

is educated or is getting educated;

is loved and is capable of forming loving relationships;

is an achiever;

is truly talented; and

has faith.

Remember that Princess Diana beat the other girls in competition for a prince while staying covered.

The Taj Mahal in India, one of the seven wonders of the world, was built by a king for his beloved who was always covered. To be beautiful, you need a little mystique to arouse curiosity.

A talent must be true in itself.
Lack of talent must not hide behind lack of clothes or sexual acts.
It must be decent and beneficial to society.

Chapter 41.   MODESTY AND DECENCY

Modesty should be in speech, clothing, and actions.

Clothing

Do not display your body to cover your lack of personality or intelligence or talent.

Immodest clothing invites a disrespectful response and even an attack.

"You are asking for it."

When a woman says she has a right to wear provocative clothing and it is up to the male to control his response, it is equivalent to a chicken saying that it has a right to parade in front of a hungry lion.

You are never liked because you have a large chest or big buttocks or swing your hips. That attraction, if any, will last a couple of months. But the charm of your personality can be lifelong. Remember that the Taj Mahal was made for a woman who was covered, and Princess Diana was fascinating to the world even though she was covered. Your attraction has to come through your personality, charm, and manners.

You do not bare your breasts or your cleavage.

You do not wear transparent clothes that show your nipples or your pubic hair. You do not wear clothes that show your cleavage or cleft.

You do not wear clothes that tightly outline your chest, buttocks or panties.

Do not wear spaghetti straps to work. Sleeveless shirts should have the sleeve covering two inches of the shoulder.

Do not wear skirts three inches above the knees. Thighs in a skirt excite men.

Backless clothes for women are immodest.

Do not wear shorts that are not at least four inches below your buttocks.

Panties and swimwear should not be cut high at the hips.

Do not wear G-strings.

Men should not wear underwear or swimwear that outline their genitalia.

Men should wear boxer shorts and underwear.

Do not parade naked, or in your underwear, in front of your children.

Fathers, do not allow your daughters to parade in their underwear in front of you or their brothers once they reach puberty.

Do not bathe naked with your children. What are you accomplishing?

Speech

You are what you speak. The words have to be first formed in your brain.

So, by speaking trash, you become trash.

Do not use words for excrement.

Do not use vulgarity in speech or gestures.

Do not indulge in sexual jokes.

Actions

Girls do not sit with their legs spread apart.

You do not touch or scratch your genitalia or private parts in public.

You do not fondle or have sex in public.

You do not bathe nude in public.

Do not indulge in suggestive dances where you jiggle your breasts or put your pelvis against another person's pelvis. Do not touch other people's private parts. Do not jut your pelvis and genitalia forward. Do not put your hands or mouth on other people's chests or legs or buttocks.

Do not be nude in public.

Male and female students should be taught separately about the facts of life.
Students living at school should always be placed in separate buildings for boys and girls with curfew times.
Education is also about learning self-control, decency, and morality.

While feeding milk to one's baby, one does not expose one's breast in public or in front of the male members of one's family (father, brother, cousin etc.). This is not natural. This is immodest and indecent. If you say that animals do so than understand that firstly, you are not an animal and secondly, in the animal kingdom brothers mate with sisters and fathers mate with daughters. You cannot apply one rule and not the other.

Broadmindedness never means that we give up modesty and decency.

Chapter 42.   WHY YOU SHOULD NOT DATE BEFORE YOU ARE TWENTY

Our lives are subdivided into stages of baby, childhood, youth, adult, and old age. Each stage has its own beauty. The immature person cannot accept this. He either wants to grow up too fast or clings to his youth when it is long gone. One age cannot be put into another without harmful effects. One cannot be a baby in adulthood with freedom from responsibilities. Nor can we have a child who mimics an adult.

We seem to be most confused about the stages of youth and adult. We think it is okay to remove the boundary between the two. We think it is "broadmindedness" to treat youth as adults and to give them the same liberties that we have.
We are dead wrong. Our logic is that everyone else is doing it. This will never absolve us from our responsibilities.

Youth and adult are two very different stages.
An adult has finished his development. A youth is still developing. He is growing taller, and his body is filling out. Some of his organs are still maturing.

In adults, the sex hormones have settled into a cycle. A youth's sex hormones are erratic.

An adult has finished his education. A youth is still struggling with his/her studies and needs a lot of concentration to absorb the education needed.

An adult has developed a set of values and character. A youth is still trying to "find himself." He has no map for the road of life.

An adult understands that his actions will have consequences. A youth believes that his will not. He is invulnerable.

An adult has the financial means to handle the consequence of sex. The youth is dependent on adults financially.

An adult has overcome peer pressure. The youth is swept away by it.

The consequence an adult endures affects him and his partner. The consequence a youth endures creates havoc in two families.

Chapter 43.   THE BOY-CRAZY GIRL

The period of ages nine through eighteen is critical for a girl.
A girl will go "boy-crazy" in this stage only:
if she has been left to entertain herself with sexual shows or to
be with boys with no adult supervision, or
if her parents are sexually permissive, or
if there is no caring for her, or
if she has low self-esteem and thinks that the more boys she
can attract, the more valuable she is, or
if she has fallen in with the wrong crowd.

Be wary of this period.
Be close to your child.
Be alert to her needs of reassurance.
Set high goals and moral values. Follow them yourself.
Keep her busy with extracurricular activities.
Do not leave her alone.
Monitor what she watches on shows, reads or hears.
Do not allow her to date.
Know the company she keeps.

Chapter 44.   DATING RULES

Women, you do not dress provocatively. You do not show your breasts. Do not show your cleavage. Do not dress in a tight dress outlining your hips or breasts.

Firstly, this will arouse a man. It is like a chicken parading in front of a lion and saying, "I am your equal. Look at me but do not eat me."

Secondly, it gives him the message that you are asking for trouble or that you are cheap.

Thirdly, it draws attention away from yourself to your body. Remember that you need him to like you as a person. It is only your personality that will keep him to you. Your body can be used by him and forgotten. But your personalities will decide if you will be happy or miserable together.

No matter how "mature" you feel, do not invite a man to your room alone. Do not go to a man's room alone.

Men and women:

Date in public places.

Date with a group of friends.

Date in daylight.

Dating is to get to know each other's personalities, to see if the person can be a prospective life partner. It is not to physically explore each other. Keep your arms off each other. This is not the time for kissing. Your kisses are reserved for the person who becomes your life partner. This is not the time to jump in bed with each other.

Dating is not the time to have sexual relations. Those are to be had only after marriage. If the man says that it is okay to have sexual relations because you are going to be married or because you love each other, refuse!

Sexual relations are only to be had after marriage. If he threatens to leave you, you must have the self-esteem to let him do so. You are too valuable to give yourself to anyone without thinking of the pain ahead that will come in your life without the protection of social sanctions and without the foresight of protecting your future child.

Just because everyone else is doing it does not make it right. You will find a man who values these beliefs as well. Do not date while studying in college. You will lose your concentration and your goals. This is particularly true of women. This is the time to strengthen your foundations for knowledge and financial gains, which could later keep you alive and prevent abuse.
Men, you are not spending the money on a girl so you can get something physical in return. It is far better that you pay your meals separately or in turns. Make the rules clear in advance.

Remember that the only thing that you marry is character. Get to know the character first.
Remember also that most men will want to date so that they can play the game. He will "play at love in order to get sex, while a woman will play at sex in order to get love." Have clarity of vision. Do not play games.
If he says, "If you love me, you will say yes," say, "If you love me, you will not ask."

Chapter 45.   SPOUSE MATERIAL

Never marry a person because he / she has fallen for you. Only a person with an inferiority complex will fall for that. "You" have to fall for the person. You do not fall for a person just because he has fallen for you. That way you will end up marrying idiots and abusers. The person must be worthy of you.

If you have high self-esteem, you will first see whether the person is worthy of you.
What you marry, what will bring you happiness is character. So, study the character of the person. You never marry a person. You marry a family. So, study the family. The apple does not fall far from the tree.

See that he /she is:
honest and moral,
responsible. Dependable,
prays,
willing to share work, decisions and money,
calm,
considerate,
courageous,
caring,
clean,
neat,
organized,
fair,
faithful,
hardworking,
kind,
tries to unite,
tries to defuse,

able to control impulses and desires,
has housekeeping skills,
financially wise,
social and
balances his/her life.

See that he/she is not:
Wavering,
Depressed,
Addictive,
Greedy,
quick-tempered,
abusive,
cruel,
selfish,
possessive,
immoral,
wasteful of money,
wanting control by making all decisions over money,
a cheater,
liar,
in debt,
unable to hold a job and
one who wishes to be supported by his wife.

Understand that the person who is chasing you will change the day after marriage and start showing you his/her true colors. So how will you know what he/she is really like? You learn by watching him/her. You know by having your parents and friends ask about his/her character at work, at sports, from neighbors and from relatives. No law of privacy can be applied here.

You must have the following questions answered before you marry:

1.What are your opinions about sharing housework? What housework are you willing to do daily? What will you do if your spouse is exhausted?

Do you believe that you should not care if the spouse had no sleep or food?

Do you believe that someone should pick up after you? Are you messy or organized?

2. What are your opinions about showing all balances of money, investments and pension plans to the spouse monthly, and whenever asked, even if the spouse is not working?

Who will make the decision about spending how much money and what items can be bought? Will both parties have equal access to the money?

Do both parties have to share equal expenditure if they are not earning equally?

Will it bother you, the man, if your wife does not work?

Do you believe that a mother should stop working for the first five years of the children's lives? What about when they are teenagers?

Do you believe that when she is not working, she should still be shown all bank accounts and have a say in how the money should be spent?

3. Do you believe that the spouse should be contradicted in front of the children?

4. Who will discipline the stepchildren? The biological parent should discipline the child except in case of abuse by the parent. However, the stepparent should treat the step- children with caring and fairness at all times.

5. Do you have the right to be rude to your in-laws? Would you be willing to control your wishes for the greater good of the family? Do you believe that the family should not be divided?

6. Do you believe in having friends over every month or week? Do you believe that your spouse should go out with his/her friends alone?

7. Can you tolerate pets? Will you help in their care?

Read "marriage" and "separation and divorce" in Life skills before you marry.

Chapter 46.   MARRIAGE FOUNDATION

Do not marry until your foundation for marriage is secure.

This is done by knowing:
self-discipline,
courteous treatment of each other, in-laws, of neighbors and friends,
housekeeping skills: cleaning, sewing, cooking, repairs, laundry etc,
financial wisdom,
how to be thrift,
child- rearing skills,
entertaining skills
by having a spiritual foundation to give to each other and children and
by having a moral foundation.

Moral foundation:
Ladies you do not go out with your old men-friends. Men do not go out with their old girlfriends. You cannot say "this is my friend" if the person is of the opposite sex. This is not broadmindedness. This is immoral. You cannot have friends of the opposite sex. Do not be alone with the opposite sex for dinner or movies.
Do not flirt with others. Do not have open marriages. Do not exchange spouses. Never ask your spouse to do anything immoral.
Do not contradict each other in front of the children.
Do not insult your spouse in home or outside home
Do not hit your wife. Do not mentally or emotionally abuse wife.
Share knowledge of money
Care, share and be fair

The wife visits her parents as you visit your parents
Care for your in-laws as a son or a daughter would. Do not have double standards that you can support your parent but she cannot. It cannot be that the groom's relatives can accept gifts from the bride's family but the bride's family can receive no gift from the bridegroom side. In a festival, both sides can get gifts from each other.

Do not bring hatred and division into families. Bring them together. Treat your in-laws with love and respect. Care, share and be fair to them. Do not make them cook their own food when they are with you. It is your job to cook and clean after them

When in-laws fight, stay out of it unless it gets out of hand. Then suggest that they take a break and discuss it later. Stay calm. Treat each other's parents with love and respect. You marry the whole family.

Dress modestly. Wake up at a fixed time every morning. Empty your bowels every morning. Brush your teeth and bathe in the morning. Change your clothes.

Pray before you start your work. Teach your children to pray with you.

Lay out the night before, things for the next day.

Keep your home neat and clean. Clean the kitchen at night and make the rooms neat.

Have division of labor with your husband.

Do not watch television while eating. That is "family time". Do not let children watch television more than one hour a day. Do not force children to finish their plates. Let them listen to their satiety center in the brain that tells them that they are full.

Write what is needed to be bought every day so that by the end of the week your list is ready. Add to it by seeing what you need for breakfast, lunch, dinner, snacks, and for cleaning the house. Keep some presents ready in case you have no time to get them. If you have an unexpected guest, do not ignore him while you give the others presents. That is rude. Give some cash if you run out of presents.

Every night check the cash you have
Write what you spent so that it balances. Make your purse neat for the next day. Every month wives must check the balance in every account, see the amount in stocks, and pension plans. Do not give up this power.
Save at least ten per cent. Check all your insurances monthly and see what is the amount due, when they finish or mature.

Try to defuse the situation. Be quiet when the other person is angry and just listen without fighting back. You can always discuss it later. You do not call each other names. You do not speak at the same time. Read the chapter on
" Do you have the right to make mistakes?"
Learn the rules for fighting in "Marriage" in life skills.

Welcome new neighbors. Take some fruit or flowers and visit them. Introduce yourself and say that you will be happy to help if needed. Partake in their sorrow and joy.

Make sure you entertain every month. Keep in touch with your friends. Make new ones. Build your social network so that you are surrounded with friends into your old age and your children benefit from this extended family.

The man who treats his family with rudeness, non- caring and contempt, who does not give money, who does not care nor shares, who is not fair, who feels the fact that he earns makes him alone to be intelligent enough to decide to how spend the money, who is inconsiderate to the needs of the spouse and the family, is a fool and builds his house on sand. He will be unloved and lonely. He will have no peace.

The man who cares, share and is fair; who treats his wife with love, respect and fidelity; who shares work, money and decision, who wishes to give his children the best education, and who is social and neighborly has built a strong foundation.

Chapter 47.   MARRIAGE VOWS

Do not marry until you have a physical, mental, emotional, social and spiritual foundation as well as know housekeeping skills. You would not accept a job position without having the skills and knowledge. This affects your whole life! If you build your marriage on quicksand, it will sink. Read the chapter on marriage in *life skills*.

Marriage can be a graveyard, an open battleground, a silent warfare, a tyranny, an abandonment or a friendship. No one expects this to happen but it does. This is why you must do your homework. You cannot learn this by living together before marriage.

Marriage vows are:

A. Each other

to care, share, and be absolutely fair;

to share wealth, property and decisions including financial ones;

to respect each other as equally intelligent beings;

to be considerate of each other;

to have only one spouse (you cannot have more than one husband or wife at a time);

to be faithful and not indulge in extramarital affairs;

to pray together daily and to lead a moral life;

to not ask for a dowry (by the husband);

to not insult your spouse privately or in front of others;

to not practice physical, mental, or emotional abuse;

to never ask your spouse to do anything immodest, indecent, or immoral in the name of love;

to each have the freedom to eat and drink what he/she likes or visit one's parents when one wants;

to be available during times of need or sickness and provide medical support, comfort and care;

to help each other when the person is tired and
to provide the basic needs of rest, undisturbed sleep, food,
shelter and clothing;

B. In-laws:
to treat the parents of both spouses with respect;
to agree to take care of both sets of parents in their old age and
not allow them to be alone;
to consider each other's family as one's own and
to bring both families together and not tear them apart;

C. Social life:
to have a social life;
To have friends weekly or monthly,
To expand the network,
to see that both parties spend some time together alone daily
and
to see that the spouse can spend time with her/his friends but
not at the expense of neglecting his/her duties to the home;
Please note: do not meet people with opposite sexes alone in
the name of personal friendship once you are married.

D. Children:
to help your spouse raise the children with love and guidance;
to never contradict your spouse in front of the child;
to not insult, demean, or make fun of the spouse in front of the
child;
to lay emphasis on bringing the child toward God;
to teach the child to pray;
to give them the best possible education and
to know that it is your duty to teach them moral values and a
good character.

E. Finances

to understand that intelligence and money are not related;

to make sure that either spouse has full access to money (to agree that the money belongs to both and will be deposited in both names at all times, and there will be no power play over money—the person who earns money will not say that only he has the right to decide how to spend the money; if so, then he should not be married);

to sit down at the end of each week and go over the finances and keep your spouse completely informed of all assets and debts;

to discuss all expenditure with spouse;

to not control a spouse by taking away friends and access to money.

F. Society:

to help and protect our society, and not do anything to destroy it;

May God bless this union!

It must be declared at the time of marriage as to how much "support money" will be given by the husband to the wife if the husband and wife separate.

This amount must fully support the wife unless she remarries, or can support herself, and must support the children until the age of eighteen. This is separate from the division of assets. It must become immediately effective at the time of separation. One should not have to go to court for this.

This agreement should look like this:

"I, name, swear that in the event of a separation, I will pay the amount----- for rent, food, and clothing per month. I will support the children's clothing, food, and education until they are eighteen by this much-------amount per month per child"

.

This form must be notarized, and witnessed by two people plus the person performing the marriage ceremony. When the occasion arises, it should be submitted to the employer and the amount taken from the husband's paycheck and paid to the wife. One should not have to go to the court for this.

It cannot apply if the woman gets married again or starts living with a man.

Chapter 48.   SHOULD YOU HAVE AN EXTRAMARITAL AFFAIR?

A woman or a man who has an extramarital affair is a weak person or an immoral person. A weak person will think that she is not good enough to deserve a person who is free to be totally hers. She is willing to accept only half of what should be rightly hers. So, if a married man glances at her with attraction, her low self-esteem is grateful for the attention, and she "falls in love."

A person with high self-esteem will acknowledge the glance of attraction but will consider himself/herself too superior. He/She will only accept a total commitment from the future mate and will not settle for anything less.

Any relationship, be it with your doctor, banker, or lover, is doomed to fail if it is built on lies and deceit. It is a betrayal of trust. You will not tolerate your banker if he says that he lied because he was attracted to you. You should not tolerate this from any other person. Any relationship built on lies and deceit can bring no happiness to all concerned, will cause you to lose your self-respect, and will earn you the hatred of his or her family. It will give you a life of loneliness and pain.

If a man cannot be faithful to his wife, why should he be faithful to you?
Would you want a cruel person? What this person is doing to his/her spouse is cruel.
He will not divorce his wife because he does not want to hurt her, but what about the pain he is causing you? If he says he will not divorce his wife because he cannot destroy his children's home, understand that he is destroying your home. Understand also that any child's home is destroyed if his parents do not love

each other. If he says that he cannot get a divorce because of his reputation, but wants to have an affair instead, what about your reputation? Do you really think you deserve no better?

Do not go for physical attraction to a married person If he says he is attracted to you, tell him that a relationship based on physical attraction cannot last. You will not settle for half a person. Why would you be attracted to a man who is not honorable?

If you say you only feel good when this person is around, you are weak. If you had high self-esteem, you would feel good about life even if you were alone. Your involvement would only be to share your happiness. You would not need to cling to a person in order to feel happy.

A man has an extra –marital affair when he has no morals , nor character, or he has a severe inferiority complex. He can only feel popular by the number of conquests he makes. Rest assured that he has no peace. He is not to be pitied. He can only have our contempt.

The mature man is comfortable with one mate. There is always a fine line that one has to cross to step into immorality and the moral man will not do that. He values his family.

Read the chapter on marriage vows and marriage in *Life Skills*.

Chapter 49.   WHEN SHOULD YOU HAVE A BABY?

You never have a baby in order to express your love for a man.
You never have a baby to trap a man.
Bringing a baby into the world is a very big commitment, not only to the baby, but also to society and also to God. Do not have relations with a man until you both sign this covenant:

A. Commitment to the baby:
When you bring a baby into the world, you are making certain promises to it.
1. You are willing to stay at home and take care of it.
You do not have a baby and then turn it over to your mother, or others, and go back to work or school. You had the baby. You stay home and take care of it.
2. You are willing to be awake at night, night after night.
3. You are willing to change diapers and clothes full of vomit.
4. You are willing to have the patience to hear endless wailing.
5. You are willing to be no longer able to do what you want and are willing to take care of this infant for months and years.
6. You are willing to let its demands precede yours.
7. You are willing to put your education, career, and social life on hold.
8. You will have the money to feed it, clothe it, take care of it medically, and give it toys and education.
9. You will give it the stability of a permanent home with two parents and will not move from man to man or woman to woman.
10. You will give it society's approval in terms of a marriage license.
Understand that it is difficult with a baby to move out of an abusive situation.

B. Commitment to society

You will be responsible for the baby and will not allow it to be a burden on society to the best of your ability. You will have society's sanction in the form of a marriage license. If you are a man, you will put your education on hold and will work to provide income for your child and its mother. You will give the child your name and bring it up with moral values. You will fight to keep your society safe and moral for it.

C. Commitment to God

You understand that this baby has come with its own personality. God has given it to you for safekeeping. You will not abuse it but bring it up in love and patience, and reinforce its faith in God.

Chapter 50. IS "QUALITY TIME" RIGHT?

Your children need your time. They need "Quantity" (not quality) time.
"Quality time" was a term invented by us Westerners to hide our guilt for not behaving as parents.

Parenting does not mean that you have a bit of fun with your child and then he goes back to the caretaker.
Parenting is not about taking the child to karate classes, music lessons or the basketball field, and seeing that he did his homework.

Lots and lots of time is needed to teach them life skills, body hygiene, manners, modesty, decency, morality, fundamental beliefs, and religion.

Children only learn by being with adults and watching how they behave in hundreds of situations. Otherwise, they will learn what they can by roaming in packs of their peers or from the worst teacher of all, the television. Then they will spend years trying to "find themselves."
Do not abandon your responsibility to them. A child is told a thing hundreds of time, and then it finally sinks in. All this needs time.

If you do not teach your children prayer;
if you do not teach your children religion;
if you do not teach your children morals;
if you do not teach your children to be kind to animals;
if you do not teach your children to care, share, and be fair;
if you do not teach your children to be modest or decent;
if you do not teach your children to be helpful;

if you do not teach your children to fight abuse and unfairness;
if you do not teach your children body hygiene;
if you do not teach your children to be neat;
if you do not teach them to not be lazy;
if you do not teach them basic self-discipline;
if you do not push them to have goals;
if you do not give them a drive to achieve;
if you do not show them that you have expectations;
if you give them no frustrations to handle;
if you do not teach them to respect the family and society;
if you do not teach them friendship; and

if your idea of parenting is not to say anything to them and to not let anyone else say anything, then you, and they, will pay a terrible price.

Teaching all the above needs quantity time, and it may not be "fun" for either, as the term "quality time" applies.

If you refuse to interfere in the children's dispute because they are over eighteen, if you do not care what they do all day or how they live, if you do not care how their present actions will affect their future, then you are a hypocrite if you say that you love them. You are a non-caring parent.

Chapter 51.   WHAT TYPE OF CHILD DO YOU WANT TO RAISE?

Will it be the child who only knows karate, basketball and soccer?

Will it be one who is rude to his parents?

Will it be one who feels it is the duty of parents to entertain him?

Will it be one who cheats and lies?

Will it be one who is taught that as long as you win and make money, nothing else matters?

Will it be one who is lazy, selfish and non-caring?

Will it be one who is immodest , indecent and immoral?

Will it be the one whose teacher is the television?

Or

Will it be one who has been taught to turn to the source of strength , God, and pray?

Will it be one who has manners, modesty, decency and patience?

Will it be one who can control his desires, impulses , his anger and greed ?

Will it be one who has honesty, fairness, moral values and courage ?

Will it be one who is unselfish and caring?

Will it be one who is hard working, self-supportive and has drive and goals?

Will it be one who can also cook, clean, be neat and organized?

To teach all this is the duty of the parents.

This takes quantity time, never quality time . "Quality time" was words invented by us to hide our guilt for not fulfilling our duties as a parent.

It meant that as long as we had fun with our children , we were good parents.
This is a lie.

To teach all the above requires tremendous time.
The true definition of a parent is one whose child is best able to handle the bad times after the parent is gone.

A child is not bonded by spending an hour shopping with his mother or seeing a movie.

A child is bonded only by three things:
1. Love. The child believes that his parents love him.
2. Trust. The child believes that you will take care of him to the best of your ability; that you will teach him self-control; that you will prevent him from doing what is wrong and guide him to do what is right; and that you will be available to the child.
3. Respect. The child will respect you only if you are moral, fair and caring. This is not done in one day

The child has to be taught that family functions supersede what individuals want to do that day. You do not go sight seeing when the rest of the extended family is having a function. This is selfishness and does not teach the child family values.

If you spend your life running after money, if that is the only thing of value that you show your children, if you do not do parenting from the time your child was born, rest assured that your old age will be full of sorrow.

If you live an immoral life, rest assured that your old age will be full of sorrow.
Read the chapters on character, frustration, parenting and what makes a good human being in *Life skills*.

Chapter 52. MATURITY

Balancing
One must balance in harmony the work, the home, the children, the spouse, the relatives, the society, the self-development, and the spirituality.
Whenever one part overtakes all others in importance, you will feel the adverse effects.

Maturity does not mean old age. Maturity means wisdom. An eighty-year-old man can be completely immature, and a thirteen-year-old child can be mature beyond his years.

Our lives are subdivided into stages of a baby, childhood, youth, adult, and old age. Each stage has its own beauty. The immature person cannot accept this. Either he wants to grow up too fast, or he clings to his youth when it is long gone. One age cannot be put into another without harmful effects. One cannot be a baby in adulthood with freedom from responsibilities. Nor can we have a child who mimics an adult.

Maturity means that we must first be comfortable with ourselves. We must like and respect who we are. Then we must be comfortable with others in our family and then with others around us if we wish to be happy. We do this by caring, and by being fair and considerate.

One develops in eight ways:
There is a physical maturity.
There is a mental maturity.
There is an emotional maturity.
There is an animal maturity.
There is an educational maturity.
There is a financial maturity.

There is a social maturity.
There is a spiritual maturity.

Read about maturity in *Life Skills*.

Chapter 53.   MILESTONES IN DEVELOPMENT

We have attained milestones in our development when:

We have overcome anger. A person who cannot control anger can be led to make mistakes.
We have overcome arrogance.
We have become honest.
We have developed patience and calmness.
We know that neatness and good manners begin at home and at an early age.
We are able to handle dirt and can clean up other grown ups who are filthy.

We care, share and are fair at home, and outside, to people, animals and birds. We realize that it is this that brings peace.
We realize that animals too, need their own company and keep them in twos or more. We realize that they have the right to run, jump and move freely instead of walking slowly, tied down.
We do not take their land or water away and we do not put fences in their way.

We charge our batteries every morning by dipping into the source of our strength, our God.
Our prayers consist of listening as well as talking.

We know that our homes belong not only to us but also to our children and to our parents. We do not say that we have no room to our children and we do not say that we have no room to our parents.
We do not allow our parents to live alone in their old age but keep them with us and take care of them. This is the only way we can conquer selfishness and pay back the gift of life. And

we treat them with respect and caring. They have two things we lack, wisdom and experience, so we take their advice seriously.

It is a milestone when a man realizes that a spouse not earning is working as hard as he is. The financial reimbursement of cleaning, cooking, laundry, babysitting, grocery shopping, doing errands, being a chauffer and public relationship, not to say about love and the companionship, is quite high. His cash is equal to her "kind"(work). Therefore, he must share what he earns equally with her. He must make joint financial decisions with her. He must respect her. He must never say that she "owes" him, or that he feeds and clothes her. He must never think that because he earns in the outside world, he is more intelligent than she is. This is a milestone.

We realize that to be a good parent we have to treat the other parent with respect and fairness.
We refuse to let the fear of losing our children prevent us from speaking out and correcting their wrong behavior. It is a weak parent who hides behind the statement that everyone is doing it so it is justified. We realize that all our money is worth nothing if we are not good parents; that parenting is a lot of "quantity time" and that letting the children grow up with full freedom is not parenting.

We realize that it is in control of our impulses and desires that we progress.
We know that all our knowledge and skills are worth nothing if they are not accompanied by self-discipline, and that this should begin at an early age.

We want to offer excellence and the highest quality instead of just making money.

We value money. We become financially wise and earn what we are worth. We treat money with respect and do not throw it away but save as we go. We do not let out personal sorrows prevent us from knowing our bills and earning money to pay them. Those who treat money with disdain do not have it.

We are courteous to those beneath us.
We want to bring our families and people together, instead of dividing them.
We refuse to accept abuse of any kind. We let go of all toxic relationships. We refuse to stay where we are not treated with respect.
We believe in modesty, decency and morality.
We realize that wavering is a sign of weakness. Conquering it is a milestone.
We make decisions mentally instead of emotionally.
We can let go in peace.
We overcome loneliness.
We have a clear picture of what we want to become, what are our strengths and what are our weaknesses.

We realize that no homeowners' association, despite their rules, can curtail an individual's freedom to live as he wants, plant what he wants and have whom he wants in his home. People are not supposed to live in carbon copy homes, told what they can and cannot do, and destroy their individuality. The rights given by the nation are above all rights.

We realize that entertainment can have a powerful deleterious effect on society and must be bound by rules so that "it does no harm".
We realize that freedom of speech, dress and actions must be regulated by moral codes. There is no freedom without responsibility.

We realize that the people we elect are our servants. We do not let them run the country any which way after the elections. It is the duty of every one of us to decide how our country should be run. We get rid of the politicians who ignore the welfare of our society. We follow only one rule, "how is this action going to affect the welfare of the society, the children and the animals". We get involved when our fellow men suffer. We get up and fight against immorality, injustice and cruelty.

We bear our cross, or carry our bag of pain, with our honor and morals intact.
We overcome fear, including fear of death.
We are completely shattered, or have lost our loved ones, or we have lost everything, but we can still pick up our pieces and go forward without losing our identity. We realize that we have an identity without our loved ones, without our money, without our homes or without our country. And we go forward without neglecting our skills, without being a burden on society but by being self sufficient, helping our fellow men on the way and at all times living with honor.

We progress from caring only about ourselves to caring about our family, to caring about our society and then to caring about the world.
We move from" my family is my world" to "the world is my family".

Chapter 54.   SELF-DISCIPLINE AND SELF-CONTROL

There is a physical self-discipline.
Self-discipline is obtained by developing certain habits so that they become automatic and you no longer have to fight with your feelings at every step. That leaves you free to reach your goals.
You get up at fixed times, you finish your work before your enjoyment, e.g. your homework before you watch television, or you finish certain things at the end of the day, you get the things ready for the next day, or you do not do certain things and so on.
You get up early enough in the morning so that you do your body hygiene, bathe, pray and have ten minutes of peace before you leave. You do not just get up and rush out the door.
You fast once a week/ month through one meal.
You do the proper breathing exercise once a day.
You do your physical exercises daily or three times a week.
You finish what you start.
You stay neat and organized.
When you leave your room/house in the morning, it is neat. When you go to bed , your home is neat.

Your willpower grows through your control of sleep, food, desires, and breath.

There is a mental self-discipline:
when you control your desires,
when you think of certain things at certain fixed times,
when you do not think of certain things at certain fixed times (you need to study so you do not daydream),
when you concentrate,

when you keep yourself together in times of severe opposition and torture,

when you keep yourself calm in news of great calamity and carry on your duty, and

when you can control the bubbles of thoughts in the ocean of your mind.

Self-discipline at work is necessary to achieve certain goals and to avoid energy from being frittered in useless activity.

Self-discipline is necessary in your personal life to get strong, to avoid abuse from others, and also to allow internal knowledge to come through. Self-discipline takes your energy, which is scattered in different directions by your whims and fancies, and streamlines it so that you become in charge of it. Self-discipline allows your energy to progress in a linear stream instead of exploding in all directions.

Self-discipline also determines how you react to external temptation.

Self-discipline is different from self-control.

Self-discipline is doing something your body or mind does not want to do.

Self-control is not doing something you want to do.

Chapter 55.   WHAT IS SPIRITUALITY?

Understand very clearly that spirituality is the connection of the soul to God.
You do not get spirituality from turtles, food, or other objects.
Feeling good about something is not spirituality.

Spirituality is the path of the soul back to its creator.
Spirituality requires purity of body and mind, truth, modesty, decency, prayer, self-discipline, self-control, morality, and meditation.

There is sunlight around us, but to reap its benefits, one has to go out in the sunlight to get vitamin D or a tan.
There is water all around us, but we have to go and drink it, instead of other beverages, in order to get its beneficial effects.
There is air around us, but we must not clog our lungs with smoke if we want to be healthy.
There is electricity around us, but we have to make the connection in order to reap its benefits. It will not work unless you connect the plug.
There is a spiritual sea around us. We can make contact with it to nourish ourselves, or we can stay without it and suffer the effects like one does when one gets no sun.

You have to go into the sunlight in order to get vitamin D.
Similarly, you have to do certain things in order to contact the sea.
You have to stop smoking in order to get the beneficial effects of pure air. Similarly, you have to stop doing certain things in order to get the benefits from the sea.

What do you have to do to make contact with this spiritual sea?

Speak the truth and be honest.

Care, share, and be fair.

Do your duty for the sake of duty.

Conquer your anger.

Have no addictions.

Live a life of moderation.

Rise from being fixated on your genitals to being fixated on the higher centers of your mind.

Be decent and modest.

Fight against the display of indecency and of pornography.

Help others in secret.

Have a fixed time of solitude in order to make contact.

Have a fixed time of prayer.

Pray in silence.

Live the life of a moral being.

What must you not do in order to make contact?

You must not be controlled by anger.

You must not be greedy or cruel.

You must not be immodest, indecent or immoral.

You can control your body. Obviously then, you are not the body.

You can control your mind. You force it to study or tell it to not think of certain things. So obviously, you are not the mind.

You can control your emotions, so you are not an emotion.

Then who are you? Why do you have this amnesia?

You are a soul that has a body. You are not a body that has a soul.

Everything in the universe is governed by laws. The apple falls down because it follows the laws of gravity. We have seasons because the earth follows the laws to rotate around the sun.

Similarly, there are spiritual laws.

Some of the spiritual laws are:

You can get spiritual nourishment if you make the effort.

The good you do to others makes you a better person.

The good you do to others gets rewarded if done in secret.

If you knock on His door, it will open.

If you touch His feet, or if you greet Him with respect, you will get a blessing.

Silence at some part of the day is necessary for you to develop and become strong.

Only by leading a life of purity, moral conduct, discipline, self-control, truth, caring, freedom from anger, greed and cruelty, can you get great insights.

If you follow the above and speak only the truth, what you speak can become the truth.

The bad times are to teach us. But the good times are to test us to make sure that we do not become immoral, immodest, indecent, non-caring, and cruel. And if we do, we will have no peace.

There is a spiritual wealth, and you can keep earning it by prayer, by self-control, by helping others, by control of your desires, and by control of temper. Once you have it , you cannot be in want.

This spiritual sea is the extension of God.
As a doctor and a scientist, I attest to His presence and bow in reverence.

Chapter 56.   HOW CAN YOU HAVE PEACE?

1. By letting go when someone wants to go.

2. By realizing that all your caring cannot convert non-caring people into caring ones.

3. By treating your spouse with respect, caring and fairness.

4. By treating others with respect, caring and fairness.

5.By doing your best and leaving the rest in God's hands.

6. By realizing that winning is not everything.

5. By living your life by moral principles and the highest ideals.

6. By not doing anything that would cause shame and regret if found out.

7. By doing penance of an equal degree if you caused shame and regret.

8. By believing that the end never justifies the means. By never compromising your principles.

9. By controlling your desires. Desire is like a fire. The more you feed into it, the brighter it burns. Self-control is the key.

10. By knowing when to give up the fight.

11. By knowing that you cannot control how others behave toward you.

12. By knowing when to walk away.

13. By not having anger, greed or cruelty.

14. By knowing that death is but a door to another world.

15. By coming to a decision instead of vacillating.

16. By knowing that you cannot change someone.

17. By knowing that in acceptance, you have peace.

18. by realizing that there is a haven of peace within you. You only have to reach it. You must dip into it daily.

19. If you practice cruelty to animals, you can have no peace.

20. It is not enough to just have peace within. The next step is to leave peace where you go.

Chapter 57.   WHY SHOULD YOU BELIEVE IN RELIGION?

Religion gives you guideposts to lead your life with the least possible mistakes and therefore the least possible pain.

Religion gives you moral values, which give you strength, stability, and peace.

Religion helps you to overcome panic attacks and avoid the need for anti-depressants.

Religion minimizes your chances of developing mental problems.

Religion helps you to handle the bad times and sorrow.

Religion prevents you from being corrupted by the good times.

Religion helps you to develop your character.

Religion helps you to differentiate between right and wrong, between good and bad, between what is moral and immoral, and so has a tremendous effect on society. Religion never tells you to not think for yourself.

Its lays forward profound truths and encourages you to think about them.

Religion leads you to God and so gives you a source of power.

The man who has been brought up in religion does not take time to find himself. He is never lost.

Our leaders who say that the state is separate from God and religion are literally doing everything to destroy our society. By turning away from religion, they encourage immodesty, indecency, and immorality. They then are busy putting out fires, which they created, because nobody has moral values to follow. These leaders are hypocrites because they start praying whenever a catastrophe occurs, but in good times, they want to have prayer removed from schools.

What we need are leaders who say that they believe in God and respect all religions. The state is separate from religion only in that it allows worship of all religions. Our leaders must believe in, and insist on, moral rules. They should start their day with a short prayer. They should allow nothing in the name of freedom if it violates modesty, decency, and morality.

There is no freedom without responsibility.

We will bring God, prayer, and moral rules back to our schools.
Before you vote for a politician, ask what his/her stances on God, morality, and decency are. Do not vote for him if he has no clear convictions.

Chapter 58.   WHY DO YOU CELEBRATE CHRISTMAS?

What is the purpose of the Christmas tree, the exchange of presents, and the decorations?

It is to celebrate the birth of Christ. So why do you make a mockery of the tradition by exchanging the presents and decorating, but refusing to pray to Him?

If you do not believe in Christ then choose another day to exchange presents.

But if you celebrate Christmas, then go to church, thank Him for being born, and follow His teachings.

The purpose of Diwali is not to decorate, have firecrackers, or exchange gifts. It is to celebrate the homecoming of Ram. Go to the temple, pray to Ram, and follow His ideals.

You cannot just join in the celebrations. What are you celebrating?

You cannot be a hypocrite. You must be true to your beliefs.

Any religious festival must first start with prayers and alms to the poor.

Chapter 59.   THE TRIPLE GATES

The triple gates to hell are anger, greed, and cruelty.

The triple gates to heaven are care, share, and be fair.

The triple gates to life are modesty, decency, and morality.

The triple gates to peace are:
to do your duty for the sake of duty,
to be the same in good times and bad times, and
to do balancing.

Chapter 60. MORAL RULES

The moral rules of a family are above that of a state. This is because the family is the core unit of society. If your family does not believe that people should drink, than the fact that you are twenty-one does not mean that you can drink.

Reason for moral rules.

Moral rules are essential for the functioning of any society. They lead us from "the survival of the fittest" to " the protection of the weakest". They join the society together and give it strength. Every individual knows that he will be protected by "prevention". It leads to a society that functions with minimum pain and self- destruction. The society is then free to progress.

If everyone does what he feels like doing, if everyone believes in "freedom without responsibility", than the society will have tremendous pain and destruction.

If I say that, "I do not care what people, and my parents, think or say. This is my personal life. I can live with a woman/man without marriage, have children without wedlock and so leave when I want", then how do the women and the children get protected? Who takes care of them ? The society! Whose money will be spent when these people will go on welfare ? The rest of us ?

What character of the child will be formed as the woman gets shunted from man to man and the child gets multiple fathers who have no time for him as everyone is busy doing what he/she wants? What basic identity will this child have of his parents?

How much pain will this child have and will he be capable of having love for others? Multiply this child by thousands and you have a section of human race that develops with the only aim of self-preservation and with no caring for any human being. Now what happens when this race attacks us? After all, we helped create it. We looked the other way and said that it was none of our business as to how a person lives his private life!

Anytime, abuse is committed; it is no longer a personal affair.

Anytime a moral law of a society is broken, it is no longer a personal affair because the repercussions will be felt by all of us down the line.

Living together out of wedlock and having children out of wedlock is abuse against the woman and the child. The persons doing so must be given a choice to get married or be fined and punished. One third of their paycheck must be taken away every month and put in a "security fund" to be available for the woman and for the child if the man walks out. They must sign that all property that they have will be divided between the two the minute they split and that the man will have money removed from his paycheck for the rest of his life for the support of any child and to support the woman until she is remarried. If they refuse this, they must lose the job and pay heavy fines. This is breaking the code of society and abuse of the woman and child. They must not be eligible for federal jobs. They cannot say that this is their personal affair because we pick up the pieces when they go on welfare or foster –homes.

If they are self-employed, the state should give them the option to marry or be fined and punished. The state must take away one third of the money they declare as earnings every month and put it in the "security fund" for the woman and child. They must sign papers that property will be divided if they leave each other.

If one of them is already married, than this is adultery and they must be punished for breaking the marriage vows, breaking the moral code of society and destroying the institution of family. This deserves imprisonment for three months. The persons must pay fine for every month that they stay in such union and lose any federal employment they have. People in public position must do the same and step down from their positions. How will you know if there is adultery? The spouse or the family member has to file a case of adultery and adultery must be recognized in court as a crime.

Those people who say, or who teach in the media, that they do not care about what people will say or how society will react when they break moral laws are guilty of turning against society. They are destructive to society, and so must be punished.
All benefits of society, including police protection, must be denied to them.

They cannot say that "I will enjoy every benefit that this society offers but I owe the society nothing in return. In fact, I will actively work to destroy its moral values, its very blueprint for survival".

Families will get torn apart as the weak get trampled upon; as "might is right" is practiced by every individual; as men will go from one woman to another; as children will be born out of wedlock and be killed or will have multiple fathers; as children will have no family life because they will be shunted from one home to another; as children will be left to fend for themselves because selfish parents will take vacations by themselves; as children will lose all respect for parents and turn against them; as women will have affairs outside the marriages so the family will be destroyed; as entertainment will only consist of sexual excitement and violence and so women, children and animals will be attacked as they fall prey to the uncontrolled sexual urges that have been fanned by the media; as people will live for the moment. Then they will become increasingly isolated and will turn to the television or computer for companionship. Thus, they will become available for brainwashing.

You can see that we believe in "might is right " today because the person who has money is able to flaunt all moral rules and get away with it. He is not punished.

The leaders are, naturally, busy running around putting bandages on every wound, and there will be plenty of wounds of rape, murder, pain, theft, illegitimacy, infanticide, violence in school, violence against teachers etc. These wounds could have been prevented by their foresight and moral rules.

But they are not looking for prevention. This type of society is called a torn and self- destructive society. This is a decaying society and all its technology will not prevent its destruction and its being over taken by another society.

The basic rules of society are:
1. that there can be no freedom without responsibility; and
2. that modesty, decency and morality are crucial for this.

Only when we first do not do what we want to do, can we then do what we want to do. This is because by controlling ourselves, we develop.

The life of a man is divided into:
1.Childhood.
You shall not take away the innocence of a "child".
You shall not allow child labor.
2. Youth.

Youth is for learning to master your senses, to develop good habits, self-control and learning. Therefore learning must be taught in an atmosphere of self- discipline, self- control, morality and prayer.

3. Adulthood.

The adult who has developed his foundation can now be a productive member of society. He can marry and form the crucial unit of society, the family. He most also be prepared to defend his society from attack.

4. Retiree.

The retiree who has reached old age must get the benefits of his toil. But he should still play an active rule in becoming the watch- guard of society. He must correct those astray and pass on the learning of the values. It is the retirees who must form or join committees of morality in education, morality in politics, morality in medicine, morality in law, morality in marriage, morality in childhood and morality in television and in computers. It is the retirees who can safe- guard the society . They must meet every month, and publish their recommendation every quarter in public statements. They must alert us to what is wrong and urge us to fight to correct it.

It is crucial in society that there is no segregation.

Children should not roam in their own gangs and the elderly should not be segregated into senior citizen homes. This breaks up society. The children can play at a fixed time but then must come home to spend a few hours with their family because it is then that the character is developed. It is then that they learn household chores . It is then that they learn adjustment. It is immoral to hand over the education to the television or computers.

Television and computers must be supervised and not be allowed to be seen for more than an hour a day . Active protest must be launched by you if the television or computers have shows that are indecent and immoral or if places of learning including colleges have uncensored programs for the students. The public must have available to them, six months in advance, all programs that the places of learning will expose their children to.

The children, the family, the grandparents and the extended family is the family unit and must stay as such. The person is responsible for his child and cannot throw him out . He is also responsible for his parents in old age and must be punished for throwing them out or for abusing them. Single aunts and uncles must stay with the family. They too, have the right to be taken care of. They too, have wisdom to give.

The state has to acknowledge the value of the family by giving tax breaks to those taking care of their parents, their grandparents and their relatives. This is crucial for the state if it wants a safe society.

We must treat our God with reverence .
We will not tolerate others treating Him with disrespect.
We must first start our day with a prayer to God.
What hypocrites are our leaders if they are the first to pray when we get bombed, yet refuse to allow prayer in school?
Prayer must be taught in school.
A state can be separate from religion but it cannot be separate itself from God, Prayer and Morality.

Moral rules are separate from religion. They are an entity by themselves. They are adopted by all religions, because only by following them can a society stay meaningful and with minimum pain and disorder. They extend across all religions. This is because, like all the cosmic laws, they are universal and unchangeable. A technically superior society will ultimately crumble without rules.

The moral rules (not lack of them) of a family are superior to any laws of the society because ultimately the family values are the core values of the society.

The state can say that it respects all religions but its job is also to protect them by never allowing any immorality to flourish. This is the duty of the state. It has to uphold all moral laws and enforce their public display. It cannot say that the display of moral rules is bias toward a particular religion because moral laws are the same in all religions.

Moral laws never depend on what you feel from moment to moment to be right or wrong. They do not change. Those who say that the moral laws are within you are referring to your voice of conscience, and never to your emotions.

There is no freedom of speech if the state allows you to publicly curse God and religion but does not publicly allow you to pray to him or refer to him in songs speech and writings. This is evil.

Politicians

If your leaders do not protect morality, than you must change your leaders because the welfare of a society is at stake. Ask them clearly, what their moral beliefs are. They cannot say that their personal beliefs are separate from the work they do. A politician's beliefs, morality, faith and personal life have a profound affect on society. If he wants to keep his beliefs and personal life private, let him step down from a public office.

A leader does not say, "Do what I say". It is "do as I do. Believe as I believe. Act as I do in my personal life" What great men do, the masses will follow. Since a politician must uphold morality, his character must be above reproach. If caught being immoral, he must resign immediately. It is immoral for him to work for even one more day. If he fights this, he must be taken away and imprisoned for betraying the faith of his people in him. Do not hurt the taxpayers by using their money to fight a court battle with a politician for obvious crimes, when there is proof or he has confessed. To use the taxpayers' money for such legal battles is a crime against the people and that itself is a cause for punishment. If he is sorry only after he is caught, that is no repentance. Once caught having committed a crime and punished, a politician should not be allowed to hold an office for the next four years. He cannot say that he made a mistake because he is human. So is a murderer! A politician cannot say that he has to go to therapy to know why he did what he did. This is the defense of a cunning man out to fool the masses.

Each of has a conscience that tells us what is right and wrong. Each of us is accountable for every act that we commit. Are you going to meet God after death and say, "I need to go to therapy to tell You why I committed my sins"?
God will tell you that you had the intelligence to know what you were doing.
If you do not have the intelligence, why are you holding that post? Certainly we do not want a leader who is so confused that he does not know what is right or wrong and who is ruled by his feelings and passions. He could put the whole country at risk!

You cannot hide behind your past to excuse your present.
No human being can ever say that he needs to go to therapy to know why he behaved the way he did unless he wishes to be considered mentally retarded.
You chose to give in to your anger, your greed, your lust, your cruelty and your temptation.

No human being has to be in therapy for months in order to grow up. Conquering anger, developing patience and self-control is part of growing up that we learn from our parents and people around us. If you have not learned this as a child, all you have to do is to make a decision that you will learn patience and anger management and you will gradually learn it. The first step is will power.

You must do self- study every night to see if you were able to do so that day and how you could have handled it better. You pray for intelligence and insight and you will get it. The most powerful tools in the world are thought and will power.

You do not go to a therapist and say," let me go over my past and see why I behave as I do". The past is gone. You have today.

Your first step should be, "I gave in to anger or temptation. What I need to do is to stop this. It is irrelevant as to how I was treated as a child. I am an adult and accountable for my actions. I can only do this by will power. This comes with determination and self-discipline. Therefore, I am going to start practicing physical and mental discipline. I am going to follow the chapter on anger. I am going to run from temptation and refuse to be in such surroundings (remember the saying you advocate, " just say no"?)

Otherwise, it is plain that you have a weak character. Who wants a leader with a weak character?

If a politician has made a mistake, he has to accept the responsibility like a man. He has to resign on the spot and await his punishment. He has to resign even if the people in his department made the mistake because the responsibility is on his table. He cannot fight to hold on to his position because that shows his greed for power and that shows his low character.

If a politician has made a mistake, he must be punished more severely than an ordinary individual because:

firstly, his mistake affects the whole country, and
secondly, he has betrayed the trust of the people who elected
him.

He cannot say that he is a victim.
Anyone over eighteen years of age who could walk away, who
is not mentally retarded and who knows how to say "no" is
not a victim. Again, this is the defense of a cunning man. It is
a sign of a low character that tries to see if he can confuse the
masses. However, we are not fools.

A politician cannot say that I went to church and confessed my
sin and said I am sorry, so everything is all right now. Then a
murderer should be able to do this. You betrayed the trust of
your family and the people. Your act affected many people.
You have to be a man and accept punishment. You also have
to do penance. In addition, you have to accept the contempt of
your fellow men.

A politician must never criticize any religion. He must be
removed if he does so.

A true leader cares for his people. It is immoral if he puts his
interests and those of his children, family and party above those
of the party.
A politician who cannot fight the abuse in her house cannot be
morally fit to lead a country.

If a politician, or a member of the politician's family, commits
a crime, be it theft, rape, molestation, drugs, torture, accepting
bribe, using public funds to build his business, using the
politician's power to give land, business or post to his friends
or relatives or any other crime, the politician must be removed
in disgrace immediately. Abuse of power is also using his office
perks for personal pleasure, to use public funds for his private

needs and pleasure, to have siren on his cars, to take away other people's land, homes or business or women, to beat people and to imprison people on will without a court process.

If the politician committed the abuse, he must be imprisoned. If it was his family member, the member has to be imprisoned but the politician also has to resign immediately for allowing misuse of power. He must not be allowed to stand up for elections again for four years. He has to pay fines to the people affected.

This has to be part of the politician's oath, "I will not, nor allow my family member to abuse the power of my office".

It is your moral right to have a democratic institution.

A democratic society does not exist unless leaders are held accountable; and unless a citizen has the power to see that they keep their promises, that the country is being run correctly and that steps are taken to alleviate any distress that he has.

It is never a democratic society if the politicians once elected do what they want. They were elected as servants of the people. Your duty is not just to give them votes. Your duty is to remove them if they do not run the country the right way; and you do not wait for the next general elections to do so. You must have the right to do so every six months in general votes on topics that have bothered you!

How else do you hold them accountable? By having juries for politicians where you can bring a politician if he has ignored your cry for help. It should be the same number of jurors and should not take more than one day. If he has ignored your cry for help for no justifiable reason, he must be made to step down. For a politician to write you a glib letter, after months, thanking you for sharing your thoughts with him, and ignoring your cry for help, is immoral. He must tell you what concrete steps will be taken in what time or why he will not take them.

235

If a citizen has a distress and writes to the politician, and his distress is not looked into, this is immoral.

A copy than must be sent to the "politicians ethic committee". This committee must respond in seven days.

If the bureau cannot satisfy the citizen and his complaint is justifiable, than he should have the right to make the politician appear before a citizens' jury.

The politician must appear before a jury to explain why he did nothing. If his reply is not satisfactory, he should be made to step down, and the person who came second in election take his place. There must be juries for politicians.

If a politician does not implement the promises he made within three months of acquiring office, he has to explain this to the public..

If he has no satisfactory reason for his lack of action, he must be made to step down and the person who was second in election asked to take his place.

It is immoral for politicians to vote themselves any increase in income unless the public votes in agreement.

It is immoral for a leader to not overturn any law that allows animals to be tortured.

It is immoral for a leader to allow punishment of people who are trying to prevent cruelty to animals

It is immoral for a politician to not overturn any law that allows shows to be seen that take away the innocence of children. It is immoral for him/her to not overturn any law that allows television and computer to show things that flaunt immodesty indecency and immorality, and that show sexuality and pornography.

It is the duty of a leader:
to see that his people get justice;

to see that their poverty and distress is alleviated;
to see that they are protected from invasion from other countries;
to see that they are protected from criminals in the society and to see that they are protected from immorality within the society.

Ask a politician before you vote for him ,
Do you believe in God?
Do you believe in Prayer?
Do you believe in Moral rules, decency and modesty?
Do you believe that our environment should be modest, decent and moral?
Do you think that our current entertainment policy is having a deleterious effect on children and society?
What do you plan to do about implementing them?
Go to the chapter on , "Do our leaders believe in decency and morality" for further details.

General moral rules

Do not be a hypocrite. Do not praise someone at his face and stab him in the back.

Do not cheat. The end never justifies the means. You loose terribly in self- respect and self- power.

Do not steal.

Do not accept bribe in any form. A person accepting a bribe should be severely punished. This includes contributions demanded by politicians to hear a complaint or to handle a matter.

Do not kill except in self- defense, in grave injustice, to protect our freedom or to prevent a calamity.

Do not lie.
If you speak or act nothing but the truth, you get great power inside you. Truth can unleash a powerful force. It can lead you to great insights. Combined with prayer and willpower, it can lead to an explosion in personal development and self-esteem. If you speak only the truth and pray, what you speak can become the truth.
However, if there is a need for a higher morality, as in cases of saving the lives of innocent beings by lying, than a moral being will take the sin of lying, and accept the consequences.

Keep your word. Your word should be as good as any contract. People breaking verbal agreements should be subject to punishment as long as there are witnesses on both sides who can testify to the same thing.

Fulfill any responsibility given to you.

Speak out if your friend has been wronged. Correct the person who has wronged your friend. It takes courage to be involved when wrong is done to others. Those who tell you to not be involved are cowards.

You cannot excuse a wrongdoing because you "loved someone", or because you too have problems.

Be faithful. Resist temptation, by running away. Giving in shows a weak character. No therapy is needed to discover this.

Do not hit someone weaker than you, nor a woman, nor an animal.

You do not torture in the name of religion. You cannot kill because others do not follow your faith.

You cannot commit abuse

Your spouse, child, sibling or parent cannot carry out the revenge you had planned.

You cannot commit adultery.

Morality means you conquer anger, arrogance, greed, cruelty and desire.

Fulfill your responsibilities to those dependent on you in terms of shelter, clothing, food, rest, education, courtesy, as well as protection from abuse, immodesty, immorality and indecency.

Do not do anything that will make you feel ashamed if the world found out.

The "me first " idea is wrong. You never take your happiness at the expense of your duty. You do not go for vacations and leave your babies or children behind.

Do your duty not because you like to, and not even because it may bring results, but because you must do your duty.

Never compromise your principles. Life is never about winning or loosing. It is only about how fair you play the game

Care share and be absolutely fair.

Morality means modesty.

Do not dress with your breasts, cleavage, buttocks, clefts or panties exposed or your genitalia outlined. Not only must the parents stop you, but also the schools, colleges, stores, restaurants, malls, working places, transport system and politicians.

This is because we have to protect our society, and "indecent attire invites disrespectful behavior".

It is a fact of life that men are attracted by women's breasts, buttocks, thighs and genitalia. They would not be men if they were not. Are you telling them that they have no male hormones?

For you to parade around in immodest attire is like a chicken parading up and down in front of a lion saying "you can look but must not touch".

What do you expect the lion will do?

Modesty states that a man must not wear a swimsuit or underwear that outlines his genitalia or is not three inches below his buttocks.

Self –control in speech, dress and actions are the hallmark to self-mastery.

Morality means you practice modesty, decency and self-control in speech, actions and in your dress.

It is the moral right of any adult to correct a child and prevent him/her from making mistakes. You cannot tell the adult that he/she cannot correct you because "you are not my mother".

It is immoral to stay where you are not treated with respect or where you are abused.

You cannot tell anyone what his right or freedom is without telling him his responsibility.

If you do something wrong, you must do penance of equal degree to atone it.

If you hurt someone of a different faith, you must help someone of that faith.

To let someone else suffer the punishment for your sin is immoral.

Help the poor and the weak. Give alms to the poor. Do not ask payment to give water to a poor person.

It is immoral to allow children to marry before they are twenty.

It is immoral to say that "children cannot play here" unless safety or security is at stake or the place is a national monument.

Do not be an addict of any kind, including wealth and power. An addict has sold his soul.

It is immoral to keep what you owe others. If you did not pay when you said you would, be ashamed and apologize.

It is immoral to give up your knowledge in exchange for trust. Always know what you have.

Know that sins of omission are equal in immorality to sins of commission.

Keeping quiet instead of speaking out is cowardice and gives the perfect atmosphere for evil to flourish in. By keeping quiet when you should speak out, you give a silent permission for others to continue and expand their behavior.

Morality means that when you are overcome by feelings, you control them.

You are first a layer of emotions at base. Higher than this is the layer of your mind. Higher than this is the layer of your spirituality. Your emotions try to sway you in every direction. An intelligent person acknowledges the feelings but controls them with his/her mind and follows the path of what is right. You do not give in to your feelings whenever they occur because that leads to a fragmented personality.

You can only let your mind become stronger by having some time daily for spiritual nourishment, cutting off all sources of distractions and thinking only about what is the right thing to do. It is by believing in your own intelligence. It is done by physical and mental self- discipline and periodic fasting.

There is always a fine line in every action, that if you cross, you will be doing what is wrong, and you have to be alert about this line. You must have self-control and practice morality because by this, you develop strength, peace and courage. You then do not have panic attacks.

In morality, there are no gray areas. You do not say that you will live morally but will let others live in immoral situations, because evil will then invade your home and take over you, your family and your society. You have to fight immorality and eradicate it.

If your parent or parent- in- law is sick, you should offer them your home and help.

If your relatives' children become orphans, you should offer them your home.

It is moral to severely punish someone if he insults your God by putting His/Her picture on toilet paper, on toilet seat, on shoes, on panties, bras and underwear, bed sheets, bedcovers, or on places you will walk, sit or lie on; or if he makes lamps or other appliances out of His statues; or if he attributes carnal pleasures to Him, or makes pictures of Him in carnal pleasures; or uses His name to get carnal pleasures with others or to get addiction.

His /her business must be taken away. He/she must be fined and imprisoned.

Freedom does not give you right to do this.

You do not insult someone's parent.

You do not insult someone's God.

The very fact that you could do this shows how evil and full of greed you are.

Evil people will push freedom beyond all boundaries of modesty, decency and morality and then complain that you are taking their freedom away. Those who defend such people are evil themselves. This is abuse of freedom.

Morality states that you do not abuse freedom of speech or dress.

1. Abuse of freedom in speech occurs when you say that you can talk filth, when your language uses words of excretion or words of intercourse, when your songs or literature have description of sex, excite others to sex or to kill others.

2. Abuse of freedom in expression occurs when you show nudity, genitals, sexuality, sexual stimulation, and intercourse in TV, magazines, books, pictures, movies and computers. This violates modesty, decency and morality.

3. Abuse of freedom in dress occurs when you pass all decency and modesty, when you are nude, or you parade with your breast, cleavage or cleft or panty exposed.

If someone curses God in front of you and says he has a right to do so because this is his God too, you shall leave his company. Break all relations with him. You will not tolerate your brother cursing your father and you will not tolerate this man cursing God.

Elderly

A society in which the elderly are not treated with respect is an immoral society.

Treat the elderly in your home and outside with respect and help.
You cannot tell your parents what to do or whom to invite.
Take care of your parents in their old age. Keep them in your homes. Repay the fact that they gave you life. Treat them with respect and tend to their needs.

Do not leave them alone in their homes. They must live in your homes in old age unless they are very ill and need to go to hospitals or need care around the clock. What sort of cruel monsters have we become that we allow our old parents to live alone. You do not say that you have no room for your children. You do not say that you have no room for your parents. Just as you are responsible to take care of your children until they reach adulthood, you are responsible to take care of your parents and keep them with you until they die.

This does not mean that they become your babysitters. This is never their obligation to you. It is tiring for you to be parents. It is three times as tiring for them. Find your own babysitters. If your parents do agree to take care of your children, do not insist that this becomes a contract for so many months or years. You have to accept whatever time they are willing to give you graciously. At all times, make sure that they get a break in the day after some time and are completely free from the children.

Keeping parents with you also does not mean that they become your cooks and cleaning people. You should cook for them and cleanup after them.
At all times treat them with respect and listen to their advice before you make a decision if you do not want to keep making mistakes. They have two things you lack completely, wisdom and experience.

Do not make them work to support themselves. Send them money. This is your moral duty. Do not take their money away from them. Do not ask them for rent.
If your parents are divorced, do not say that it is the duty of the husband or the court to decide how your parent will financially survive.

It is the duty of every adult child to financially support his mother and his father and to offer them his/her home. If there is more than one child, each child should start sending his share the minute he starts earning. You have to send your share of what is needed for their upkeep. It is your duty to take care of their medical expenses.

No parent should give his/her money or house to his/her children until both the parents are dead. Your parents must live in one home and not shift from child to child unless they want to. The rest of the children must send money to the parents. Do not separate your parents from one another.

Make sure that your parents have access to a social life or ability to move outside your home and visit places when they are with you.

Treat your parents with respect. You do not call them stupid or other names. You do not say that what they did was stupid or dumb. You do not tell them to shut up. You do not hurt their feelings. You do not order them around.

You never sit around while your parents are working unless you are ill.

Do not be a parasite on your parents after reaching the age of twenty-two. Gain knowledge and skills to survive on your own. You should be bringing in money after twenty-two to support them. Also, give them money in their time of need and their old age. Do not ask them to explain how they spent the money. This is disrespectful. If you live with your parents after twenty-two you must share with expenses, cooking, chores and cleaning.

It is immoral to ask your parents, non-working relatives and your children in college to pay money for staying with you. Do not ask them to buy their own groceries.
By the same token, relatives and children who have finished their education, or do not wish to study anymore and are holding a full time job, must give one third of their salary to the home they are staying in. They should also buy groceries once or twice a month and help with household chores.

You do not sacrifice your nuclear family to impress others. You should always be fair and give each person his due. Never hurt those dependent on you because of a misguided sense of generosity or sacrifice.

Read the "abuse by children to parents" in chapter of abuse.

Love and wealth

Love too, has to be moral. You cannot be swept by feelings. You cannot steal someone's love or destroy your or someone else's family. You cannot say that this is between you and your lover, or you and your wife. You cannot say that you do not care about what people think.

Your love affair is the affair of the society if it crosses the moral boundaries.

If you go against society than you should lose all rights to get the benefits of society including police protection, federal housing, fire services, pension plans, federal grants and college, and other, loans.
This is because society is not just built on technology. Society must blend technology with modesty, decency and morality in order to prevent self-destruction.

Just as bigamy is a crime and involves a jail sentence because it is immoral and destroys family life, so too should extramarital affair be considered a crime and be punished. One should be able to file a charge against one's spouse that he/she is having an extra- marital affair and thus has broken the vows of fidelity and morality and that this is spouse abuse. It is a ground for immediate divorce.

A society that looks away when its rich people and movie stars have multiple wives and husbands weakens itself. It must punish these people and show that wealth is not above the law. They must go to jail, pay fines and lose protection from society.

Every act has a moral boundary around it. Never cross it.

Love also means that you do not destroy people or property to get who you love.

Love cannot be had through murder or destruction. It will not be complete, pure or honest.

You cannot force someone to love you. You cannot force someone to live with you if that person does not love you or if that person loves someone else.

You cannot say that if " you do not love me than you cannot love someone else".

You cannot hurt or kill someone because he/she does not love you.

It is the fastest way to destroy the peace within you.

True love is the ability to let go of someone. True love is being happy if that person is happy.

True love never means that you give up your baby so you can live with someone else. You gave birth to a child. That means you made a contract with the baby to take care of it, help it grow, give it love and caring, and protect it with your life. That supersedes any contract with an adult.

Broadmindedness, being so called advanced in your thinking, is never a sanction for immodesty, indecency and immorality.

Having wealth and power is never an excuse for being immoral.

Power and money are the final test to see that you can still keep your modesty, decency and morality.

Power and money are never the permission for you to rise above morality for if you do, you will have no peace.

You do not have affairs with your son, daughter, mother, father, sister, first cousin, brother, niece, nephew, step-son, step-daughter, brother- in- law, sister- in- law, your daughter's friend, son's friend, with your friend's boyfriend or girlfriend or husband/wife. You do not have affairs with anyone else if you are married. This is immoral.

Your desires should always be within your control and never hurt others.
Understand that desire is like a flame. The more you feed it, the brighter it burns.

You do not invite a man alone to your room nor do you go to his room alone.

It immoral to live with someone before getting married. It also takes away the woman's rights to protection from society in terms of assets etc. It takes away the protection for your children. It lowers your self-respect as well as respect from others.

You can live in a chaotic world drifting from man to man with no peace within; or you can have some principles to live by. You do not jump into bed because you are attracted to someone. Instead, you practice morality and self-control, and first study this person to see if he or she is an appropriate mate for you. You do not jump into bed saying that you will get married anyway. You marry him and then jump into bed.

Remember the only thing that will give you happiness is not his running after you or his appearance. It will be his character. Your relationship depends on character. Remember that the only thing you marry is character. Also, you marry a family, not a person. It is your moral duty to keep this family together and not divide them.

A woman after marriage does not go out with another man alone for entertainment.
She does not go out alone for dinner with a man unless it is for office purposes.

Any woman does not embrace a man other than her husband, uncle, father, grandfather, cousin and brother in greeting. She does not kiss another man in greeting.

Entertainment

Being eighteen years of age does not give people permission to watch sexual films. This is offering addiction. This is immoral.

Sexual films are for the depraved people. They cause untold harm in destroying the very fabric of our society.

They cause families to break up and an inability for men to perform at home. They are a source of distraction, incitement, addiction and lack of peace.

They cause disrespect to women, as well as attacks on women.

They cause children to become sexually active at younger and younger age.

They cause illegitimate and teenage pregnancies with accompanying infanticides.

It is immoral for ships, trains, hotels, airports or any public place to offer nude areas or entertainment with sexual actions or innuendoes. Such places should have their licenses taken away.

Remember that for centuries people lived without sexually exciting shows and had good families as well as societies with no fall in population.

Entertainment is not synonymous with sexual excitement and must be completely separated from it. This separation is clarity of vision.

Greedy entertainers have tried to cross all limits of modesty, decency and morality in search of wealth. A person cannot say that he has the right to perform as indecent or immoral action as he likes and you have to shut your eyes and ears if you are offended. This is immoral.

The first rule for any industry is that you will not harm society.
The second rule for any industry is that there is no freedom without responsibility.

The entertainment industry has to follow these rules just like any industry.
1. It cannot harm society
2. There can be no nudity. There can be no obscenity. There can be no vulgarity.
3. It cannot cross the limits of modesty and decency in speech dress and action. See the chapter on entertainment for the speech and dress code.
4. It cannot advocate a philosophy that violates any of the moral rules of society, e.g. it cannot show that it is okay to be disrespectful and non-caring to our parents, or to live out of wedlock, or to have children out of wedlock, etc.
5. It cannot murder the innocence of our children and youth.
6. It cannot show that our traditions do not matter or are wrong.
7. It cannot show cruel acts or violence
8. Entertainment does not mean sexual excitement. When a director says that he wants to engage the public's senses he cannot mean sensuality and sexual excitement. This is immoral. There can be no sexual scenes, jokes or innuendoes. There can be no feeding to lust in the scenes.
This has to apply to magazines, books, radios, videos, movies, television computers etc.

It is immoral for a politician to ignore the power of entertainment.

Entertainment can influence the speech, dress and attitudes of our society. It is a powerful propaganda tool. It can drastically change the philosophy and moral code of a nation.

Pornography is a harmful addiction like drugs and must be banned.

Read the chapters on pornography and addiction.

Parents and children

A parent who runs after money and ignores parenting is immoral and will have sorrow in old age.

It is immoral in a separation or a divorce to not give the children to the mother unless she is physically incapable, an addict or mentally ill.

The mother is biologically created to be the nurturing parent. Do not blur the lines.

She holds the child for nine months in her body.

She gives milk to the child.

She nurtures the child.

She will give preference to the child over her job. A man will give preference to the job over the day-to-day care of his children.

Her world revolves around the children. A man's world revolves around his job.

The mother passes on the moral rules and traditions of her family and society.

The mother must have the child.

A child needs lots and lots of quantity time, and never just quality time.

It is immoral not to teach a child character, modesty, decency and morality. This can only be done by tremendous input of time.

Morality is understanding that childhood is a time to develop neatness, organization, manners, modesty, decency and morality to prepare for adulthood.

A child will do what the adult does. Never forget this

It is immoral to give a child to homosexual parents.

It is immoral to give away your child for adoption if you are living and well. It is an act of complete abandonment. Never give up your children for adoption unless you are ill or dying. This is not love, nor sacrifice. This is breaking of your covenant to God when you give birth. Any abandonment of child is not only abuse, but also a violation of its trust and right to have its biological parents.

No animal abandons its young.

To take money for having children to give to others is equivalent to selling children and is completely immoral. It shows how low you have sunk. If a person cannot have children he she should adopt orphans.

Never sell you children or put them in hardship so you can survive. This is immoral.

It is immoral to use child labor.

A society that takes away the power of the parents and makes them impotent and helpless spectators is immoral.

What makes a weak parent?

1.Society, by taking away our powers to punish;

2.Other parent or family member by contradicting us and belittling us;

3.Television by becoming the teacher of speech code, dress code and of philosophy thus guiding our children's actions;

4. Computers, magazines, books and movies in the same way as the television does.

5. Our fear of losing the love of our child if we tell him that what he is doing is wrong, or our weakness to speak out when other parents are allowing what is wrong.

It is far better that you face the fear of losing the child but say what you feel to be morally right. In the end, your child will respect you for not being a coward and thank you for showing him the right path. If you do not do so, you will spend you old age crying because of them.

In addition, you must be moral yourself. You cannot tell your children," Do what I say". It is, " Do what I do. Believe what I believe".

The parents have the moral right:

to be treated with respect by the child;

to not be shouted at, to not be disobeyed , to not be insulted, to not be called names;

to know where the child is at all times;

to know the company that the child keeps;

to have the child follow the rules of the home;

to have the child help with household chores , including cooking and cleaning.

to make the decisions about what medications the child should or should not get (the child should not be allowed to make this decision by society until he is twenty).

to go into the children's room at any time;

to go through the child's belongings;

to punish the child if the child does wrong;

to be able to spank the child; As long as no bones are broken and no sticks are used, spanking is not cruel and is even needed at times. No police should interfere in this.

The parent has the right to remove the child from school for a year if the child is doing badly and to transfer him to a vocational, or other school, or even keep him home for a year; This is because there are two types of education, the one that is taught in school, and the life skills. You cannot have the school over the other.

The parents have the right to know the grades of the child even if the child is over eighteen as long as the parent is paying for the school fees. They have the right :

to not allow the school or the university to teach or expose the child to anything that is against the family ethics and morality or that outrages the sense of modesty or decency of the parent;

to be able to admit a child to any public school;

to be able to see that the child is free from temptation and addiction. They must be assured that the building his child lives in at college is only for boys or girls; that the opposite sex is not allowed freely to come in; that they can only meet in the official lounges at fixed times.

The parents have the right to be assured that his child is not exposed to addiction in terms of drugs, alcohol, homosexuality or pornography and sexual themes in literature, radios, magazines, pictures and movies. The parents have the right to be assured that the campus of learning has an atmosphere of morality.

"Alternate life styles" are immoral and those who teach them are immoral. They must be outlawed. Do not forget that this was so for the past five hundred years until our politicians threw all family and educational values out of the windows.

This is why you must ask before you vote for politicians as to whether they will elect the laws we need. See the chapter on laws that must be formed.

Parents, do not keep bad company. Relationships and friendships have the power to create evil, or good, in your family. Do not mix, or allow your child to mix, with immoral people nor bring them into your homes out of a mistaken sense of sympathy. Whatever help you want to give has to be from far.

It is immoral to bring a child into this world just because you love a man.
A child is a human being in his own right; and should not be had unless you are willing to take care of him, wash his soiled clothes, spend sleepless nights and endless hours in affording him protection and guiding him in life.
You should be able to give him a home, toys, food, clothing and education.
All this requires money. Before you bring a child into the world, you must know how you will provide all this and have the money saved to do so.

You are signing a silent contract when you bring a human being into the world:
that you will help it to develop to its highest potential,
that you will surround it with love and caring,
that you will see that it is treated fairly and with love,
that you will always protect it and give your life for it and
that you will never abandon it until it grows up.

A parent has a tremendous responsibility to set the right example to his children.
A parent does not attend parties where half clad females/males dance provocatively.
It is immoral to bring boyfriends and girlfriends to sleep in your house if you are a single parent.
Broadmindedness does not mean you crack indecent and sexual jokes around the house, or allow sexual magazines to be read.

It is immoral to allow your children to see pictures of nude people, or sexual films, because this cause feelings of arousal, disrespect and the need to become sexually active.

It is immoral to take a child's innocence from him.

It is immoral to have your children date before they are twenty.

You are putting them in situations where, you as an adult, cannot control yourself. How then can they?

It makes them act as adults when they are not ready.

Because of their immaturity, this leads to distraction away from education to focusing on relationships and their complications.

It also leads to wrong values at an early age, that they will be valued only if they have a boyfriend or girlfriend. They do not get a chance to realize they must attain maturity before they enter into relationships; and that maturity also means being comfortable by themselves.

It leads to multiple sex partners and loss of values, unwanted pregnancies and therefore loss of ability to have higher education, and hence a lower income bracket, having children before forming the maturity for parenting and therefore child abuse and infanticides. Read the chapter on, "should you date before you are twenty?"

Know the difference between youth and adult.

A child must not be left alone at home unsupervised until she/ he is fifteen.

A parent or adult must always be around watching what she watches on television or computer or what she/ he reads. If the child is a girl, the adult must not be a man, even if the adult is family member.

The child must talk on the telephone publicly in the family room. The child has no rights to privacy as far as the phone is concerned. Never step out because the child wants to talk on the phone. This is about forming the character and the safety of the child.

Do not listen to the child when he /she says, " Do you not trust me?"

It is not the job of the parent to trust the child. That will come only when the child has become an adult with a developed character. Never burden the child with your trust. If the child asks whether you trust him/her, say that that is not your job and so you refuse to answer the question. Your job is to protect the child and not put him in the clutches of others who are not trustworthy. No child should be allowed to feel that he/she can handle temptations and threats.

You do not send your child to the beach, hotel or other places unsupervised after the junior prom, because "everyone else is doing so". However, youth can and should meet together in groups for fun activities under supervision of adults.

The child should not be wandering out alone or in gangs at night. The child should not be left alone at malls because he/she is " bored at home". Malls are for shopping and if the child needs to shop, an adult goes with him/her. Do not drop off the child at malls and pick him/her up later. Malls are not for entertainment for children. Evil people are looking out for unsupervised children. Do not abandon your responsibility.

The child should not be allowed to "sleep over". All doctors can tell you of the number of sexual molestations that occur and the invitations to see sexual literature or films. Once it has happened, the scars are there for life. Children rehearsing for plays or having parties are not left alone in basement or homes while the parents are upstairs or out. It is your duty to supervise them.

A child cannot be allowed to wear provocative clothing.
A child cannot be allowed to see shows that have nudity, sexual jokes, innuendoes or scenes. This is not broadmindedness.

Using children for pornography must be punished by death

Schools
It is immoral for schools to ask parents for donations to admit a child, besides the fees. Such schools should not be allowed to exist.

It is immoral for the teacher to be paid to give extra help/tuition to his/her student, as it becomes a conflict of interest. If the teachers wish to help their own students they must do it free. If more than two children in a class needs extra help, than something is wrong with that teacher.

It is immoral for a teacher to have an affair with a student. This is not broadmindedness. This is exploitation and breech of trust of the child and his parents. It must be punished.
It is immoral for a teacher to talk to a student about sexuality.
There must be no books in schools with sexual literature.
The atmosphere of the school must always be modest, decent and moral.
It must be free from any addiction.
Books about great men and women must be taught in elementary, middle and high schools.
Moral rules must be taught in elementary, middle and high schools

All books for courses in schools and colleges must be available to the public six months before the course starts.

There must be no teaching of "alternate life styles" in any school or colleges.

There must not be allowed any teaching of a topic that goes against the moral values of a child's family even if the child wishes so. No child can make decisions of what is in his/her interest until he / she is twenty.

It is the duty of the educational institution to send the report card to the parent as long as the parent is paying for the education.

Duties of a child

To be considered one's child:
a child must treat the parent with respect,
a child must listen to the parent,
a child must keep contact with the parent,
a child must worry about the welfare of the parent and
a child must follow the moral values and beliefs of the parent.

It is immoral for a child to:
to treat his parents as his equal instead of his seniors,
to consider himself wiser than a parent
to not listen to the parent,
to treat parents with disrespect: to shout at his parents, to tell the parents to shut up,
to say that he was speaking first, to tell his parents that they are over- reacting, to call the parent names,
to do the opposite of the parent says,
to not do chores in the house,
to not help his parents in work and when needed,
to keep no contact with the parent,

to consider the parent his cook, servant or baby sitter
to order the parent to work,
to see that the parent is working and not get up and work with the parent,
to take away the money of the parent, his pension or earnings,
to ask for money when he is an adult and should be supporting himself,
to not give money to the parents for their support
to give money and then become rude, arrogant and think that he is wiser because he gives money for their support and so should now be considered senior to them,
to not offer his home for the parents to live in,
to let his parents live alone,
to force the parents to live where they are not happy,
to not take care of his parents in their illness,
to take away his parent's house while the parent lives,
to make the parent live elsewhere, while he lives in the parent's house,
to throw away those belongings or items of the parent that he does not like,
to throw his sibling out and live in the parent's house himself,
to separate his parents,
to tell the parents to leave the house,
to do his own marriage ceremony instead of going by what the parents want to do,
to order his parents to listen to his spouse,
to judge how they should talk or behave with his spouse,
to not insist that his spouse treat his parents with respect,
to give preference to his spouse over them and
to abandon his parents and adopt other people for money.

Marital status

Marriage is a union between a man and a woman only.
At any time, a man can only have one wife.
At any time, a woman can have only one husband.

It is immoral to marry your daughter, son, sister, brother, niece, nephew, or grand children.

It is immoral to have more than one spouse.

It is immoral to have a divorce just by saying the words without having legal sanction and without having made provision for the welfare of the spouse and children as well as division of property.

Property must be divided equally between all children

It is immoral to ask for dowry. Dowry is associated with greed, and greed is completely immoral. People accepting any gifts from the bride's relatives over a thousand dollars in local currency of that country must be fined double the amount immediately. Only an educated bride can put her foot down and blow the whistle. Know that if your in-laws are greedy enough to want dowry, they will be very cruel to you and will probably kill you. There is no end to greed. You must only marry a noble character. People who do not want to give dowry and cannot find their prospective matches should leave their name with local social agencies organized by state for marriage purposes.

It is moral to see that the woman is protected in case of abandonment. Provision must be made at the very time of marriage that the husband will have this much money agreed to be taken out of his paycheck per month in case of abandonment or if the woman leaves because of abuse. Alternatively, he can give a fixed amount at the separation. However this must be sufficient to support the woman until the woman remarries or becomes self- supportive. It must support the children until they are eighteen.

It is immoral for a man to not give money to run the house or support his family unless he is physically or mentally ill. He does not look towards the wife to support the family.

It is immoral for a man to hide his money from his wife.

It is his job to see that his family has the basic comforts of shelter, temperature, clothing, rest, food and social recreation.

Husband and wife should not equally share the expenditures of the house if they are not earning equally

It is immoral for him to insult his wife in the house or outside the house.

It is immoral for him to have affairs with another woman while he is married.

It is immoral to mentally, physically or emotionally abuse her. Then he has no right to remain married.

A man's wife is not his property to barter with.

A man cannot ask his wife to do anything immoral.

It is immoral for a husband to live off the income of his wife unless he is hired in her office. Such a man should lose all respect of his fellow man. No woman should stay with him.

A man or woman cannot have extra-marital affairs. A man or a woman cannot say that because the spouse was away, or because of the pressure of his life , job, illness etc., he/she "became closer to another person". This is completely immoral. If your affection and self-control disappears the minute your spouse is away, you do not deserve to be called a human being. Such type of philosophy should be banned from being shown on the television. If you are not mature enough to practice self-control, you deserve every contempt and punishment.

It is immoral to marry someone because your parents told you to, and then abandon him or her. The vows of marriage are not to be taken lightly. You need to be punished to for destroying another person's life, for taking the vows lightly and for making fun of society.

It is the moral duty of every human being to give shelter to any human being or animal that is being abused and not send him/her/it back.

Parents, if your child comes to you physically, mentally and emotionally abused, it is your moral duty to give her shelter, protection and financial support. The child and her family must stay with you. Do not send your child back. It is immoral to say to the child that she must stay in abusive surroundings until she is dead. That belief encourages men to act like monsters and this is immoral.

The whole society must take the woman back and take care of her if she has no parents. The society must see through the court that half the paycheck of her husband is turned over to her for the rest of her life unless she remarries or can support herself. This must be started immediately on separation and not wait until the divorce comes through. Shelters must be offered to her if she cannot stay with relatives or friends. She must be offered job skills.

It is the moral duty of an employer that if he is told that his employee is abusing his wife, he must warn the employee that this behavior is not acceptable. The employer must tell the employee that a repetition of abuse will get the employee fired. He must insist on knowing that the wife has a bank account in her name alone. He must have the wife meet the personnel department or a social worker who can see that she has funds to support herself; and the next check should be in her name. He must immediately see that all pension plans and investments are in both the husband and wife's names. This is moral.

Abuse of a human being is never a personal affair. It is everyone's affair.

If a wife files a charge of abuse, it is the moral duty of the court to first send a letter to the husband telling him to stay away from his wife and children until further orders.

The court should then immediately send a second letter to the employer stating that his employee has committed abuse and that, until further notice, all paychecks should be split in equal amounts between the husband and wife. The checks in the name of the wife should be sent to the court address until further orders. She can pick them up there. The court hearing should be by the next week.

These two actions of public knowledge and division of checks are powerful deterrent to a man.

It is the moral duty of a society to send checks to married couples in both the husband and wife's names. This honors the union of matrimony and deters abuse.

It is immoral to not realize that man and woman are unequal in the fact that the man is physically stronger, and that the woman bears the child and feeds the child from her body. She has the genetic makeup to care for and nourish the child, to worry about its welfare at the expense of her job, if any.

It is she who passes down the majority of moral and social values and beliefs.

Therefore, she must be allowed to have the physical relief from strenuous activity in pregnancy and the first two years of child rearing. In the interest of the child, she must be available to it for the first ten years. In this vulnerable period, she must be protected financially if the society needs to benefit from her child as a good citizen.

Because a man is physically stronger than a woman, he must take over physically arduous activities.

Homosexuality

Sexual relations are allowed only between a man and a woman.

Sexual relations are not allowed with a child, nor with an animal.

Having sex with the same sex is immoral.

Gay marriages are immoral.

Do not allow children to have gay parents.

Do not teach that homosexuality is right.

Broadmindedness never means that you become immoral or accept as normal what is a sin.

Sexual harassment

It is immoral to demand that a woman sleep with someone to keep her job or to be promoted. This must be severely punished. It is immoral to subject a woman to sexual taunts at work or when she is walking or sitting near you. "Eve-teasing" must be severely punished. It is immoral to expose her to pictures or literature of nudity or sexuality.

Animals

You cannot be considered human if you do not love animals.

Giving any electric shock to animals is immoral.

It is immoral to kill animals for sports.

It is immoral for the state to sanction hunting as a sport.

Would you tolerate it if people were allowed to hunt your young ones, cause them endless pain, kill them, destroy families and deprive young ones of their parents, all for a few minutes of "feeling good"?

Only when hunting is banned as a sport, can we say that we have climbed another step in moral and emotional development.

If the population of China is very high, does that mean that we resort to hunting the people?

It is immoral to take away land from the animals and use it for humans.
It belonged to them before us. It is immoral to have no land allocated for animals or birds in any town.

We must allow animals to live and exist freely on this planet. It is immoral to insist that an animal can only walk slowly tied to a chain. Would you like it if I insisted that your children could walk only tied to a chain?

An animal had this planet before you. It has as much right as you to jump, run freely and play as you do. How do you expect it to do that when it is only allowed to move tied to a chain? In third world countries animals move freely. By becoming technically superior, have we morally regressed?

An animal must be allowed to run and play freely as long as its owners or responsible people are nearby.
It is immoral to keep an animal tied or kept in a cage all day.

It is immoral to say that the animals must be locked inside the house all day and only be allowed to come out to go for a walk. Every townhouse should have an enclosure where the animal can stay outside. It is immoral for any housing development to say that pets are not allowed.

When you take a land for building, you must first make a public announcement for sixty days. At that time, you must also state what you are going to do about the birds, the animals and humans that are going to be displaced. How will you re- settle them? How much you will pay for their support until they are rehabilitated. You must have public sanction with their reasons from PETA and ASPCA for animals, and the human rights bureau for humans. They must be given an equal amount of land elsewhere and helped to be replaced.

It is immoral to put a fence around a pond or feeding area of animals and so cut off their water and food supply. You must also make sure that the animals will have no fence to stop them from their migration, and that their water and food supply will remain intact.

It is immoral for you to insist that animals do not pass bowel movements or urine or that they can only do it at certain times. Should you be allowed to pass urine or stool only when I tell you to? They cannot control themselves either and should never be punished for that. They should not be allowed to pass urine only in the morning and evening.

It is immoral to separate animals when you separate from your spouse. One spouse should have both animals.

It is immoral to abandon animals after you have them. No animal abandons its owner. Are you of a worse character than them?

It is your moral duty to take in an abandoned animal and no one should be able to stop you from that. If you cannot afford professional medical care and can only give it shelter and food, you are still doing the right thing.

It is immoral to take away babies of animals before they are weaned.

It is immoral to sanction hunting trips by a society. It is the highest cruelty against defenseless creatures.

Giving an animal its rights is part of our moral development.

It is immoral to punish people who fight against cruelty towards animals.

Read the chapter on animals.

It is immoral to keep your environment filthy and full of garbage and so unfit for humans and animals. No aid should be given to a society until it is actively trying to keep its areas clean.

Death

It is not inhumane to give death penalty to those who are inhuman.

It is moral to kill those who commit terrible crimes like sex crimes against children and women, kidnapping, rapes, torture of animals, children and human beings, murders and using harmful additives in food. It is moral to kill a person if he has committed a heinous crime or to prevent a heinous crime. It is moral to kill in the name of freedom, or to fight tyranny, injustice or immorality.
It is moral to kill your child if she is going to be raped or tortured and you cannot save her.

It is moral to ask for euthanasia when there is no cure for a devastating illness.
It is moral to give euthanasia to those who ask for it and who have no cure for their tremendous suffering.

Homicide, patricide, matricide and infanticide are immoral.
Your giving birth to someone does not give you the right to kill that person.

It is immoral to die because someone does not return your love or has left you. It is immoral to die because some one else has died, or because you became a widow or widower. It is immoral to kill yourself because you did not get your wish. It is also selfish, as you do not worry about how your dependents will survive.

It is immoral to not allow widows to remarry or to dress like everyone else and partake in fun once the mourning period of six months is over.

It is not moral to give only three days for bereavement. Death is a milestone in our lives with devastating effect. Four weeks of leave should be given for deaths in immediate family.

Law

It is immoral to claim insanity as defense for murder.

It is immoral to have frivolous lawsuits. Both, the person filing the lawsuit and his lawyer, should be fully responsible for the fees and the time lost by the defendant if he is proven innocent.

It is immoral to ask for compensation for emotional suffering. Human emotional suffering cannot be measured. People in war zones, and earthquakes suffer tremendously and then go forward without getting a dime in compensation. Compensation should be asked for only for physical damages, medical treatment and loss of wages.

Now we have beauty contests in prisons! Have we taken leave of our senses? Rehabilitation does not mean that people who commit crime against the societies get parties, beauty contests and televisions. The taxpayers' money is being spent on entertaining those who hurt them!
This is madness and is abuse by the jailors of his powers.

This is immoral.

The prisoners are there to be punished. Rehabilitation means that they are taught the wrongness of their behavior and are taught work skills so that they will not resort to their original method of making a living. That is it! People who come up with different ideas of rehabilitation must get it sanctioned by the public before they can act.

It is immoral to persecute the one who tries to help others.

People should not get gastrostomies and be forced to live longer if they are mentally retarded or cannot make decisions about themselves.

It is immoral for the hospital to ask for money first when a person is brought in from an accident or seriously ill. The patient must become stable first.

It is immoral for a doctor to ask that you fill up reports before he touches a patient in case of crime or accident. That puts the life of a patient at risk and makes the doctor guilty of inhumanity and murder. His license should be taken away. His first duty is to see that the patient is stable.

The state

It is the moral duty of the state to offer free water, toilets on the roads; shelters for abused women, animals and the homeless, orphanages and hospitals with fulltime-employed physicians for the poor.

Orphanages are better then foster homes because a child in a single home cannot be protected whereas in an institution he can be periodically checked. He is protected from greed. He has the companionship and support of the other children.

A state must have marriage- agencies where eligible people can leave their names if they wish to get married. These lists must be offered to prospective suitors. The state must help in these marriages if it wishes to eradicate the dowry system.

It is immoral for the state to ask the citizen to pay toll each time he crosses and drives across a piece of road. The earth is his right. He has a right to walk on it, sleep on it, sit on it and drive on it without paying taxes each time he does so.
Taxes can only be taken once a year from a citizen for this.

It is immoral for the state to not put guidelines for entertainment.

It is immoral to say that you will only send or accept a document through fax, or Internet or from an institution and not from a person. A document must be accepted by any person or institution by mail, by hand, or by the way that the simplest illiterate person can send it.

It is immoral for the bank to say that it will no longer return bank checks. A bank and every institution have to accommodate the computer illiterate person.

It is immoral to expect people to pay their bills before the beginning of the month when they get their salaries on the first of the month.

It is immoral for rich countries to have a veto power when it is the poor country that is always more moral. Veto power should be banned.

It is immoral to assist countries that trample on the rights of their citizens or those of citizens of other countries.

It is immoral for the state to take away prayer from school or to forbid public display of moral rules.

It is immoral for the state to allow compensation for emotional damages.
It is immoral for any person in a jury to award compensation for emotional damages.

Insurance company

It is immoral for the insurance companies to increase the premium after the first accident or incidence. That is what we had brought the insurance for.
It is immoral for an insurance companies to increase a malpractice premium of a doctor after he is proved innocent.

It is immoral for any type of insurance company or a hospital to give guidelines to a doctor telling him/her when a patient can be admitted, how long the patient can be admitted, how the patient should be treated, what medications the doctor can and should use, and when the patient should be discharged.

It is immoral for a state to allow insurance companies to form contracts with doctors, laboratories, x-ray facilities, hospitals or to hire their own contractors. This must be totally banned. The quality of work suffers tremendously. Read the chapter on health maintenance organizations. This also applies to insurance companies trying to hire their own repair shops. They should never be allowed to do so.

It is immoral to take away the freedom of a human being to go to any doctor, laboratory or hospital. Contracts of insurance companies with doctors, laboratories, physical therapy centers and hospitals violate this right.

The contracts also violate the right of a citizen to have the same doctor all his life. As insurance companies join and terminate clients, this right is grossly violated.

It is immoral for any doctor or insurance company to deny the need for a patient to have a test, treatment, or hospitalization without examining the patient. Insurance companies violate this every minute.

It is immoral for insurance companies to send guidelines to doctors of how to treat patients. Insurance companies do this every day.

It is immoral for insurance company to determine the length of stay for any patient.

It is immoral to state that you will not be paid for a service rendered unless it is described in a code and that the code is justified in the payer's mind.

A service, if performed, has to be paid even if it is written on a piece of cloth and should be in the in the language of the common person.

It is immoral to deny any payment because a code does not match the "ICD" code (A human body is so unique it cannot always match the code), or because it did not have fifth digit or was not the code the insurance company had in mind.

It is immoral to demand notes to justify the code. Do not waste the doctor's time.

If you suspect the doctor of fraud, take him to court or to an independent panel of doctors from the medical schools. If you are found to have been wrong, you are guilty of harassment and must pay all fees.

Suppose you were the owner of a grocery store. A customer brought a banana, and the insurance company had to pay for it. The insurance company did not pay for this because you used five digits instead of six or it did not like your code for any reason and refused to tell you why.

Or the description of the banana did not match the company code and it will not tell you what its description is. It will tell you to keep guessing and send the bill repeatedly.

Or it will not allow the customer to buy the same banana within six months

Or it wants proof, a picture or a note, that you actually sold that banana because it considers you a cheat. Asking notes for proof of service is same as calling a doctor a liar and cheat and the insurance company should be sued for defamation.

Then it will do this for three months hoping that you will get too busy to remember that it owed you a payment or will get too discouraged to keep trying.
This is what insurance companies do. This is immoral and unethical.

No lawyer, no politician, no storeowner, no plumber, no one will be willing to be paid this way. Yet, the doctors in USA are made to do so and all the protests to the politicians falls on deaf ears. This has happened only in the last ten years and the health maintenance organizations have emerged as powerful rich companies because they cannot be sued if the doctor listens to them and yet the doctor cannot move without their permission. They will change their rules whenever they like and no one can say anything to them as politicians have ignored one hearing after another from doctors. But whose health suffers? The patients. Who allows this immorality to persist? The politician.

The lawyers must be made to receive payment for their services based on fifth digit codes so that they understand the craziness of the system.

What can a citizen do about anything that is immoral?

You can join with your neighbors and form societies called "modemos".
You can form state and then national societies.
You can ask every politician the questions in the chapter, "questions to ask your politician".
You can elect seniors as your watchdogs
You can put up candidates who believe in morality and vote for them.

Evil people will push freedom beyond all boundaries of modesty, decency and morality and then complain that you are taking away their freedom.

One is not fair to those who are unfair because they flourish on your fairness.

Chapter 61.   THE ULTIMATE TEST

The bad times are to teach us but the good times are always to test us that we keep our morals.

The ultimate test is to give us fame and fortune.

We are tested to see whether we retain our morals or do we get intoxicated with power.

If we get intoxicated with fame and fortune than we feel that we do not have to be modest or decent; that we can break all morals; that we can become cruel, inconsiderate and non-caring. But we will also lose all sense of peace. We will feel a hypocrisy within us that has to be maintained at a great cost.

We can say we passed the test of wealth and fame when:

We remained the way we were before we had fame and fortune.

We did not become arrogant, selfish and cruel.

We retained our faith and spiritual foundation.

We retained our physical and mental self-discipline.

We retained modesty, decency and morality.

We cared, shared and were always fair

We did not abuse others physically, mentally and emotionally.

We did not become addicted to wealth and fame so that the more we had, the more we wanted. In addition, we retained our equanimity when we lost our fame or wealth.

We used our wealth and fame to help others and to spread modesty and morality.

Chapter 62.   HOMOSEXUALITY

As a doctor, I can very clearly tell you that no center in the brain has ever been identified as a homosexual center.
There is no medical basis, no scientific proof, for homosexuality? There is no proof, whatsoever, that people are born that way.

1. Mental
Just because the Association of Psychiatry, this year, (and only this year, for the first time) decided to make homosexuality acceptable, does not make it acceptable.
All these years homosexuality was taught as an aberrant behavior in medicine. What a few people, forming the psychiatric association, decided to do now, all of a sudden, does not make it right. They have no basis for their action except social pressure. No center was biologically discovered. Perhaps some members had a different leaning themselves.

2. Religion
Every religion in the world condemns homosexuality.
The bible speaks of Sodom and Gomorrah, and God turned against them.
This is in the Old Testament, which is read by both the Jews and the Christians.

Islam condemns it.

Hinduism is against it. Hinduism stresses a purity of body and mind. There is a clear-cut distinction of man and woman. Homosexuality goes against the moral development of man. Sexuality is only for the purpose of creation, and therefore needs both a man and a woman.

In Buddhism, homosexuality goes against the "Right way of thinking" in the eightfold path.

Why would every religion for the past five thousand years condemn homosexuality?
Because it destroyed the basic Law of God, the family unit, and therefore society.

Any priest who performs a gay marriage is an outcast from his respective religion. He has nothing in his religion to support his action

3. **Physical**
Homosexuals say that we are men and woman only because we think we are; and that there is no basis for defining that we are men and women.
This is an outrageous lie.
Do we "think" that we have female and male organs? Is that a figment of our imagination? Do they not actually function?

As a doctor, I will tell you that right down to the basic cell of your body, you are defined as a man or as a woman.
In every basic cell, there is a code bar called chromosome. On it is a gene called xy for male and xx for female.
These genes can be seen under the microscope. There is no gray area in this.
In an example of genetic illness called hemophilia, only the males will get the illness, and the females will be silent carrier of the disease.
You cannot "think" that you are a male and so will get the disease.
So, God was very clear in distinguishing females from males.
We cannot think that we are male or female and so become one. It is in our genes.

Animals will act homosexual only when they have no access to females.

Every part of the human body, the liver, the heart, the lung, is the same in the male and the female, except the sexual organs. The sexual organs are made so that they are a pipe in the male and a hollow tube in the female so that they can fit like a lock and a key.
The rectum is medically designed to store our stools and absorb water. It is not biologically designed to be a sexual organ.

So we were biologically designed to be heterosexuals.
So, it is "normal" only to be heterosexual.

Homosexuality is not normal behavior. It is a chosen aberrant lifestyle by a few. That does not give them the right to say to my children that it is an acceptable alternate life style. That does not give them the right to invade my society as an accepted norm.

4. Sexual

It was to be expected in the extreme sexual permissiveness condoned by our leaders that we would get bored by what is available, and would like to try new types of sexuality.
And so, we will progress from "straight" sexuality to homosexuality, then to pedophilia, and then to sex with animals.
We have gone right back to the cities of Sodom and Gomorrah. And even the fact that AIDS raised its head did not deter us from our immoral path.

And our leaders joined the march in the name of "broadmindedness".
They did not once stop to think that they were destroying family units and our society, which was so valued by our forefathers.

They could not care less. What do we speak of their clarity of vision or foresight?

5. **Clarity of vision**

So now, we have two men (or women) who tell us that they wish to enjoy each other's physical body.
This is against our morals and religion, but we do not know what they do and when in their private room. We do not even care.

But now they are not satisfied with enjoying each other's body in private.
Now they want to hear it from us that it is right and that we sanction it.
Why?
And why should we sanction it?

Then they start to invade our schools and colleges telling our children that it is alright to become a homosexual and that we are men and woman because we think we are so (a mandatory course in Rutgers' University, NJ, USA, called "shaping a life". One cannot graduate without passing it).

So now, they want to wipe out five thousand years of religious teaching and contradict the very values we wish to pass on to our children. They are brainwashing them. And they want them, and us, to ignore the scientific proof of genetic makeup of our bodies. And they want to take over our children. And our leaders sign that it is okay.

Then they push further and demand that two men (or women) who are staying together just to enjoy each other physically should be given the same benefits as a family.
Do you see the invasion?

If the homosexuals insist on having a "different" lifestyle than us, than why should they be given the "same" benefits as a family unit?

If the homosexuals do not want us to teach them that our style of living is right, than how can they invade our schools and colleges to teach our children that their lifestyle is right?

In a family unit, a man and a woman do not just get together to enjoy each other's physical body. They stay together to form a unit to take care of each other "and to procreate", to extend ourselves, to pass on to a new generation what our knowledge, faith and values are.
The homosexuals cannot do so. Therefore, this is aberrant. So why does the aberrant behavior get the same benefits of a family?

They say that they love each other but love between two people of the same sexes is called friendship. It is only when the physical body is enjoyed that it is called homosexuality.

Then they push further and say that since they cannot have children, we should let them adopt our children who they can raise with their beliefs.

Why would we do that?
And our leaders agree to every such thing in the name of broadmindedness.

Does broadmindedness mean:
that we accept the abnormal behavior over the normal?
that we accept the indecent behavior over the decent?
that we accept the immoral behavior over the moral ?

Tolerance or broadmindedness never means that we accept abnormal for normal, indecent over decent or immoral for moral.

So by the same token, I can say to you that I enjoy the physical body of my dog and it enjoys mine.

So please, please in the name of "broadmindedness":

1. Acknowledge that it is right for me to feel so.

2. Allow me to go to your schools and colleges so that I can tell your children that this is right.

3. Give my dog and me all the benefits you give to a family unit.

4. Since I cannot produce a child, please give me your children so that I can raise them with my beliefs.

And our leaders will say it is okay to do so.

But you and I, who are fighting for a clean and moral world for our children, will not say it is okay.

You and I, who are fighting to retain five thousand years of religious learning and wisdom, will not say it is okay.

You and I, who are fighting to preserve decency and family values, will not say it is okay.

Look at what our country has produced by becoming separate from religion.

Our leaders in the past strongly believed in decency and family values.

What about our current leaders? They are putting an axe to our society.

Do we want such leaders in office?

If you read history, you will see that before a society destroys itself, it loses all moral values. Study the Roman Empire.

We, every one of us, have to take a stand right now as to which side we are on.

We will ask every politician who stands for election, whether in a small town, or in the White House, what his stand is on homosexuality.

We will not vote for any politician who says he is for homosexuality.

We will not vote for any politician who says he is neutral.

We will stand at noon, on the first Monday of every month, on the main streets of our town, wearing our blue and orange ribbon in support of morality.

We will unite in every town forming a network of decency and morality,
and meet every month.

We will meet in our schools, in our churches, temples and synagogues. Then we will contact other schools, churches, temples and synagogues.

We will network with the people of every town in our state through our website.

We will put forward in these meetings what type of society we vision for our children in terms of decency and morality, profanity and pornography.

We will consider what is taught in school, what is spoken on the radios, what is sold in magazine shops and books, what is displayed on televisions and computers, in movies; and what should be allowed in name of freedom.

We will note what type of society we have become when the State separates itself from God and will consider whether we are in favor of the State doing so.

We will demand that there is no freedom without responsibility to us, to our children and to our society. We will not be impotent anymore.

We will see who in our meetings has leadership qualities and can bring back these qualities, and will consider putting him/her up as political candidate. We will do so in every state.

You do not say that you were struggling with your identity. There is never an identity crisis. You are who you are as a worker, as a spouse, as a child and as a parent. All this contributes to your identity and determines who you are. What you are struggling with is your conscience as you chose to prefer sexual deviation as a source of pleasure and entertainment. You are taking a source of entertainment of your genitalia to determine your whole identity.
This is absurd.

Having sex with the same sex is immoral. Gay marriages are immoral.
Do not allow children to have gay parents.

Let the homosexuals form their own society. They have no right to infiltrate our homes, our schools, our entertainment and our defense forces in the name of broadmindedness.

Chapter 63.   DEATH

The greatest thing you can do for a dead person is to live life as fully as you can in his/her name so that he/she is proud of you.
If you cannot do that, then it is still okay to live life one day at a time.
Accept his death as part of life. Death does not mean that you sit in a corner and turn your back on life, and hurt others around you. By easing others' pain, you ease yours.

The greatest tragedy is people spending the rest of their time crying for the departed one, not knowing that their own time is limited here and soon they too will have to leave. The only thing that is certain in this world is that you are going to die.

You do not need a grief counselor to get through grief. Death and sorrows are part of life.

You make a mistake when you say that you did the so-—called "closure" or that you could not do the "closure" because there was no body to be found.

There is no closure. You do not say that it is over and now you have to go forward. Your brain does not have doors that can automatically close on a person. The movies are lies.
However forward you go, this grief will go on within you. With it will be guilt, pain, anger, regret, despair, and a host of different emotions at different times. Different persons will react differently.
Separation and grieving is a process that will take years. Anyone who thinks that a person is pathological because he/she is still depressed or crying after some months of a death is mistaken. Some people will have the fight taken out of them.

The best thing you can do as a friend or relative is to visit the person in grief again, and again. Talk about the departed one. Shed a few tears in sympathy.

Do not avoid the topic. Take over some tasks that the bereaved cannot do. The best medicine is love, caring and time. One does not need a grief counselor to handle grief. One needs love, friendship, work, distraction and time.

Read the chapter on death in *Life Skills*.

Chapter 64.   TERRORISM

Terrorism is to be condemned, but just think about the following.

As long as heads of powerful nations will be friends with nations that oppress other countries, terrorism will prevail. Morality states that if your friend is doing something wrong and you cannot persuade him to change, you should leave him.

If a powerful nation attacks a defenseless nation and nobody wants to listen to the defenseless nation or come to its aid, what do you expect it to do?
The fact that one's ancestors were oppressed does not give one the right to violate the freedom of other people and take away their land and fundamental rights.

The terrorism would end immediately if our wise leaders would behave absolutely fairly; if they would bring the defenseless nation in front of all countries to be heard and to see that its people are treated fairly; their fundamental rights returned and its land given back. Yet, we do not offer this! We refuse to care. Would we tolerate it if we were oppressed? If our lands were taken away? If our rights were taken away and no one would listen to us?

The United Nations was made for countries to make joint decisions.
It is an ironic fact that it is always the poorer persons and the poorer nations that will be more moral than the more powerful ones, and their decisions will be more just. Yet they do not have veto powers! The passion of power makes one forget that one should always have moral principles. The very fact that nations refuse to give up their veto power shows that their thirst for

power is not quenched. This veto power makes a farce of the United Nations and makes it impotent. The veto power must be given up.

But terrorism is still to be condemned. You do not take innocent people and kill them to highlight your needs. That is cold-blooded murder and can never be justified. Terrorists must be dealt with severely. To create terror, pain and suffering in innocent beings just to make your demands public is selfish and immoral and one cannot consider you a human being. Then why should we care about your pain?

Chapter 65.   LIFE SKILLS: A Synopsis

You should:

1. Be smiling when you wake up.
2. Give a welcome smile when you first see someone or if you see someone after a while.
3. Be cheerful. Make others feel glad that you came and sad that you left.
4. Be optimistic. Have hope.
5. Have fun. Have the gift of laughter. Use humor to handle life.
6. Communicate. People cannot read your mind. Tell them what you want. Do not assume.
7. Be a good listener. Listen between lines. Do not interrupt others.
8. Be polite and well mannered. Do not talk back. Do not whine. Accept a "no" by the third time. Courtesy is not a sign of weakness.
9. Be gentle in your speech, not arrogant or aggressive. Do not use foul language or obscene words. To use obscene words, you have to first think them in your brain and so you will become obscene, undeveloped, and unrefined. You will have no peace.
10. Handle criticism. Do not fight back. Do not counter- attack. Being quiet does not mean that you are passive. It shows your maturity. Hear quietly. Later think over what was said. If unjustified, go back after some time to discuss it.
11. Be open-minded. There are other ways of doing things. Tolerate freedom of speech in those who oppose you.
12. Defuse situations. Calm people. Keep your cool when others cannot.
13. Be on time.
14. Be organized. Be neat in your work and surroundings.
15. Lay out all your tools before you start anything.

16. Help in chores at home. You do not sit while one person does the work. Never let an older person work while you sit.

17. Do your homework. Prepare for situations.

18. Be hardworking. Do not be lazy. If you do a thing, do it to the best of your ability, or do not do it at all; and do it fast.

19. Be steadfast. Finish what you start. Do not flit from job to job, or from person to person.

20. Never make fun of others because they have a different color, speech or appearance. A flower of a different color is equally good. Make friends with someone different.

21. Treat all men equally regardless of color, race, or creed. Men and women are to be treated equally for their mental abilities.

22. Practice modesty, decency, and morality in all aspects of life.

If you have no self-confidence in your looks or personality, you will bare your breasts, cleavage or buttocks, hoping that this will make you attractive.

But if you are comfortable with your looks and personality, you will practice modesty at all times in your dress, speech and actions.

Know that immodest dress or behavior will invite an indecent or disrespectful response. A woman who dresses provocatively is like a chicken who parades in front of a lion and then says that it cannot eat her.

23. You should care, share and be fair.

Care. Have the courage to be involved in other people's problems. Do not listen to your superiors or others who tell you not to be involved. They lack humanity, caring, and courage. Do not say, "This is not my problem." Above all, be fair.

24. Never stand by while people are making fun of another, insulting him, accusing him unjustifiably, treating him unfairly, or attacking him. Tell them to stop it. Defend him. Defend even an animal/bird thus being treated.

25. Know that the bully understands only the language of the bully. Stand up to him. Do not placate him.

26. Fulfill your responsibilities. Keep your word. Be dependable.

27. Take responsibility for your actions. Do not say, "He did it too," or "I am not the only one to blame." Do not spread the blame.

28. Apologize quickly if you are wrong. It makes you bigger. Do penance for your sins.

29. Be considerate.

If someone is sleeping or studying, be quiet.

If someone shall be coming home tired, do his chores.

Do not keep doing things that bother others.

30. Treat others, as you would want to be treated.

31. Pass on a kindness daily without expecting anything in return.

32. Enter a house graciously. Leave a house graciously.

33. Just because you earn money outside the house does not make you more intelligent than your wife. Make joint decisions with your spouse.

34. Value honest people highly. It takes courage to follow truth. It takes courage to expose and condemn a wrongdoing by a friend or relative or to defend an enemy if he has done no wrong. Do what is right.

35. Develop patience. It is a milestone in your development. Master temper and frustration if you want to avoid painful mistakes. Read these chapters and "What Makes a Good Human Being" in *Life Skills*.

36. Know that you cannot succeed without self-discipline and self-control.

37. Save ten percent. Donate ten percent.

38. Your job is to be a parent to your child, not to be his/her friend.

39. Know that a child who is abused together with the spouse will side with the mother. However, a child who is pampered

while the mother is abused will turn into a bully. The child in turn will then abuse others or become non-caring. He will listen to no one.

40. Do not have children if you will not raise them. Even animals do not abandon their young. Do not give up your children for adoption. It is abandonment. It is also violation of the child's birthright to have his/her own parents.

41. The job of the parent is to teach his/her children so that they can survive the bad times. This requires quantity time.

42. There is nothing so trusting as a child. To hurt a child by molestation or pornography is a crime that should be punished by death.

43. Know the children in your building, street, and neighborhood. Watch out for their safety. Risk your life for them.

44. Allowing your child to drive alone before he/she is eighteen is offering him/her a death sentence.

45. Do not use anything made by child labor.

46. Do not allow child labor.

47. Your children need your time. They need quantity (not quality) time.

Lots of time is needed to teach them life skills, body hygiene, manners, modesty, decency, morality, fundamental beliefs and religion.

Children only learn by being with adults and watching how they behave in hundreds of situations. Otherwise, they will learn what they can by roaming in packs of their peers or from the worst teacher of all, the television. Then they will spend years trying to "find themselves."

Do not abandon your responsibility to them.

"Quality time" was a term invented by us Westerners to hide our guilt for not behaving as parents.

48. In a divorce, a child must not be traumatized by going back and forth between two homes. The child must go to the mother unless she is proven unfit.

49. Do not overburden your children with your trust. Care enough to hover over them, to go through their things, to walk into their rooms, to search their rooms, and to know where they are and what they are doing.

Do not listen when they ask, "Do you not trust me?" This is not the time to give them privacy. The protection of your children and their character as well as their future is at stake. You have every right as a parent to be aware of what is going on with their lives. It is your duty to remove them from temptation and to fight for what is to their benefit.

50. Care about your neighbors. Help them carry heavy loads. Help them in repairs. See if they need anything. Step in to talk to them occasionally. Check on them if you do not see them. Share their sorrow and happiness. Do not become cold-hearted monsters.

51. There is no freedom without responsibility.

52. Offer your home to your parents in their old age and in illness. Do not let them live alone. This is cruelty. Treat them with respect and care. Do not say, "I have no room." If you have room in your heart, you will find a way. Put two children in a room if necessary. The debt of life that you owe them can only be paid by offering them your home and taking care of them in their old age. They helped you with your first steps. It is your duty to help them with their last steps. They did not leave you alone when you were frail and helpless. It is now your turn. Never tell your elders or in-laws that they are fed because of you. You do not have arrogance.

53. Be hospitable to your guests. Do not begrudge them food and lodgings.

54. Give alms to the poor.

55. Know that the bad times are to teach us and the good times are to test us. What can you learn from the bad times? That you should act to prevent their recurrence, get strong, fight abuse, develop what was lacking, appreciate what you have or do not have, become more sensitive and caring, realize your

mistakes, become more appreciative of the beauty around you and develop true values.

56. If you eat too much or too little, sleep too much or too little, you cannot be wise. Practice moderation.

57. Dinnertime is not the time to discuss things that can lead to fights.

58. Take time to rest. Listen to your body.

59. It is better to have no apple than to have half a rotten apple, which will then corrupt others.

60. Regardless of the fact that you are paying for the wedding, the wedding should be in the tradition favored by the parents unless you have no respect or caring for them.

61. Believe in building social supports and a network of friends.

62. A man who insults his wife in the house, who insults his wife outside the house, who does not give money to his spouse to run the house and who hides his money from his spouse; such a man has no right to be married.

63. There are evil people. Be wary of them. They follow no rules.

64. You do not practice fairness when you deal with evil because firstly, evil is unfair, and secondly, evil is depending on your fairness to survive and flourish.

65. There should be minimum lights at night because it affects the sleep cycle of the plants.

66. A town that does not take care of the garbage endangers the health of its people. All garbage must be removed to a fixed site daily and not just swept to the side of the street. Do not aid a nation until it has sanitation rules.

67. If you are selfish, cruel and rude at home, but show good manners outside with people you consider equal or superior, you are a coward with an inferiority complex. Good manners begin at home and then spread out to others.

68. Any relationship with a person can only succeed if it is based on honesty and trust. There can be no lies said in order

to protect someone's feelings or in the name of love. Trust once betrayed can never be replaced.

69. Just as you are careful initially with the stranger or neighbor until the trust is built, so must you be careful with the person you marry until you know his character and can trust him. To trust someone who betrayed you is asking to be kicked again. Do not go by the future promises. Go only by the past actions.

70. Life is a door that opens to this world. Death is a door that opens to another world. One of the greatest tragedies is that of people spending the rest of their lives mourning the departed one. They do not know that their own time is limited, and soon, they too will leave.

71. There should be no lawsuits for actions that your common sense should have prevented. It does not have to be written on a product that steam can scald.

72. Toy stores should not be allowed to write what toy is appropriate at what age. Can we not think for ourselves? A parent should decide what his/her child can use.

73. A child needs toys that can also move his muscles. You should not buy a motorized vehicle that runs on electricity. How then does a child move his muscles? A motorized vehicle should be only allowed on public roads at the age of eighteen.

74. Treat your parents and all elders with respect. Any person older than you has the right to correct you. Do not say, "You are not my mother so you cannot correct me."

75. You have been given only one brain, and it is very delicate. Do not damage it with drugs, alcohol, smoke, or other addictions. An addict has handed his life to others and has sold his soul. He is no longer in control.

76. Being psychologically traumatized after an event depends entirely on your outlook on life. Great people have emerged from awful conditions.

77. Think big, plan well but start small. What good is a large building if it is not productive? Intelligence is to know that you start small and grow big.

78. You are who you are without your spouse, children, family, job, house, country or money. You can be complete only when you believe this.

79. If your spouse shows anger whenever you wish to know your financial situation, you can be assured that he is cheating you financially. Even if you are not earning , it is your right to know what your financial balance is every month.

80. If a person cannot walk away from the abuse in his/her home, he/she is too weak to lead a nation.

81. All of the education cannot make a leader. A leader can only be born. So do not pass your mantle to your child. Give it to someone who is capable.

82. Education is not enough to succeed. One must also have goals with time limits, self-discipline, inter-personal skills and financial maturity. One must work fast, offer excellence, fairness, honesty, courtesy, follow-up and check every detail. And still there will be the element of luck.

83. If you show lust and violence, you promote lust and violence. If you show decency, you promote decency.

84. If you accept something, then you are duty bound to give something or do something in return.

85. You cannot stay away from people in sorrow because you cannot stand the pain. Morality demands that you go and comfort the bereaved to the best of your ability in order to be called a human being.

The "Do Nots":

Do not lie.

Do not steal.

Do not covet what is not yours.

Do not dress immodestly.

Do not be a hypocrite. Do not smile at a person and stab him in the back. That makes you the lowest of lows.

Do not run from problems. Face them.

Do not hit a woman or someone weaker than you.

Do not be greedy.

Do not be cruel.

Do not take risks to impress people.

Do not do anything with the expectation of getting something in return.

Do not procrastinate.

Do not give up until you have tried everything.

Do not do anything wrong because your superiors, relatives, or friends told you to do so. Think for yourself. Do not condone what is wrong because it involves your friends or relatives. Never do a thing if it is wrong because others are doing it and you are afraid of being left alone. Stand up for what is right.

Never do anything that you would regret, nothing that would make you lose your self-respect or act as a hypocrite, nothing that would make you ashamed if the world found out.

Do not stay where there is no love or respect for you.

Do not stay where the people are toxic to your soul.

Do not waste love on those who do not value it. All of your caring cannot turn non-caring people into caring ones.

True love is the ability to let go of the person if he chooses another.

Do not do anything wrong or immoral in the name of love.

Never be in denial at what is happening around you. Have clarity of vision.

Do not repeat a mistake more than twice. Learn from other people's mistakes. Do not waste your time repeating their mistakes.

Do not mourn your yesterdays or dread your tomorrows. Today is all you have.

Do not vacillate. Weigh the benefits versus risks ratio and make a decision.

When you visit someone, do not criticize them or their loved ones. Nor do you impose your will on people you visit.

Do not criticize anything in your house until you have come in and sat down for ten minutes and had a pleasant exchange with people in your home.

Do not discuss things that can cause arguments during mealtime.

Do not watch television while eating.

Do not walk with ear plugs in, listening to music. Your ears warn you of danger. Use the time to think.

Do not spend time crying over how badly you were treated in the past. Talking about it a few times brings relief to repressed emotions. But after this, crying about it only evokes a cycle that creates pain and anger and does not release you to go forward.

Do not remove moral rules from public places, no matter from which religion they are. Moral rules are an entity by themselves. A government that does so is immoral and must be removed immediately.

Do not vote for politicians who ignore modesty, decency, morality and prayers.

You have been put on this earth with your fellow creatures, the animals.

Protect them and their environment. Give them the environment they need. Do not shut off their water supply by putting fences around ponds or convert their pond into parks as they did in Edison, New Jersey. Just because there is no law against it does not mean that God will forgive such cruelty.

Do not kill them for fun, sport, clothing, beauty, or experimentation. Do not use such beauty products or clothing. Even animals you eat should be kept in humane, natural surroundings free from cruelty. They must be allowed to move free. They must not be force-fed. They must have enough room to move around. They must not always be kept in light. It is your responsibility to find out how they are kept. Such places must allow you to visit them at any time. Your schools must take you once to them. Listen to organizations like PETA, but check out such places once for yourself in your lifetime. This is your duty to them. If you are not allowed to visit such locations, do not use their products. Do not close your eyes and ears.

Do not drive away birds and animals because their droppings and sounds bother you. God will not forgive you. Give them food and water. A town cannot tell its citizens that they cannot offer food or water to an animal or that an animal cannot run, jump, or play but must be tied with a leash in order to move. An animal must move freely as long as the owner is nearby.
If you have pets, keep two of them so they can have their own kind for company as well. Exercise them daily, giving them enough freedom to move around at their leisure. Do not drag them or hold the leash so tightly that they cannot sniff around. Do not keep them tied up or in filthy conditions. Do not mutilate them in the name of beauty or because you do not want your furniture to be damaged.
Do not vote for politicians who are not animal-friendly.
No person should be fined or punished if he harasses or fights with people who are cruel to animals. Being kind to animals will help your soul to progress.

If you do not teach your children to be neat and organized,
if you do not teach them to be caring to animals and humans,
if you do not teach them to be helpful,

if you do not teach them to not be lazy,
if you do not teach them basic self-discipline,
if you do not push them to have goals,
if you do not give them a drive to achieve,
if you do not show them that you have expectations,
if you give them no frustrations to handle,
if you do not teach them to respect the family and society,
if you do not teach them the rules of friendship,
if you do not teach them morals, or
if your idea of parenting is to not say anything to them and not
let anyone else say anything to them,
then you, and they, will pay a terrible price.

A parent does not show himself/herself to be a weakling,
making mistakes. A parent who only cares that his/her child
should not cry is not a parent. A parent is one who guides the
children to grow up as responsible, moral and disciplined adults
despite their tears and pouts. To be a good parent, you must be
respectful, caring and fair to the other parent. If you do not pass
on your moral and religious beliefs to your child, than you are
not a parent.

Set aside the same time every day to pray. It releases great
strength.
Pray in the morning after you get clean and in the evenings.
Teach the children to pray in your home and schools.
Do not pray only when you want something. Pray regularly
just to be connected. Use any prayer you like.
You should bow first to Him in reverence and start with a
respectful greeting. You can say that you just want to be
connected. Or, you can ask for courage and blessings to start
the day. You can ask for guidance or clarity of vision. You can
thank Him for what you have. You can leave your troubles at
God's door. You can ask for strength to handle the pain. You
can ask Him to heal your soul. You can ask for forgiveness

for your sins. Then sit quietly for five minutes to make the connection. When you finish, thank Him and bow again. Read the chapter on prayer.

What hypocrites are our leaders if they are the first ones to pray whenever there is a calamity, yet they ban prayer in school? Our forefathers were wiser than they are. We must bring prayer back into school.

Learn all religions. Know that they all lead to one God.

All religions should be taught in schools. Someday there will be multisided temples with each side representing a religion, and the center will be empty to represent one God.

Do not ever hurt or kill in order to spread your religion.

There is a physical maturity.
There is a mental maturity.
There is an emotional maturity.
There is an animal maturity.
There is a financial maturity.
There is a social maturity.
There is a spiritual maturity.
A man has to develop in all these spheres and balance them. Of what good is it if you are good at your work but neglect your sister, child, parent, spouse etc.
Read "Maturity" in *Life Skills*.

Understand very clearly that spirituality is a soul's connection to God.

You do not get spirituality from turtles or food. Feeling good about something is not spirituality. It is the path of the soul back to its creator and requires body purity, modesty, decency, morality, self-discipline, self-control, and prayer.

Chapter 66.   ADDICTION, SEX AND PORNOGRAPHY

Understand very clearly that watching pornography is an addiction just as is smoking, alcohol, drugs, money, or power. You become a sexaholic.

You do not offer drugs to your children when they are eighteen.
You do not offer them nudity, sexual scenes or pornography when they are eighteen.

Even below eighteen, a child should never be allowed to watch these shows because "they are too young to understand anyway". It damages them profoundly.

An addiction is a situation:
In which you become a slave to your passion;
In which the more you have, the more you want;
In which you need a higher dose to get the same euphoric feeling;
In which you need a stronger combination to get the same euphoric feeling;
In which your sense of right and wrong is destroyed, as is clarity of vision;
In which all sense of moral responsibility is lost;
In which children and innocent beings are hurt;
In which others get hurt as selfishness, cruelty, and immorality creeps in;
In which normal relationships in the family can no longer be achieved;
In which the family is destroyed;
In which the society is damaged; and
In which you are ultimately destroyed in terms of happiness.

It is mind boggling that our leaders have allowed pornography, nudity, and sexuality to pervade every aspect of our lives in the name of freedom.

We do not want such leaders. Be very careful whom you give your vote to if you wish to protect your children.

Entertainment is NOT synonymous with sexual excitation.

In any industry, including entertainment, there can be no freedom without responsibility.

If a singer, writer, or producer has to show nudity or sexual scenes in his production, it is because he tries to cover the fact that he has no talent. Look in the past, and you will see, throughout the ages, fantastic shows and masterpieces without any profanity, immodesty, nudity, or sexual content. These people knew they were talented.

Our forefathers, who gave the concept of freedom of speech, believed very strongly in decency, modesty, and morality. Our current leaders have completely ignored what is happening in the name of freedom in our society. They are trying to destroy our society, as everything that is modest, decent, or moral is being thrown out in the name of freedom. All shows are given permission to show nudity and sexual content, and there is no end to the depravity as we progress from clothes to nudity, and sexual content to homosexuality, pedophilia, and the involvement of animals.

Strong messages are constantly being sent that this is the only way you can feel good; and then everyone is shocked when priests, children, and men are going around raping and molesting everyone. This is madness.

Who is responsible every time someone is raped?

It is the person you voted for who is ignoring the chaos around him/her.

Stores, radios, televisions, computers, and movies cannot have the freedom to show any books, talks, or scenes that violate modesty, decency, and morality. There can be no freedom that violates these, because this destroys our society. There can be no freedom without responsibility. Any law that allows this is immoral.

Universities, like Rutgers of New Jersey, that allow pornography and teach homosexuality on their campuses in the name of freedom of speech, pander to these addictions. Such educators must be removed. We spend hard-earned money and send our children to these institutions to receive education, not to become immoral and addicts. These educators and these institutions exist because of our money.
Read the chapter on entertainment.

A leader, or a person in a prominent government position, if caught in an immoral act, viewing or committing pornography, commits the worst act of all because he influences millions. It is a breach of trust. He must immediately be stripped of his title without any court procedures. He must pay a hefty fine and be barred from any future positions in the government.

Stand on the main streets of your towns on the first Monday of the month at lunchtime wearing your blue and orange ribbons to support decency, morality, and animal welfare.

Above all laws are the laws of your conscience, common sense, and morality.

Chapter 67. ENTERTAINMENT

Entertainment should follow the same rule as any industry:
that it should do no harm to
adults, children, animals, or the environment.

It should also not violate any modesty, decency, or morality
in
speech, clothing, appearance, and actions.

Entertainment has a profound effect on changing our way
of thinking, speaking and dressing.

Pornography, like drugs and alcohol, is an addiction

The politician who ignores the effect of entertainment on
society
is
an enemy of the society.

There is only one rule for any publisher or entertainer to follow:
What he presents must not violate modesty, decency, or morality.
It must not have an adverse effect on our children.

He cannot say that this violates his freedom, because there is no freedom without responsibility.

He/she cannot ignore the first rule that every other industry has to follow, that "YOU SHALL DO NO HARM."

He cannot say that he can do as he pleases, because he is not living on an island. Just as the wave in the ocean cannot move without causing a ripple effect, so each individual affects the society that he lives in.

We have an enormous amount of literature in our past that is astoundingly beautiful but has no nudity, vulgarity, or sexual scenes.

Not one of our politicians has cared to worry about the enormous harm being done to our social and moral fiber by the entertainment society. Not one of them has bothered to study its impact. These people hold such stringent rules for other industries for the safety of our people, yet put their heads in the sand when it comes to entertainment. Has one of them bothered to put forth an amendment in the Constitution to bring the entertainment industry under control?

The world laughs at us. Do you want such leaders? The next time you vote, ask the politician in every town and city, "How do you plan to regulate the entertainment industry so that it is decent for my child?"

If he has no plan, refuse to vote for him.

The entertainment and the publishing industries have gone completely out of control and have violated all rules of decency, morality, and modesty in speech, dress, and actions. They have become an environment of filth for our children and us. They parade filth, garbage, depraved values, and sex for entertainment. They are only motivated by ruthless greed.

And they have done this in the name of freedom of speech.

The harm being done to our social and moral fiber by these greedy people with no conscience is tremendous.

The entertainment and publishing industries have forgotten that when our forefathers insisted on this freedom of expression, they above all were most careful about not violating any sense of morality, modesty, and decency. When our forefathers spoke of freedom of speech, they never agreed to public displays of indecent and immodest speech. They were very careful of what was presented as family entertainment. Just watch any old shows.

These industries have forgotten that the purpose of entertainment is to relax.
The purpose never, ever is sexual excitement or to arouse our baser feelings of lust, cruelty and violence and non-caring. Entertainment is not to excite the bottom part of your body. It is to relax your brain and your heart. For centuries, people were entertained without sex, cruelty, and violence.

There can be no freedom without responsibility. There can be no compromises with immorality.

The unforgivable harm done by the entertainment industry to our children and to the moral fabric of our society:
is in the violations of every sense of decency, modesty, and morality;
is in taking away the innocence of children and their faith in the protection by adults and in their respect for adults;
is in creating an environment in which others, particularly the weaker sex and the children, get hurt as selfishness, cruelty, and perversion creeps in;
is in terms of increasing illegitimate children;

is in terms of younger and younger children becoming sexually active;
is in terms of increasing sexual attacks and rapes on women;
is in the lack of ability for men to have a satisfying home life;
is in the breakdown of family life and society; and
is in making us feel that entertainment and sexual excitement are synonymous.
This is unforgivable.

For a court to sanction the show of pornography is incomprehensible.

But history is full of unjust laws in every country from the sanction of the slaughter of the Jews, or the ability to have slaves or the denial of rights of women to vote or the laws of apartheid.

It takes courage to speak out against unjust and immoral laws. No court law is above the law of morality. A society is built on character, morality, decency, and modesty. Why are we regressing to the cave age?

Entertainment with nudity, immodesty, and sexual entertainment is an addiction just like drugs and alcohol.

An addiction is a situation:
In which the more you have, the more you want;
In which you need a higher dose to get the same euphoric feeling;
In which your sense of right and wrong is destroyed, as is clarity of vision;
In which all sense of responsibility to others, to your children, to women, to animals, and to your society is lost;
In which your values are lost;
In which the family is destroyed and

In which you are ultimately destroyed.

We run around trying to get a euphoric feeling. We become alcoholics and drug addicts. For a long time, it was not recognized that smoking and drinking was an addiction.
Now we are becoming sexaholics.

No entertainment should be allowed to be performed unless it is clean, family entertainment with no sexual or indecent innuendoes, jokes, nudity, stripping to undergarments, or indecency. One question should be asked:

"Would I want my child to watch this?"

It is wrong to have plays or movies that show:
1.people nude or in underclothes or in sexually provocative clothing or in brief clothes just covering the chest and exposing the thighs in skirts, or in bras and panties;
2.people performing a sexual act or a rape scene; or
3.a man kissing a woman anywhere else but the cheek or her hand, and with no tongue protrusion.

Nor can it be allowed to show provocative dancing that consists of nudity, provocative clothing, bending forward so that breasts are seen, or pushing elbows back so that the chest juts forward.
It is wrong to show a pelvis being thrust forward in any dance.
A woman or a man who uses these movements or shows her/his body in order to promote her/his so-called talents is nothing better than a prostitute.

Nor can the movies be allowed to show anything that is not decent; that has curses; that has violence; that has cruelty; that has any hint of fondling, arousal or intercourse; or that has off-colored jokes, vulgar words or gestures, words for excrement, or profanity. There should be no scenes about urinating, defecating, or farting.

There should be no movies showing prostitution or sexually deviant behavior or homosexual behavior.

Nor can they be allowed to tell stories or jokes with sexual innuendoes.

Nor can this be allowed on the computers.

Such entertainment must be outlawed.

Do not allow shows that break down moral values, that state it is okay to be rude to your parents or treat elders with disrespect, or that approve of having children out of wedlock or of being promiscuous or of going to bed without being married.

No show can depict parents as weaklings making mistakes and the children being wiser than them.

No show can show that the traditions of a society can be changed in terms of decorations on body or around the homes, in clothing and behavior.

No show can depict that the moral values of a society should be broken.

No actors can be shown wearing clothing that is indecent or contrary to the society around. Backless blouses or with spaghetti straps instead of sleeves have to be banned. The entertainment industry does not have carte blanche to let its imagination run wild without any responsibility to society.

Talk shows cannot discuss indecent or immoral topics.

No books or magazines should be allowed to be displayed in public if they have any nude or immodest pictures or have any reference to sexual activity.

Books writing about sexual activities or inducing sexual excitement have to be destroyed and cannot be displayed in public places. It is not adult to read pornographic literature. So-called adult bookstores should not be allowed to exist in towns, and it is not broadmindedness to tolerate them.

The word *sex* should be banned in the entertainment, publishing, and computer industries. It should not be allowed on public display on billboards.

There can be no songs referring to lovemaking or private body parts or curses.

You do not show any advertisement on television, radio, or computers that include medicines that affect sexuality or periods, or violate modesty, decency, or morality.
It should be illegal for ships, trains, hotels, airports, or any public place to offer nude areas or entertainment with sexual innuendoes or actions. Such places should have their licenses taken away.

Evil will fight with you on grounds of freedom, broadmindedness, and fairness. But evil is only interested in greed.
There is no freedom for evil. There is no broadmindedness with evil. There is no fairness when dealing with evil. It has to be ruthlessly eradicated.

The first rule in the entertainment and publishing industries has to be modesty and decency, not greed.
Let the entertainers have the courage to write and sell stories without sexual activities or innuendoes.
A show must have decency and modesty in words, dress, and actions. If you show a low character, you must also show a character that follows the ideals.

Your desires should always be within your control and never hurt others. Understand that desire is like a flame. The more you feed it, the brighter it burns, and at the cost of your peace.

Entertainment is not about showing every act of life but to help people to relax. This is never synonymous with sexual excitement. Relaxation and excitement are opposites.

Just because everyone else is doing it never makes a thing right.

Understand clearly that it is not maturity to say that every man should be able to do his own thing if that thing invades your very home and takes over your children and family.
You do not say that you will perform but that if I do not like it I should shut my eyes and ears. Your freedom to perform is only present if you do not violate the standards of modesty, decency and morality.

Understand very clearly that the freedom to protect our children is above every other freedom.

Our politicians have blatantly ignored such issues and closed their eyes and ears at a tremendous cost to society.
Form societies of decency and morality. Join hands with other societies and collect signatures to replace the current politicians if they will not protect us, as well as change the current laws.
Vote to remove politicians if they will not listen because they too have become immoral. Put up your own candidates.
Let the entertainment industry understand very clearly that
THERE IS NO FREEDOM WITHOUT RESPONSIBILITY.

Chapter 68.   IS OUR GOVERNMENT ANIMAL-FRIENDLY?

Does our government believe in the prevention of cruelty to animals?

Does our government believe that we should share our planet with the animals and birds?

Does it prevent the pharmaceutical companies from torturing the animals in the name of research?

Does it hold harmless people who protest such rights or fight against such companies?

Is there an Animal Humane Treatment Act/Department in the government?

Does the government put fences around the ponds so that the animals cannot drink, causing them to stay thirsty and eventually die (Roosevelt Park, Edison, New Jersey)?

Does the government take away ponds that animals use and convert it into people's parks?

Does the government have prohibitions guarding the water supply of animals?

Does our government allow putting fences up so that animals cannot reach their food supply or migrate?

Does our government have punishments for those treating animals cruelly?

Does our government have fines for drivers who run over animals?

Does our government have open protected areas for the animals to live in?

Do builders have to get approval from an animal humane society like PETA before they cruelly take away any land from the animals to build on?

Does every township have a representative on board from the animal humane society whose sanction is taken and made public before allocating land to builders?

What provision does our government have to place such animals that are driven out of their land?

Does the government work with animal humane societies to enforce their recommendations?

Does our government prohibit the hunting of animals for sport?

Before you vote for a politician, ask him/her these questions. Then decide if he/she deserves your vote.

Remember that if a person cannot be kind to animals, he cannot care about humanity. And politicians are supposed to care about humanity.

Chapter 69.   DOES OUR GOVERNMENT BELIEVE IN MODESTY, DECENCY AND MORALITY?

The greatest "danger that a democracy can face is becoming licentious in the name of broadmindedness."
Every society has a moral fiber.
Our media and the entertainment industry are doing everything possible to destroy this fiber and make this country a terrible place for our children to be in.
Why is our government looking the other way?
It must not believe in modesty, decency, and morality.

We need a government that applies the same rule to the entertainment industry as it does to any other industry: "You shall do no harm to society." Understand very clearly that entertainment is NOT synonymous with sexual excitement. These are two separate things. They must never be put together.

We have a right to clean, family entertainment.
History has shown us again and again that before a society destroys itself, it becomes morally depraved.
We must fight to preserve our children's innocence and protect our society from these morally depraved people who are only ruled by greed.

A moral amendment must be passed in our Constitution.
It must state the following:

1. You cannot be in public in immodest dress. Women must not be topless. Men and women must not have any clothes

that reveal breasts, cleavage, buttocks, cleft, or pubic hair, or outline the genitalia.

2. There can be no public touching of genitalia or breasts, nor any sexual activity in public.

3. In public speech, profanity or words pertaining to sexual organs, sexual performances, or body excretions will not be permitted.

4. No store, dealing with bodies being offered for physical pleasure or engaged in sexual activities, can put up a public sign.

No such store can be within fifty miles of a residential or downtown area.

5. No magazine or bookstore can sell magazines with nudity, sexual descriptions, pictures of people having sex, or items affecting one sexually. There can be no articles about sex. The word *sex* cannot be on any cover.

6. No library, bus, train, airport, hotel, ship, or public place can offer any magazines, pictures, shows, or movies with nudity or sexual references, descriptions, or scenes. They cannot offer places for nudity to be practiced.

7. No radio shows should have talks or jokes with sexual connotations or hints. No radio shows should have references to undergarments or sexual arousal or descriptions of nudity or sex. No radio shows should have advertisements by any companies of products that affect genital and sexual performance or enhancement. This is decency.

8. No song will be allowed to be on air or sold publicly if it has profanity, references to male and female organs, or references to sexual activity.

9. Products for sexual activity or for enhancing sexual pleasure cannot be publicly displayed.

10. Computers and televisions cannot have advertisements dealing with female and male organs, their enhancement or performances, nudity, or sexual scenes.

11. Comedy shows cannot have jokes or talks with sexual nuances.

12. Movies and shows cannot have scantily dressed actors and actresses; nudity; sexual jokes; the touching of each other's breasts, hips, or genitalia; or scenes depicting sexual arousals or sexual activities or rape. Kissing anywhere other than cheeks and head should not occur.

13. Shows cannot affect a society adversely, such as depicting the right to live together without marriage, or having children without marriage, depicting homosexuality, advocating cruelty to humans and animals, or treating parents with disrespect. Children on the show will not ask immodest questions like asking adults if they are pregnant.

14. Clothing worn by actors and actresses must be decent and modest.

Male clothing cannot outline the genitalia.

Actresses cannot wear bras and panties alone. Buttocks cannot be exposed.

They must not be in backless or strapless dresses or wear spaghetti straps in place of sleeves. Cleavage of breasts or gluteal clefts cannot be exposed.

Their clothes must cover them to below the knees. Breasts tightly outlined must be covered with a veil. A swimsuit should cover an actress from above the cleavage to below the gluteal fold of her buttock.

Ask your politician before you vote for him whether he advocates the above and plans to implement it. Your vote is the only way you can protect your children and your society.

Chapter 70.   HEALTH INSURANCE COMPANIES

You must know how health insurance companies jeopardize your health. Therefore, this too, is a life skill. Otherwise, you may fare poorly or even die.

In the last ten years, in United States of America powerful insurance companies have come up called HMOS. These companies have compromised the health care of the country. They became powerful only because they were allowed to form contracts with hospitals, doctors and healthcare facilities and diagnostic services.

Insurance companies should not be allowed to form contracts with doctors hospitals, laboratories, diagnostic services or any health facility.

They must not be allowed to have contracts with repair companies.

This damages the quality of care delivered to patient or client.

The only one who gets rich is the insurance company.

The ones who suffer are the patients.

It is your moral right go to any doctor or hospital you chose for your life.

Who has taken away this right?

The insurance company by forming contracts with doctors, hospital and therapy places. Ten years ago, this was not the case. The citizen enjoyed full freedom to go to any doctor, hospital or laboratory he wanted to. People with Medicare insurance still have this right.

So, the HMOS are stepping on your rights.

Before this, you had a family doctor who knew you and your family for generations. You had a rapport with him and you stopped seeing him when you moved or he died. This trust and confidence in him helped your immune system. Now every year as insurance companies drop or change clients, you have to find a new doctor and see if you can form a rapport all over again. You have to start your life history with this person all over again. See how stressful this is? How unethical?

Insurance companies ask for medical necessity of a test ordered by the doctor. Thus, they can put it off for few more days.
Does not the doctor order a test because it is medically necessary? After all, it is not a layman who is ordering it.

Before they approve a test, they want notes to be submitted about when the previous medication was ordered, how long it was ordered for, what were the symptoms, what then happened and then they will think about deciding to pay for it.
This is calling the doctor a cheat and asking him to defend his decisions.
No doctor has the time for this harassment. Therefore, this affects the patient care adversely. Do not forget that it is the doctor who examines the patient, not the insurance company. If the doctor feels that the patient needs the test, that should be good enough.

If the insurance company feels that the doctor is a fraud, it should appeal to an independent panel of doctors from medical schools , but never to doctors on its payroll. That is fraud. Do you think that its employed doctors are going to bite the hand that feeds them?

Then the insurance company wants seventy-two hours to reply. It does not care how much the patient suffers in the interim. Even after seventy-two hours, it says that "its systems are down and now it is the beginning of a long weekend so it will not be able to do give us any approval for four more days ".

Does it care about what happens to the patient? Is this ethical?

The insurance companies say that they will approve a test over the phone but will not give anything in writing so that later they can say that it was never agreed to.
Is this ethical?

They throw out a woman after one day of delivery regardless of what the doctor thinks. Is this ethical?

It is malpractice to see if a patient needs treatment by going over the notes.
If this was good medicine, all doctors could go home and not examine the patients. Yet, day in and day out, the insurance companies do this malpractice. Without once seeing the patient, without talking to the patient and worse, without examining the patients, their nurses, (not doctors), make decisions about the need of the treatment, test, therapy and hospital stay.
Is this ethical? This is medical malpractice.

Does a nurse sitting hundreds of miles away know more about your needs than the doctor who examined you does? What gave her the right to go over your doctor's head? The insurance company! This is unethical.

Insurance companies decide how long a patient stays in the hospital and not the doctor. Your life is at stake here. Then why did the doctor study medicine? Is this ethical?
Their deciding that they will not pay for further stay " because it is not necessary" is arbitrary and they are never held accountable for this. People have gone homes and died. People have been discharged because of them only to be admitted again the next day because they were too ill to be discharged. The insurance companies do not care.

Is this ethical? Who has given gave them the power to make these decisions.
The politicians! Why are the insurance companies not held accountable?

The Insurance companies now send guidelines to doctors as to how to treat hypertension and other diseases, how to do check ups and what questions he should ask the patients.
Is this ethical?

Why did the doctor go to medical school to learn? Why should we have the medical schools? The insurance company could send lay people to treat patients.
The insurance company hires some doctors, pays them top dollars and then tells them to send guidelines to other doctors as to how a patient should be treated. Your doctor may have much more experience than these doctors yet is forced to listen to these companies otherwise he will not be paid.
Whose care is affected? Yours. Is this ethical?

The insurance companies tell the doctor each month what medication he can use and for how long.
Is this ethical?

The insurance companies are forcing the doctor to use a cookbook recipe for each disease. All patients are to be treated the same way, for the same days, by the same medicine, by the same protocol or they will not pay. The doctor has no business to think or make his own decisions.

Now the hospitals are getting into the act. They are sending letters to the doctor every month saying that "last month you kept a patient with pneumonia for four days, but Dr. Smith kept it for three days (It does not matter my patient may be weaker

or run down); and by the way Medicare says that in California the patient for pneumonia stays only for two days."
Therefore, you are a bad doctor and must not have admitting privileges in the hospital".

.

Is this not horrifying? Is this good medicine? Is this ethical? Who suffers? You do? Why are the hospitals doing it ? They do not want the insurance companies to not pay them . Is that excusable? No.

The hospitals now are also sending out guidelines to doctors as to how to treat the patient, what medicine to give, what protocol to follow, what questions to ask the patient.
"If you stray from this line then you will lose your privileges to admit patients to our hospitals."
This is not only horrifying but malpractice and downright unethical.
All the education and experience of the doctor is to be ignored

.

Your doctor knows that each person is a highly unique individual with unique problems based on his genetic make-up, his family history, his past history, and his sensitization to medicine. He will not allow the same medicine across the board to all the same patients for the same disease. He will also use his intuition in different circumstances.
Each patient has a different genetic background, different stamina, with a different set of medical conditions, different life span and different resistance pattern. Patients are not identical cookies. Each one is unique. One cannot treat them with cookbook formulas.
You may have traveled to an area that affected you with other illnesses. You may have picked up secondary things that the other patient may not have. You may have different sensitivities.

You may have a depression that lowers you immune system and so are different from the next person. You may smoke and so may not have as good a circulation as the next person.

Only your doctor knows what to do with you, not the hospital and not the insurance companies. They have no business telling your doctor how to treat you.

The insurance companies cannot be sued for denying tests, therapy, treatment or length of stay in hospitals .
Is that ethical?

If the patient sees the doctor again for the same problem, the insurance company says that "doctor, the patient saw you more than once in so many days. This is not right." It does not matter that he needed to. Is this ethical?

If you examine a patient in a motor vehicle accident for the insurance company and say that the patient may need another specialist, perhaps a neurologist, the insurance company orders you not to say that in the report. Is this ethical ? The patient may need that and no one may have thought of it. Whose health suffers?

If you have had surgery by a doctor for an emergency, but the doctor is not in your insurance plan, the insurance company will say that you should go for a follow- up to a surgeon who is in their plan.
This is malpractice and downright dangerous. The new surgeon did not operate on you. He does not know how your insides look and yet must decide what your treatment should be.
Is this ethical?

Every day the insurance companies are on the back of doctors and hospitals saying that the patient should be discharged faster, and faster, so that a hip replacement that was allowed to say for four weeks, has been cut down to three, then two and now one week. They say it is alright to do so. Who are they to decide? Of course, the insurance companies and the hospitals will say it is fine. They are saving a lot of money.

It is your body, not theirs.

Because of these HMOS a whole breed of so called "physician assistants have emerged. Now you get to be seen by them instead of the doctors and they can do everything that the doctor can with one-tenth the training. Is this ethical ?

The nurses have gotten into the act. They can now see you examine you and write your medical prescriptions and they do not need to go to medical schools to do this!

So why have the doctor? Why have a person who studied seven years of medicine and then seven years of residency if you are not allowed to see him and you have to be treated by physician aides and nurses instead ?

And your lawmakers allowing this complete unethical state of affairs!

Soon we will have law-makers assistants with one year diploma practicing laws.

Now the insurance companies are comparing your bodies to cars. They say that just as the car can have one part fixed at a time, they will allow only one part of the body to be fixed at an admission. Have you heard of anything so unethical. Are we cars with no feelings? Do we run off the assembly line? So if you are admitted for pneumonia but develop abdominal pain, the insurance company will refuse to pay for the abdominal pain. All along your doctor believed in treating the patient as a whole . Your one part affects the other. We used to talk of holistic medicine. A human body cannot be compared to a motor vehicle ! That is inhumane!

All these problems have been told to the senate health committees again and again and the politicians have looked the other way as they have received contributions from the insurance companies.
Is this ethical? Whose health is affected?

Did you ever think or ask how much the CEO of an insurance company makes?

Tell your politician that you want to be treated like an individual and that you have a right for an individual approach. Say that you will only vote for him if he passes the following laws:

No insurance company can form individual contracts with the doctor or hospital, therapy centers or diagnostic services.

It is the fundamental and moral right of an individual to go to any doctor he wants and any hospital he wants, and you want this right back

No insurance company can send literature telling the doctor how to practice medicine.

No insurance company can decide the treatment plan by reviewing notes but must examine the patient personally.

No insurance company can say that they will justify each day's stay after reviewing the notes and laboratory values. Either they come and treat the patient, and physically examine him daily or they leave the doctor alone.

If the insurance company has a concern over a doctor's treatment, it should take him to court, or to a panel of doctors appointed by the medical school. But it cannot take him to its own hired doctors for a second opinion.

No insurance company can tell the doctor that they will stop paying for the hospital stay after this day

No insurance company or hospital can tell the doctor what medicine he can order and for how long.

No insurance company can have the right to do a pre- approval before a test or a treatment is started. It cannot question a doctor's judgment.

No insurance company or a hospital can tell the doctor what questions he should ask the patient, what advice he should give the patient and what treatment he should give the patient.

No insurance company can ask the doctor to list how many minutes he spent examining the patient.
No payment can be denied because the c.p.t. codes do not match I.C.D. codes. codes; or the codes are not of the highest specificity or sensitivity; or they need a fifth or sixth digit; or not the code that the insurance company wants but will not tell the doctor; or a truncated code .
Codes are changed annually to add to the confusion . A multi-million dollar industry has sprung up because of these codes and immense time of the doctor is wasted as he wanders through a bewildering maze of codes. He has to hire extra staff to get through these codes and even then he is unsuccessful. No lawyer or a congressman would agree to be paid for his services this way. They should agree to a trial of being paid themselves this way before they apply it on doctors.

Payment cannot depend on codes. In our nation, once someone has performed honest labor, it is his birthright to be paid as long as he describes his services in the simplest manner that the most illiterate person can understand.

All codes have to be banned. A simple description of doctor's visit, or the service performed, can be given with the name of the disease in letters.

If the insurance company has spent money to devise payment in their favor, it can spend money to do it the right way.

No insurance company can have more than one billing office for a geographical area.

Tell your lawmakers that you do not want your insurance companies to have the power to form their own rules. Rules for the human bodies can only be made by medical schools.

It is time you voted for people only after they tell you what they will do about which problem and if they give you the right to remove them in six months if they do not keep their word.

Chapter 71.   WHAT DESTROYS A SOCIETY

To allow cruelty to animals, or to allow hunting as a sport, destroys the morality of a society, and the society itself, in the end.

To not care about what society thinks about your actions destroys society.

To refuse to allow worship of God destroys society. To refuse to allow prayers in schools destroys society. Prayer should be directed to God. Thus, it is not favoring any particular religion. Never forget that the people who separated the State from religion were people who believed in God and prayers. You cannot take part of what they said and ignore how they believed in God , prayers and morality. It is immoral people who will do so.

To allow immodesty, indecency and immorality in the name of broadmindedness is dangerous to society. To not protect women children and animals thus affected destroys society.

Why do you not learn from the Roman Empire? The mightiest society, it crumbled once it became immoral.

To say that you will not allow display of moral rules because they may represent a religion destroys a society. Morality is the way one should live a life so that society and its citizens can survive. It ensures the protection of the weakest instead of the strongest (or the richest). It ensures the highest development of man. This is irrelevant to which religion you call your own.

A secular state must recognize morality as separate from religion. All moral rules are universal cosmic rules. That is why they are present in every religion.

A State that does not do so is giving permission for immodesty, indecency and immorality, the destruction of the weaker sections and ultimately of the society as the "dog eat dog" rule creeps in.

A state that does not do so also infringes on the rights of the people to live in an atmosphere of modesty, decency and morality, and must be overturned.

All moral rules should be publicly displayed and taught in schools and colleges.
A state must declare that it respects all religions and allows their display equally.
No politician should criticize a religion. If he does, he should be made to resign.

To not enforce that schools and colleges should have a moral atmosphere destroys society. Learning has to go side by side with the wisdom of morality, self -control of desires and self-discipline so that society can be safe.

To not recognize pornography and sexuality as an addiction; to not understand their dangers for women, children, animals and family life; to not understand that they are not synonymous with entertainment; to not ban them in television, movies the literature and computers destroys society.

To take away the powers of parents, and to hand them over to the children destroys society.

To take away the innocence of our children destroys society.

To prey on a race because of its ethnicity destroys society.

To prey on one working class and have separate general rules for its working conditions and payment destroys society.

Unregulated entertainment can destroy society.
Entertainment can profoundly affect the speech code, the dress code, the modesty code, the morality code and the philosophy of a society. Entertainment is a powerful propaganda tool.

The politician who ignores this is the worst enemy of society. There can be no freedom without responsibility. Like every industry, entertainment must be regulated. Like every industry, it must follow the rules that it shall not harm society. It must have a speech code, a dress code and a philosophy code that should not violate that of the society or that of decency, modesty or morality.

By not allowing an individual to participate in the government, except to vote, you destroy society. It is the birthright of every individual to recognize that the politicians are elected as servants of the people. They must be watched daily that they do not ignore the public, nor their promises to it, nor misuse their powers. If they do so, they must be removed immediately and not wait until the next election time. Votes must be allowed every six months to remove politicians who did not keep their word.

To insist that people live in carbon- copy homes; to have a watchdog to see how they live; to see how many people they live with; how many pets they have; whether they can open their doors or windows; or what they can dry outside; what they can put out on their porch; to make sure that they can only plant certain items or put only certain decorations, or how they can entertain etc is a gross violation of a human being's freedom.

This destroys the individuality and the creativity of a human being, his freedom and thus ultimately destroys society.

No homeowners' association can do this and take away the freedom of an individual. No homeowners' association can have private laws that violate the laws of the country.

Understand that a state rules by dividing its people. No matter how horrified you are at a news you watch, you feel helpless because you are an individual who no one will listen to.

This is why you must go to monthly meetings in your town and state your opposition to unethical issues. You should organize these meetings if none exist. You must count the votes and make contact with similar citizens' meetings in different towns and ask their reaction to the issues mentioned. You must join together in stating your concern in the newspaper and make sure that your demand for six monthly voting rights is agreed to. The leaders from every town meeting must then meet, collect all the votes and see that these issues are protested and fight to over turn them.

Chapter 72.   LAWS THAT NEED TO BE FORMED

Knowing what laws are needed is a life-skill.
In any society, laws and departments are needed for food and agriculture; water; air, environment and waste disposal; electricity and energy distribution; transport; defense; police, law and order; handling of disasters; education; entertainment; economy and taxes; animal welfare; and prayer and morality. Technology must blend with modesty, morality, and spirituality.

Any national and state function must start with a moment of silent prayer to God followed by prayers from every religion. It is the duty of the State to display moral values publicly.

Those people who say, or who teach in the media, that they do not care about what people will say or how society will react when they break moral laws are guilty of turning against society. They are destructive to society. All benefits of society must be denied to them. You cannot just have benefits from society without doing anything in return to protect it.

Severe punishment in terms of fine and imprisonment should be applied if someone insults your God by putting His picture on toilet paper, on toilet seat, in the toilet room, on shoes, on panties, bras and underwear; bed sheets, bedcovers, or on places you will walk, sit or lie on; or if he makes lamps or other appliances out of His statues; or if he attributes carnal pleasures to Him, or makes pictures of Him in carnal pleasures, or uses His name to get carnal pleasures with others or to get addiction.

MODESTY

You cannot dress with your breasts, cleavage, buttocks, clefts or panties exposed or your genitalia outlined. This is violation of modesty and must be punished.

A man must not wear a swimsuit or underwear that outlines his genitalia or is not three inches below his buttocks.

CHILD

In a divorce, the mother must get the custody of the child unless she is physically or mentally unfit to do so. You cannot compound the destruction of a child's family by making him/her shuttle between two homes. This is traumatic and unstable.

A child cannot have homosexual parents.

It is not abuse for a parent to hit a child as long as he is not hit for more than a few times. Spanking or punishment is necessary for discipline. A child cannot be allowed to call the police for this. This is violation of a parent's right to discipline his/her child and the state has no right to do that. No state can make a parent powerless if it wants to have a moral, safe and strong society. A teacher should be able to hit a child twice over an incident. But he should not cause internal injuries or rupture an eardrum.

The only people who must report a case of child abuse are the health-workers, the doctors and nurses, the educators, the neighbors and the social workers. It should not be the child. The child can go to the teachers, doctors, neighbors or health-workers.

The police should only be called by the people mentioned above. Otherwise, this prevents the discipline of the child.

Because few children were abused does not mean that majority of parents should pay the price of becoming powerless. It is how the majority is affected that leads to rules. You cannot take away the power of the parent.

A child should not be left alone at home or anywhere until he/she is fifteen. Otherwise you are endangering his/her life. A girl should never be left alone with an adult male at home or outside (even if the male is a relative) until she can defend herself.

People employing child labor must be imprisoned and fined.

EDUCATION

In schools, in colleges and universities, the parents must get the report card as long as they pay for the fees.
A parent has the right to stop the education of the child for up to one year if the child has fallen into bad company.

The parent should have the right to see that the child can have education at home or that the child can have education at an aunt or uncle's town in order to remove him/her from bad influences. The parent can put the child in vocational or other schools.

A child should not be forced to attend a school determined by the location of his home but should be able to attend any public school.

The federal aid given to a school will be determined by the number of children, which is kept balanced by the student-teacher ratio. There should not be more than fifteen children to a teacher in elementary school and not more than thirty in middle and high school. Understand that the larger the number of students, the more difficult it is to enforce discipline or safety.

There should be no pre-schools. A child should enter school only at five and should spend the time before with his/her family. Those who want others, including grandparents, to take care of the children and want the mother to work in the first five years of life, or in the teenage years, should not have children.

A child should not be made to take any tests in order to enter a school until middle school, that is after fifth grade. It is madness to have little children at the age of five or six taking pre-admission tests.

Children in day-cares must be offered milk, instead of juice, with snacks at snack time. Juice is completely non-filling for a small child.
Children in elementary schools until third grade must be offered milk by the state.

No school, or place of learning, can ask for donations in order to admit a child. The people in charge must be severely punished if they do so. Only fees can be asked for and these fees must be available to anyone who asks for them.

A child should not carry more than one note-book and a pencil box until the fifth grade. His/her books should be at school or at home. From the fourth grade through eighth grade, a child must not carry school bags that weigh more than two to three pounds. This hurts their backs, as well as shoulders, and causes problems in later life. Even afterward the bag cannot be more than eight pounds.

It is the right of a principal to remove any child from education if he/she is a bad influence on others, or is disruptive or disrespectful or shows lack of self- control.

Education has to include life skills, moral values, self-discipline and prayer from beginning. Without these the purpose of education(to prepare one for life) is lost.

A teacher cannot take payment for giving extra help to student of his/her own class.

A teacher must be evaluated for competency if more than two students in his/her class need help to pass.

A teacher who has affair with a student must be removed. This is violation of the ethics of education.

It is imperative that education is taught in an atmosphere of morality, self-control and self-discipline. These three things are part of education and protect the citizen, the family and ultimately the society.

The schools , colleges and universities must be shut down if they offer or allow on their premises, gangs advocating hatred to a race, smoking , alcohol, drugs, sexual description, sexual permissiveness or freedom in literature, shows or actions.
One cannot have magazines, books, literature, cassettes, tapes, videos, songs, plays or shows with nudity, sexual jokes, sexual scenes or innuendoes, in schools, colleges, universities or in student's rooms. The authorities have the right to search any room, confiscate such material and expel the students.

No college, school or university is allowed to publish any such materials. The authorities must be removed if they permit this or if they teach any kind of sexual lifestyle. No sexuality should be taught in school, colleges or university A biological description of the sex organs and their functions should be taught in biology.

The reason a soldier can defend our nation is because he is taught self- discipline.
It makes him tough and motivated. Self- discipline helps in depression. Our students need to get tough and motivated.

Waking up in college campus has to be by a fixed time and no student should be found in his/her room during daytime hours except in case of illness. This helps in self-discipline.

The education must start in the morning with a daily prayer. In a democracy, the prayer has to be directed to God, to greet Him, to thank Him for the day, to ask for His blessing and His help. A general prayer does not violate any religion. Emphasis must be laid to respect all religions as the paths to God. By middle schools, all religions should be taught.

Living quarters have to be in separate buildings for boys and girls. They must only meet in public lounges (not in their rooms) during visiting hours. All students have to be back in their rooms by ten pm.

Dress has to follow codes of decency and modesty.

Schools must have clubs dealing with welfare of animals.

No school should teach the child anything that is against the moral and ethical beliefs of any religion.

Computers in colleges and universities must be censored for any sexuality, nudity or pornography.

All books and curriculum for schools, colleges and universities must be available to the public six months before the courses start.

ANIMALS

Hunting has to be banned.

Giving electric shocks to animals is inhuman and is totally banned.

An animal cannot be kicked, stoned, whipped, beaten or poked in its private parts. It cannot be made to go without water or food. It cannot be run over. It cannot be made to suffer pain. All these are crimes that need to be severely punished.

An animal must be allowed to run, jump and play freely as long as its owners or responsible people are there. It has a right to use its voice.

One cannot keep an animal or a bird tied or kept in a cage all day. It must be allowed to exercise.
All cages must be two and a half times the length and height of the animals. In a fish tank, fishes must be able to swim at least two feet over their body length if under six inches and three times the length if over two feet. Birds must have at least two to three feet of area around. Pet shops that keep fishes and animals in shorter cages and fishbowls must be fined.

An animal must not be locked inside the house all day and only be allowed to come out to go for a walk. Every townhouse should have an enclosure where the animal can stay outside. Animal can stay in the enclosure even if the owners are not home. No housing development can say that pets are not allowed.

When you take a land for building, you must first make a public announcement for sixty days. At that time, you must also state what you are going to do about the birds and the animals that are going to be displaced. How will you re- settle them? They must be given an equal amount of land elsewhere and helped to be replaced.

You must pay for their support until they are rehabilitated. You must have public sanction with their reasons from PETA and ASPCA.

If humans are displaced then you must satisfy the human rights bureau.

You cannot abandon animals after you have them. You can take in an abandoned animal. You cannot take away babies of animals before they are weaned.

Abuse of animals and torture of animals must be severely punished with imprisonments and fines.

You cannot torture an animal for experimentation.

You cannot put a fence around a pond or feeding area of animals and so cut off their water and food supply. No city or state can do that. You must also make sure that the animals will have no fence to stop them from their migration, and that their water and food supply will remain intact. You cannot take away ponds and convert them into parks when they are the nesting grounds and water supply of animals or birds.

You cannot eat babies of animals. You cannot cook animals alive. You cannot eat animals that just had babies.

You cannot kill them for clothing. You cannot torture them for beauty or other products. Any company using animal products must allow visitors to visit their site anytime to see that no animals are suffering. It is the job of every one of you to visit such places at least once unannounced.

Animals that you use for your trade are to be kept in the most humane conditions, given food and water, never overburdened and given adequate rest. They should not be beaten, whipped or poked in sensitive areas.

Animals cannot be made to race or fight for our pleasure.

Even animals you eat have to be kept in natural and humane surroundings. They cannot be kept tied up, but must have freedom to walk about, even run, and play with their own kind.
They cannot be kept in over- crowded conditions.
They cannot be force- fed.
They cannot be given hormones.
They cannot see other animals being slaughtered in front of them.
They cannot have their young ones taken away from them before they are weaned.
They cannot be carried while tied up in a painful manner.
They cannot be kept hungry or thirsty.
They cannot be beaten or tortured.

Do not use an electric fence. It is inhumane. Do not use electric shocks to control animals.

Animals cannot have their babies tied where they cannot reach them. The babies must be free to drink the milk before the human beings take them.

Animals cannot be turned out when they have outlived their usefulness, but must be taken care of in their old age.

You cannot make them perform show after show and give them no rest. No animal should perform more than once in two days and never if it is sick or acting listless. You cannot inject them with drugs to make them perform.

You cannot tie an animal's mouth. It controls its heat from its mouth by panting.

You cannot have railings around any pond or lake. This prevents the animals from getting their water supply. A person knows that he/she or his/her dependents can fall into water and must be responsible to prevent this. This is not done by putting railings.

All schools must have animal clubs and must be members of ASPCA, Green peace or PETA.
Towns must have parks for the play of children and for running and play of pets.

Any land given to builders by the town must have the approval of these humane societies.

Animals should stay in their natural surroundings. In every town there should be set aside at least twenty square miles for animals to exist in their natural surroundings, and vehicles should not be allowed to speed around it. The roads should be on bridges so that the animals can walk under it.

You cannot punish people who fight against cruelty towards animals.

You cannot mutilate an animal in the name of beauty.

You cannot persecute anyone because an animal passed feces on your grounds.

You cannot lock an animal in garage and go away on a trip. You cannot lock an animal in a basement.

You cannot keep a single guard dog. You cannot keep it chained all day

You cannot leave an animal in a car for even a few minutes without opening the windows.

You cannot use collars with prongs

You must stop if an animal is trying to cross the road. Let him get across. Places where animals frequent must have an overpass so that cars can go on the top and the animals can cross below.

MARITAL STATUS

Marriage is recognized by the state as a union between a man and a woman only.

The state must honor the marriage institution by making the paychecks in the name of the husband and wife. If a spouse objects, he/she should not be married. Both husband and wife need to sign these checks in order to deposit them.

If a woman lives with a man without marrying him, she will forfeit all federal aid. She will lose all benefits of society including scholarships and police protection. She cannot appear on public programs or publish books. The same applies to the man.

At the time of marriage, the husband must sign how much money will be turned over to the wife if he abandons her or if she walks out because of abuse. If she has no children, this money must support her until she can support herself. If she has children, she must continue to get child support until she remarries. This is to be decided at the time of marriage and witnessed by two people from both sides of the families. This basic amount is not to be fought over in the court and is irrespective of any other money that the spouse may be entitled to.

Asking for dowry is a crime that is punished with fines and imprisonment.

Living together out of wedlock and having children out of wedlock is abuse against the woman and the child. The persons doing so must be given a choice to get married. Otherwise one-third of the paychecks must be taken away every month and put in a "security fund" to be available for the woman and for the child if the man walks out. They must sign that all the property that each has will be divided between the two of them the minute they split and that the man will have money removed from his paycheck for the support of any child and to support the woman until she is married or can support herself in terms of shelter, clothing, food and basic necessities.

By living together, they are breaking the code of society and causing potential abuse of the woman and child. Therefore, they should not be eligible for federal employment.

If they are self-employed, the state should give them the option to marry or take away one third of the money that they declare as earnings every month and put it in the "security fund" for the woman and child. They must sign papers that property will be divided if they leave each other.

If one of them is already married, than this is adultery and they must be punished for breaking the marriage vows, breaking the moral code of society and destroying the institution of family. This deserves imprisonment for three months. The person must pay fine and lose any federal employment he has. People in public position must pay fine and step down from their positions.

How will you know if there is adultery? The spouse or the family member has to file a case of adultery.

ABUSE

Abuse of a human being is never a personal affair. It is everyone's affair.

When you are abused, or if your husband is having an affair and he refuses to mend his ways, you should be able to file a complaint against the abuser in the family/domestic court immediately. Laws should pass that this should also be done automatically once the police or your doctor forwards your file to the court.

If a wife files a charge of abuse, or if a doctor or police forwards a case of abuse, the court should immediately send a letter to the husband telling him to stay away from his wife and children until further orders. This has to be automatic without waiting to have hearings. At the same time, a female social worker must be sent by the court to arrange the safety and protection of the wife and children and see that she has money to feed herself and the children.

If she has no money, the court can order the husband to give her money. This money must feed her for one month.

The court should immediately send a second letter to the employer stating that his employee has committed abuse and that until further notice, all paychecks should be split in equal amounts between the husband and wife. The checks in the name of the wife should be sent to the court address until further orders. She can pick them up there after signing in front of a witness.

The employer must warn the employee that a case of abuse has been filed against him in the employee folder and that a second incident will cause termination of employment.

The court hearing should be by the next week. The wife should stay either with relatives or in a shelter. In the preliminary hearing, when abuse is established, the employer must be directed by the court to contact the wife and divide all pension plans and investments equally in both husband and wife's name. These must be turned over to the wife without further battle.

In case of self- employment by the husband, and where the wife was not earning, the court must order the husband to send the next paycheck the same way to the court in the wife's name. Until further orders, half of all his paychecks should be sent in the wife's name to the court address. The pension plans and investments must be spilt the same way.

PARENTS

In case of abuse of parents by the children, or where no one wants to keep the parents, the parent or neighbor can file charges.

The child or all the children must be ordered before the court and a case of "parent abuse" charged against them.

They each must be fined. One child should be chosen to keep the parent and the others must contribute in proportion to their earnings. The social worker must go every two weeks for the next two months to see that there is no further abuse.

A person is responsible for his children until they are twenty-one. He/ she is responsible for his/parents until they are dead. Persons cannot be left alone to live after they are sixty-five, or younger but ill, unless they specifically desire so. Children must be punished for abandoning their elder parents.

Tax shelters must be given to those who keep their parents and relatives.

DEATH

One can ask for euthanasia when there is no cure for a devastating or painful illness.

There will be death penalty for heinous crimes.

Abortion will be legalized.

One cannot plead insanity to avoid punishment.

It is not right to give only three days for bereavement. Death is a milestone in our lives with devastating effect. Four weeks of leave must be given for deaths in immediate family.

People should not get gastrostomies and be forced to live longer if they are mentally retarded or cannot make decisions for themselves after thirty days. One does not keep a person alive hoping that science will come up with a miracle. We have to deal with the present. If the person is unable to communicate his/her wishes or needs, interact with his/her surroundings and make decisions for himself/herself, than he/she must be allowed to move on to another world. Death has to be accepted as part of life. When a person is married, it is the spouse who has to be authorized to   request this decision over the parents because in marriage two people become one.

But any two doctors should be able to come to this decision.

LAW

You cannot have frivolous lawsuits. Both, the person filing the lawsuit and his lawyer, should be fully responsible for the fees and the time lost by the defendant if he is proven innocent.

You cannot persecute the one who tries to help others.

It is immoral for people in the jury to award compensation for emotional suffering. Compensation can only be given for physical damages, medical treatment and loss of wages.

There must be a cap/ limit for all malpractice suits.

Lawyers cannot insist that a doctor " cannot use his judgment but must conform to community standards." This is absolutely horrifying. It is telling another human being, "You cannot think. You cannot use your experience, wisdom, intuition or insight. You must blindly follow what everyone is doing."
This is mind control. No human being should ever be told not to think for himself and not use his judgment. A lawyer suggesting thus should be banned from practicing law.

STATE

It is the moral duty of the state to offer free water, toilets on the roads; shelters for abused women and the homeless, orphanages and hospitals with fulltime-employed physicians for the poor. The state must also have shelters for abused animals.

All cities must have orphanages, which must be periodically checked

No company can ask that we pay their bills before the beginning of the month when we get our salaries on the first of the month.

The state should not ask the citizen to pay toll each time he crosses and drives across a piece of road. The earth is his right. He has a right to walk on it, sleep on it, sit on it and drive on it without paying taxes each time he does so. Taxes should be paid once a year for the road.

A document does not have to be sent only through fax, internet or from an institution in order to be accepted. A person or institution must accept a document by mail, by hand, or by the way that the simplest, illiterate person can send it.

A bank cannot say that it will no longer return bank checks. A bank and other institutions have to accommodate the computer- illiterate person.

Homosexuality, pedophilia and sex with animals are illegal.

The state recognizes the right of a person to go to any doctor, pharmacy or hospital that he/she wants.
The state, therefore, will not allow hospitals, pharmacies, physical therapy centers, laboratories, diagnostic centers and doctors to form contracts with insurance companies.

It also recognizes the right of a patient to see a doctor instead of a nurse practitioner or physician assistant if he or she so wishes.

The state also recognizes that a physician assistant or a nurse practitioner has much less hours of education and training than a doctor and therefore must not be allowed to carry out the same procedures as a doctor nor write prescriptions for medicines.

The state should declare that no nurse or anyone, other than a doctor, can be hired to review a doctor's performance.

No insurance company can demand to review doctor's notes before approving a test or a hospital stay. When a doctor orders a test or a hospitalization, it is medically necessary. If the insurance company suspects fraud it should take the doctor to a tribunal formed by professors of medical schools and never by doctors on its payrolls.

Male nurses or male technicians cannot take care of female patients. This violates the modesty of a woman.

MEDICINE

A doctor cannot ask that in case of a crime, you must fill up report forms before he touches a patient. This makes the doctor guilty of inhumanity and murder. His license should be suspended. His first duty is to see that the patient is stable.

A medical school must enforce that its students take the Hippocratic oath on graduating. We must never ignore the ethics of our profession.

A doctor who hits his patient because she/he is screaming with pain,
A doctor who makes fun or allows nurses, and others, to make fun of a woman in pain from childbirth,
A doctor who ignores a patient crying in pain and goes away or starts talking socially to others,
A doctor who drives past a person in accident, or ill on the ground and
A doctor who does not offer his services when someone becomes ill on the road or in a social gathering,
must have his license suspended on grounds of cruelty.
Cruelty and non-caring cannot be part of the medical profession.

A doctor must practice the highest ethics. A doctor must be aware of the wrong things happening in his society and fight to remove them.

INSURANCE
It is immoral for the insurance companies to increase the premium after the first accident or incidence. That is what we had brought the insurance for.
It is immoral for an insurance companies to increase a malpractice premium of a doctor after he is proved innocent.

Insurance companies cannot form contracts with doctors, pharmacies, hospitals or laboratories/x-ray facilities as this violates the above right and jeopardizes medical care.
Insurance companies cannot form contracts with repair shops.

Insurance companies cannot tell the doctor what medication he can use and or for how long.

They cannot decide the payment of a doctor's service based on codes
A service, if performed, has to be paid even if it is written on a piece of cloth and in the language of the common person.

They cannot send guidelines to the doctor as to how to treat diseases or do checkups.

No insurance company can decide how long a patient can stay in the hospital or what treatment or test the patient can have without itself physically examining the patient. No insurance companies can send children home with tracheostomy tubes. This is malpractice.
No insurance company can say that it will only pay for one medical problem in the hospital.

All appeals about the necessity of a test or treatment have to go to an independent panel of doctors from medical schools. No insurance company can ask that appeal be directed to doctors it has hired.

See further rules in the chapter on HMOs.

HOSPITALS

A hospital cannot ask for money first when a person is brought in from an accident or seriously ill. The patient must become stable first.

A hospital cannot charge parking fees from the patients and visitors.

A hospital cannot tell a doctor that he must discharge his patients earlier or he will lose admitting privileges in the hospital.

No hospital can insist that a doctor can only have privileges to admit patients in its hospital after he has admitted twenty- five patients under supervision. Five patients should be enough to judge if the doctor is competent.

A hospital cannot harass the doctor, and say that in California a patient is discharged for pneumonia in three days, and ask why he is keeping his patient for four. This is highly unethical! No patient can be compared to another. Each patient has a different genetic background, different stamina, different set of medical conditions, different life span and different resistance pattern. Patients are not identical cookies. You can treat them with cookbook formulas.

Hospitals cannot send doctors monthly "length of stay" sheets telling them that they kept their patient for so many days.

No hospital can send guidelines to the doctors telling him what medications he must use, how he must treat patients and what advice he must give his patients.

The job of the hospital is only to provide room and nursing care.

Why did the doctor go to medical school if he cannot use his judgment?

No hospital can demand that whenever a patient is admitted, the doctor must ask the patient if he has a living will. This is highly insensitive and tactless. It makes the patient feel frightened that he must be very ill. The hospital forces the doctor to do so purely for financial reasons. The hospital mails advertisement to patients. It can also mail requests asking if the patient has a living will. Since this is done when the patient is well, it is less threatening.

Hospitals have to be sensitive to the fact that doctors need full concentration with their patients otherwise the patient care will suffer. Hospitals must show that they have policies that when a doctor is reviewing charts in nurses stations or medical records, or is in the library, there are no radios on.

The hospitals must also have a policy which makes sure that the staff does not continue to insensitively discuss their private life over the head of the doctor while the doctor tries to review the chart, decides treatment or performs a procedure, e.g. a colonoscopy, a delivery or surgery. This is not only rude; it is downright dangerous to the patient.

The hospital cannot ask for donations before a doctor is allowed to work there.

A hospital must see that the patients in its clinics are not waiting for over an hour and the doctor is not around. The administrator must arrange for alternate doctors to cover immediately.

ENTERTAINMENT

Computers, movies and televisions cannot have shows of nudity, sexuality or advertisement of drugs that affect genitalia or potency.

No drug company can advertise products affecting genital organs and potency in computers, radios, televisions or public magazines. This is the height of indecency.
No company can advertise products concerning menstruation or brassieres. This is not broadmindedness.

No billboard in any city can have the word "sex" advertised.

No sex shops can have billboard advertising what they do.

The first rule for any industry is that you will not harm society.
The second rule for any industry is that there is no freedom without responsibility.
The entertainment industry has to follow these rules just like any industry.

Entertainment rules:
1. It must be clearly understood that entertainment is not synonymous with sexual excitement. The job of the entertainment is to relax your mind. It is not to stimulate the genital organs at your other end. They are at the opposite end from your mind.

2. There can be no nudity. There can be no sexual scenes. There can be no obscenity. There can be no vulgarity. The show cannot say that it feeds your lust or desire, nor can it do so. When a director says that he wants to engage the public's senses, he cannot mean sensuality and sexual excitement.

3. It cannot cross the limits of modesty and decency in speech, dress, and action. See the chapter on entertainment for the codes on speech, dress, modesty and decency.

4. It cannot advocate a philosophy that violates any one of the moral rules of society.

5. It cannot murder the innocence of our children and youth.

6. It cannot show that our traditions do not matter or are wrong.

7. It cannot show people discussing problems or situations on the cell phones while driving. Cell phones are to be used only for emergencies.

8.Topics of rape, or sexual harassment cannot be discussed on family entertainment.

9. There can be no sexual description, jokes or innuendoes. This has to apply to magazines, books, radios, videos, movies, television and computers etc.

People who show sexual films, photographs, cards or literature publicly must be punished. This include the restaurants, general stores, bookstores, hotels, ships, airports and trains besides the movie halls and theaters

.

No bookstore or any store can sell magazines with sex topics or nudity. The cover of any book cannot have the word "sex" displayed. Magazines cannot have the word "sex" on the front cover, nor can it have topics related to sex.

Magazines like "playboy, penthouse" or any other showing nudity or sexual topics cannot be sold in public stores. This violates the innocence of our children.

No hotels, no ships and no public places can offer sexual pictures, movies or pornography. No public places, no ships and no hotels can offer nude areas or shows, televisions or movies that have sexual jokes or innuendoes.

No talk shows, including radios, can give any remark that is immodest, indecent or hints at lust, nudity or intercourse, breasts or genitalia. There can be no sexual innuendoes.

Homosexuality, pedophilia or sex with animals cannot be shown in entertainment.

The entertainment industry does not have carte blanche to let its imagination run wild without any responsibility to society. Entertainment cannot cross the limits of modesty and decency in speech, dress, and action. Artists who have no talent rely on nudity and sex to sell their products. A true artist does not. He does not bring in nude people, people in their underwear or women in scant dresses, bras and panties. He must not be allowed to do so.

ENTERTAINMENT RULES

1. There can be no nudity.
2. There can be no scenes of a man undressing a woman or untying her clothes.
3. There can be no scenes of a woman undressing a man.
4. There can be no scenes of a woman undressing or bathing.
5. There can be no sexual scenes. There can be no scenes of sexual acts being performed. There can be no scenes of homosexuality or any other sexual perversion.
6. There can be no fondling of each other's body.
7. There can be no scenes of man and woman lying naked, or appear to be lying naked, in bed. Women cannot be topless.
8. There can be no scenes of a man on top of a woman, or a woman on top of a man.
9. There can be no scenes of a man and a woman rolling over each other.
10. There can be no scenes showing a rape act.
11. There can be no scenes of birth or a miscarriage.
12. A male cannot run his face over or above the body of a woman .This arouses lust. A male cannot put his face near the pelvis of a woman.
13. Testing for talents for acting cannot involve sexual scenes or dialogues or provocative dances with semi-nude clothes.
14. A pregnant woman cannot have her stomach tightly outlined. She cannot walk around holding her stomach. A man cannot touch her stomach, kiss it or put his face next to it.
15. There will be no un-zippering of pants.

Understand that those who yell "broadmindedness" are only concerned with financial profit. It is only because of these people that we have descended from modesty to immodesty, from decency to indecency and from morality to immorality.

16. Kissing code:

There can be no kissing anywhere except on the forehead or hand, and with no tongue protrusion. This is to be shown only in affection and not because of advertisement of products.
There can be no kissing of the pregnant stomach.

17.Touching code:

There can be no touching of a woman on her neck, chest, breasts, buttocks, thighs and legs. There can be no kissing of her legs or feet. There can be no touching of her pregnant stomach by a man.
A woman cannot touch a man below his waist, on his thighs, legs and buttocks.

There can be an embrace.

18. Dress code:

A woman cannot wear a backless dress or a backless blouse. Blouses must be four inches below the breast. If blouses tightly outline the breasts than they must be covered.
Dresses, shirts or blouses cannot have spaghetti straps instead of sleeves.
Women and men cannot act or dance in under-clothes. Women cannot act or dance in bikinis or bras and panties. They cannot be in clothes of the size of bras and panties, or in clothes just covering the breasts or exposing the thighs.
Breasts or their cleavage cannot be exposed. Buttocks and their clefts must be covered.
All dresses have to be below the knees. The waist of a skirt or pant must cover the cleft of the buttock and be above the hip bone. It cannot be more than two fingers below the belly-button.

Clothes cannot be transparent over the breasts, chest, back, buttocks, genitalia or legs in women. They cannot be transparent over the buttock and genitalia in men.

A woman cannot be shown in wet, drenched clothes outlining her body.

Men cannot wear swimsuits outlining their genitalia. They must wear boxer shorts which are three inches below the fold where the thighs start.

A pregnant woman's stomach should not be outlined but should be draped over with lose clothes This is decency

If the tradition of your country is loose clothing in the majority, than you cannot show girls in shirts and tight pants

Men and women are not shown in swim suits. There is no justification. Your stories are not supposed to show women exposed.

19. Dancing code :

Women cannot dance nude or in bras and panties . The blouse must cover the waist. It must not be backless. It must not show the breast or the cleavage of breasts. The clothes must follow the same dress code as in acting.

There can be no dancing where a woman bends forward so that her breast is exposed or pushes her shoulders or elbows back so that her breasts jut forwards.

Women cannot point to their breasts or touch them in a dance. They cannot rotate their hips. They cannot expose their thighs in a dance. They cannot jiggle their breasts.

A man cannot bring his face near a woman's breast, pelvis or hip in a dance.

In the male and the female, the pelvis cannot be thrust forward in a dance.

Both men and women cannot kick their legs up in a dance so that their panties or crotch is exposed.

Man and women cannot dance so that their pelvis, hips or thighs touch.

There should be no dances where you touch other people's breasts, genitals, hips or buttocks.

20. Speech code:

There can be no sexual jokes or innuendoes. There can be no off- colored jokes.

One cannot use words for excrement, sexual excitement, intercourse or profanity.

One does not use the words, "pregnant, breasts, or words referring to male and female genitalia. Use euphemism.

One cannot discuss the size of genitalia or contraceptives.

A child cannot ask a woman if she is pregnant. This is indecent.

21. Code of decency and modesty:

A man cannot have a woman straddle him so that her legs are around him while he is lying, sitting or standing.

He cannot carry her on his back so that he is holding her legs and buttocks.

He cannot carry her over his shoulder with his hand on her hips. He cannot hit her on her hips.

A woman cannot sit on the shoulders of the man with her legs around his neck.

A woman cannot jump up to straddle him in a dance.

There can be no showing of anyone defecating, urinating or farting.

22. Cruelty or Violence

There can be no showing of burning of an individual, a decapitating, mutilating, or blinding of an individual. It cannot show an individual being cut to pieces or boiled, or any part of him being blown off. It cannot show a person killing a person and enjoying it. It cannot show cruelty.

It can not show rape.

It cannot show the torture of persons or animals.

Any violence cannot occupy more than ten minutes of the whole show.

Understand that violence in entertainment leads to violence in society.

23. Philosophy

A show has a profound influence on the philosophy of a nation and its youth and therefore must always be checked to see that it does not lead its youth astray.

Those who cry censorship must understand the difference . Censorship is when you do not allow a writing or entertainment that can make a society revolt against its rulers. But checking an entertainment's philosophy is the same way that you would check what a school or a stranger tells your child to see that your child is not being led on the wrong path.

We must protect the moral values that safe guard a society and that have taken thousands of years to develop. An entertainer is only ruled by greed.

a. A show cannot advocate a philosophy that violates any of the moral rules of society. See moral rules.

It cannot show that it is okay to live out of wedlock, or to have children out of wedlock, or to show disrespect to elders, that it is alright for a teacher to have an affair with a student etc. or to not care about how society feels. It cannot make fun of people following society as having a middle- class mentality.

b. It cannot break with our traditions. If we have a respectful name for our brother-in -law, than it cannot shorten that name. It cannot change the way we do our makeup and show that this is the standard way of doing it. This is against tradition.

c. It cannot say that following our traditions and moral values is being narrow- minded or is having a " middle-class" mentality.

d. It cannot show children as being wiser than adults. It cannot show children ordering adults, scolding adults, telling adults how to behave, or asking adults to go to their rooms so that the children can see their friends.

e. It cannot show that children have a right to live in a mess or that parents have no right to check on children. It cannot show that children have a right to privacy.

f. It cannot advocate the rights of children over the rights of their parents. This breaks up families. Understand that children are not a separate minority race that have to be protected from parents. Those who advocate that destroy families and ultimately the society.

g. It cannot show adults stupid as compared to children and meekly listening to them. It cannot show adults apologizing to children.

h. It cannot murder the innocence of our children and youth.

i. It cannot show people discussing problems or situations on the cell phones while driving. Cell phones are to be used only for emergencies.

j. Topics of rape, or sexual harassment cannot be discussed on family entertainment.

A politician cannot ignore the power of entertainment. Entertainment can influence the speech, dress and attitudes of our society. It is a powerful propaganda tool. It can drastically change the philosophy and moral code of a nation.

POLITICIAN

A politician must state whether he believes in God, modesty, decency and morality in his/her curriculum vitae.
He must answer the questions in the chapter of " questions to ask your politician".

If a politician has been caught doing something wrong, he must resign on the spot and not a few weeks later. If he refuses to do so, it should be the right of the opposition party leader to have him forcibly removed.

There can be "no transition" money for politicians leaving office to help them get resettled. Do we get transition money when we leave a job?

In a true democracy, a month before elections the salary of every category of politician should be announced as well as their perks. During election, the citizen should also be given a paper with these salaries. Each salary and perk should have three columns marked next to it . These columns should say too much , too little or sufficient. The citizen should also mark one of these columns.
Politicians cannot vote themselves any increase in income unless the public votes in agreement.

The voter should be doing three tasks during election. One is to vote for the candidate.

Secondly he should check their salaries and perks.

Thirdly when he comes in to vote, he should be given a piece of paper where he puts down his grievance, say "high prices". He then votes for or against it. This grievance also then goes on a black board . The next citizen is again asked to list his grievance.

If it is the same as the previous citizen, the number of votes for high prices is added. If it is a new grievance, say "injustice", this is added on the sheet and on the black board and the vote is taken.

At the end of the day when the votes are counted , the grievances should also be counted and the number of people complaining as well. A copy is given to the local library and it is announced on the television

Ultimately these are added for the state and the nation. It is the job of the elected politicians to form policies regarding these grievances immediately on forming a government.

Six months down the road a second election is held where the voters vote against each grievance and see if they were removed. If not, the national leader for that department must step down and the person who had stood second in his election must take his place. This person must also be checked in election in six months to see that he removed the grievances. If he fails too, or if there are still more than three grievances, then general elections must be held.

Why the national leader?
Because the responsibility ends on his desk. He can fire the state leaders or others responsible with him. A politician is the servant of the people. He must be accountable to the public.

The public must be able to hear all meetings of the government. It must be allowed to hold votes every six months giving its approval or disapproval for every new law that is made. A federal vote has to be held for a federal law and a town vote has to be held for a town law. A state vote has to be held for a state law.

A citizen should also be able to file a complaint in the court that it does not agree with the present law and feels that it violates his right and the right of his family for a safe, decent and moral atmosphere or that it violates his freedom even when he has not done anything immodest, indecent or immoral.

Any filing in the court must be given to the newspaper and all newspapers must be made to give notice to the public to that effect with votes marked 'yes' and 'no' on the front page.

The votes then take place in the next six- month cycle. The newspaper cuttings can be put in the boxes or the people can vote by other means. This should be regulated by independent bodies.

If the majority of the votes are in favor of the citizen or if another town picks up the same complaint, then the state must hold the election. If the election in the state is in favor of the citizen, than the law should be opened to votes in the whole country.

How else do you hold politicians accountable?

By having juries for politicians where a politician can be brought if he has ignored your cry for help.

It should be the same number of jurors, chosen the same way, and should not take more than one day. If he has ignored your cry for help for no justifiable reason, he should step down.

For a politician to write you a glib letter, after months, thanking you for sharing your thoughts with him, and ignoring your cry for help, is immoral.

He must tell you what concrete steps will be taken in what time, or why he will not take them. You must get a reply within a fortnight.

If a citizen has a distress and writes to the politician, and his distress is ignored, or a glib letter is sent to the citizen thanking him and not giving any concrete plan of action, a complaint must be lodged with the "politicians ethic committee" made of ordinary citizens. This committee must respond in seven days.

If the bureau cannot explain the ignorance, and he is not satisfied, than he should have the right to make the politician appear before a citizens' jury.

The politician must appear before a jury to explain why he did nothing. If his reply is not satisfactory, he should be made to step down and the person who came in second should take his place.

A politician can not demand contributions to listen to your problem. That is equivalent to taking a bribe. Any leader taking a bribe must go to jail. A politician abusing his powers and perks must resign and be punished.

If a politician does not implement the promises he made within six months of acquiring office, he has to explain this to the public. If he has no satisfactory reason for his lack of action, he must step down and the person who was second in election asked to take his place.

See the chapter " Moral Rules" on politicians.

TOWNHOUSES

No homeowners' association can insist that people live in carbon copy homes; that there is a watchdog to see how they live, to see how many people they live with, how many pets they have, whether they can open their doors or windows, or what they can dry outside, to make sure they can only plant certain items or put only certain decorations, what they can put out on their porch or how they can entertain etc. This is a gross violation of a human being's freedom. This destroys the individuality of the human, his freedom and creativity and thus ultimately destroys society. The laws of the homeowner's association can never be superior to the laws of the country.

Children should not drive battery-driven vehicles on public roads until they are eighteen and obey all the traffic laws.
No toy company should put label on its toys specifying what age a toy should be for. A parent knows what his child can handle.
The toy company does not have to spend money informing the public to be careful about plastic etc. because anything a person is to know by commonsense should not be allowed to form a basis for lawsuits.

RIGHTS OF CHILDREN

The state cannot advocate the rights of children over the rights of their parents. This breaks up families and takes away the power of the parents. Understand that the children are not a separate minority race that have to be protected from parents. Those who advocate that destroy families and ultimately the society. Just because there are a few thieves does not mean that I treat every individual as a thief. Just because a few parents have abused their children does not mean that we set up children as a minority and parents as their enemies.

This is only done by people who are driven by power and who want to rule the society by dividing one person against another and by turning a child against his/her parent. This is like communism and like Hitler's people, who wanted to turn the children against their parents so they could control them.

But the person who genuinely loves his people and his society will value the family unit and not take away the power of the parent. He will not advocate posting of minority rights in the hospitals, schools and public places.

A minority is to be considered a minority only when it has fully attained adulthood. But these are our children who have not yet developed fully; who have not attained their full physical, mental and emotional growth and who need to be guided by us.

A minority is not loved by others. But we love our children more than anything else. We will give our life for them.

A minority is to be protected because they are not given basic things to survive. But we want to give our children whatever they need and we want to impart to them all our wisdom.

A minority is to be protected because they do not know whom to turn to in need.
But our children run to us when they need anything.

People who advocate rights of children are our enemies.

It has to be illegal to post the "rights of children" in any place including schools, hospitals, libraries etc.

It is not the right of a child to decide what medicine or treatment he/ or she can have until he or she is twenty years of age. That is the duty of the parent.

PRAYER, MORALITY AND RELIGION

The state must believe in God. It must allow public references to God and any religion in words, writings, songs and on government paper.

The state should be run by people who believe in God, no matter which religion they belong to.

The state recognizes that it has a duty to allow all religions to flourish and not to subdue their public expressions.

The state must protect all religions as long as they stay moral.

The state recognizes that all moral rules are the same in every religion and are vital for a society to flourish. The state must allow public display of moral rules.

The state must insist that moral rules are taught in schools.

The state must allow prayer in public schools. The prayer must be the oldest one used in the country in the prevailing language of the region with reference to God as God and not as the name used by any religion.

FREEDOM OF SPEECH

There is no freedom of speech when a nation presents only one-sided news to its people. We see this every day.

There is no freedom of speech if we are told that we cannot make any loving or respectful references to God or religion in our words, writings or songs; and yet we are given freedom to curse God. This is evil.

There is no freedom without responsibility.

Freedom of speech cannot allow one to use in public:

1. words that incite hatred or insults towards a race or religion;
2. words that are blasphemy or profanity;
3. words that have obscenity;
4. words that have terms of excrement or intercourse and
5. words that cause sexual excitement .

JUDGES AND LAW

A judge or few judges cannot have the right to either make a law or over- turn a law that has a profound affect on the nation's children, animals, women or people. This has to be voted upon by the people who alone can decide if the law should be placed, re-instated or overturned.

The face that a judge could overturn a thirty- year law banning the hunting of bears in New Jersey is horrifying.
The fact that a judge could decide that pornography should be allowed in computers in United States is not only horrifying but also shows that democracy is dead in our country!

Any new law affecting the people must be placed before the people and they must be allowed to vote on them. People must be given the right to vote on public issues every six months.

A democracy does not make its people helpless. The rights of the people are not limited to voting persons to power. In a democracy the people must be involved in decision making. That is what democracy is about.

Once something horrifies a citizen, he/she should have the right to file this in a court. It should be mandatory that the court forwards this as an announcement in all the newspapers. This question should then be put to a vote in that town in the next six month voting cycle. If it is changed in the citizen's favor it has to become legal in that state. It then must be a topic to put to vote nationally in the next six month voting cycle.

Every six months the people must be allowed to vote on topics that bother them or on politicians that have not kept their promises.

Understand that a state rules by dividing its people. No matter how horrified you are at the news, you feel helpless because you are an individual and so are not powerful to change anything.

This is why you must go to monthly meeting in your towns and raise question on an ethical topics. There should be monthly meeting of citizens in every town and they should contact each others and join in fighting for or against a cause.

This is why there must be six months voting rights of citizens on laws and issues that disturb them.

Chapter 73.   QUESTIONS TO ASK YOUR POLITICIANS

Send these letters to your political candidates. Insist on a response!
This is your life skill to see that you chose the right candidates.

"Dear candidate,
Before I vote for you, I need to know how you stand on the following issues.
Please answer each question and mail this back to me at the following address: (put your address here)

1.Do you believe in God?
Do you aim to remove His name from public statements?

2.Do you believe that prayer should be brought back into public schools?

3a. Do you believe that the State may separate itself from religion but it should not separate itself from moral rules that are the same in every religion?
b. Do you believe that moral rules should be taught in schools?
c. Do you believe in public display of moral rules?

4. Do you believe in prevention of cruelty to animals even in the name of industry or science?
b. What laws are you going to pass to see that this happens?
c. Do you believe that there should be an Animal Humane Act and a Department for Humane Treatment of Animals to see that the animals are treated humanely?

d. Do you believe that people fighting to "prevent" cruelty to animals should be protected from persecution?

e. Are you going to pass a law to that effect?

f. What is your stand on hunting as a sport?

5. What is your stand on homosexuality?

b. If homosexuals have a "different " lifestyle than us, then why should they have the "same " benefits as us?

c. Did you know that there is no medical basis, no scientific proof and no center in the brain for homosexuality?

d. Did you know that that right down to the basic cell of your body, you are defined as a man or as a woman?

In every basic cell, there is a code bar called chromosome. On it is a gene called xy for male and xx for female.

e. Did you know that every part of the human body, the liver, the heart, the lung, is the same in the male and the female, except the sexual organs?

The sexual organs are made so that they are a pipe in the male and a hollow tube in the female so that they can fit like a lock and a key. The rectum is medically designed to store our stools and absorb water. It is not biologically designed to be a sexual organ. So, the normal behavior is to be heterosexuals.

Homosexuality is not normal behavior. It is condemned by every religion. It is a chosen aberrant lifestyle by a few.

f. Does that give Homosexuals the right to say to my children that it is an acceptable alternate life style?

g. Does that give Homosexuals the right to invade my society as an accepted norm?

h.. Why must my children be forced to learn about this in schools?

i. Are you going to overturn domestic benefits to homosexuals?

j. What sort of democracy is this that states that my child will be forced to be brainwashed and taught homosexuality in schools and universities (Rutgers university course called "shaping a life". It is mandatory. One cannot graduate without it).

k. Will you ban any teaching of homosexuality in schools and colleges?

l. Will you ban showing of any homosexuality in television, movies and entertainment?

m. Are you going to ban the teaching of any learning that goes against moral and ethical values of any religion?
Tolerance or broadmindedness never means that we accept abnormal for normal or immoral for moral.

n. Will you make it mandatory that all curriculums are open to public six months before the course starts so that no one can quietly start brain washing our children again?

6. In a divorce, do you agree that the child should be allowed to stay with the mother?
Do you think we should compound the fact that the home of a child is broken by making him /her shuttle between two homes?
Does this not damage his/her stability?

7. How can three days leave be sufficient for death when it is such a devastating milestone?

8. Do you think that entertainment is synonymous with sexual excitement?

b. Do you think that we should take away the innocence of our children?
Do you think that the current entertainment is beneficial for my children to watch and hear?

c. Will you ban showing of nudity and sexual scenes in books, magazines, television and movies?

When our forefathers believed in the freedom of speech, were they not very careful about modesty, decency and morality in entertainment?
You just have to look at the old television and movies of that time. Why did they not feel that freedom of speech did not entitle one to violate modesty and decency?

f. How do you plan to regulate the entertainment industry so that it is safe for my children?

g. Do you believe that there should be a department of Entertainment and moral welfare?

h. Do you think that the entertainment industry should follow the same rule as every industry does, that it should not harm society?
i. Do you believe that every one should follow the rule that there is no freedom without responsibility? This includes the entertainment industry.

j. Are you going to put restrictive guidelines on the entertainment industry?

k. Do you believe that entertainment should follow rules of modesty, decency, and morality?

9.. Do you think that the drug companies should be allowed to advertise over the radio, television, computers, and any public media, about drugs that affect sexuality or genital organs?

10. If I pay for my children's education, I should be entitled to get their report card even in college. Are you going to make sure that I can do so?

b. Do you believe that learning in schools and colleges benefit from a moral atmosphere?

c. Do you believe that the campus and living quarters for girls and boys should be separate?

d. If you do not believe in separate living quarters, how do you plan to account for increased permissiveness in sexuality and its effect on society?

e. Do you believe that schools or colleges should be allowed to have lectures, magazines, shows, movies, television or computers showing nudity or sexuality in the name of freedom of speech?

f. Do you believe that our students in universities should be allowed to view pornography?

g. The purpose of education is that a person gains knowledge about the world around him and is best equipped to handle it. How does offering a student drugs and pornography achieve this?

h. Do you think that when our forefathers advocated freedom of speech, they were for pornography.

i. Do you think a panel of judges has a right to overthrow a law to protect my children from pornography on computers?

j. What are you going to do about protecting my children and preventing them from seeing pornography in computers, televisions and movies?

11. I should have the right to go to any doctor, laboratory or hospital that I want. Why do I have to wait until I am sixty-five years of age to get this opportunity from Medicare? This is because of health maintenance organizations. Are you going to pass a law that bans health organizations from having contracts with laboratories, doctors and hospitals? This is the only way our healthcare can improve.

b. The health insurance companies are not supposed to tell my doctor how to treat patients. Are you going to pass a law so that they cannot send any guidelines to them?

c. Are you going to pass a law so that they cannot tell the doctor what medicine he can prescribe and for how long?

d. The health insurance company denies my treatment without examining me. Are you going to pass a law that it is immoral and malpractice for anyone, including the insurance company, to decide the treatment or necessity of a test without examining the patient?

e. Are you going to pass the law that no insurance company can decide how long a patient can stay in a hospital or whether a patient needs a treatment, test or therapy? This decision belongs to my doctor.

f. Are you going to pass a law that no insurance company can ask for documentation to approve a test or treatment. If they think that my doctor is a cheat, they can appeal to an independent panel of doctors from medical schools only. They should never be allowed to hire their own doctors to make these decisions. This is unethical.

12. Do you think the power of the parents should be taken away from them?

13. What do you think of the following?
"It is the duty of a leader to see that everyone gets justice, to protect his people from invaders, from the criminals inside the society and from immorality".

14. Do you agree to step down in three months if you do not keep your promises?

Final words

Education has to be given in a moral atmosphere free from addiction, drugs, alcohol, sexuality and pornography on its premises.

For a leader to invade a wildlife sanctuary for any reason is cruelty and immorality.

For a nation to lead others in science and technology but to fall behind in morality and fairness is unforgivable.

The end

About The Author

The author is a doctor with over thirty years of practice in two continents.

Because her father was in Foreign Service, she has lived in many countries and has been exposed to different cultures. She has learned all religions.

She strongly believes in two sets of education. The one in school teaches us about our environment. The second one gives us "a map for the road of life". Both should be given simultaneously.

This book was written to complete the need for the second type of education for her children and her patients.

Printed in the United States
40733LVS00004B/109-111